THE METAPHYSICS OF THE INCARNATION

The Metaphysics of the Incarnation

ANNA MARMODORO AND JONATHAN HILL

UNIVERSITY PRESS

Great Clarendon Street, Oxford OX2 6DP

Oxford University Press is a department of the University of Oxford.
It furthers the University's objective of excellence in research, scholarship,
and education by publishing worldwide in

Oxford New York

Auckland   Cape Town   Dar es Salaam   Hong Kong   Karachi
Kuala Lumpur   Madrid   Melbourne   Mexico City   Nairobi
New Delhi   Shanghai   Taipei   Toronto

With offices in

Argentina   Austria   Brazil   Chile   Czech Republic   France   Greece
Guatemala   Hungary   Italy   Japan   South Korea   Poland   Portugal
Singapore   Switzerland   Thailand   Turkey   Ukraine   Vietnam

Oxford is a registered trade mark of Oxford University Press
in the UK and in certain other countries

Published in the United States
by Oxford University Press Inc., New York

© Oxford University Press 2011

The moral rights of the author have been asserted

Database right Oxford University Press (maker)

Reprinted 2011

All rights reserved. No part of this publication may be reproduced,
stored in a retrieval system, or transmitted, in any form or by any means,
without the prior permission in writing of Oxford University Press,
or as expressly permitted by law, or under terms agreed with the appropriate
reprographics rights organization. Enquiries concerning reproduction
outside the scope of the above should be sent to the Rights Department,
Oxford University Press, at the address above

You must not circulate this book in any other binding or cover
And you must impose this same condition on any acquirer

ISBN 978-0-19-958316-4

Printed in the United Kingdom by
Lightning Source UK Ltd., Milton Keynes

Preface

Incarnation has always been a central idea in world religion. Ever since the rulers of the ancient Persians, Egyptians, and Romans claimed to be gods in human form, the notion that a human can be one with a divine being has been a major motif in religions from Christianity to Hinduism. There seems to be a pull, in the religious mindset, towards such a belief. Yet at the same time there is a tug in the opposite direction too. Many people regard such a belief as unjustifiable or incoherent, and none of the many attempts so far made to articulate it philosophically has earned general acceptance as something that is even possible.

Today the push and the pull are both stronger than ever. The growth of both philosophy of mind and cognitive science has developed our understanding of the human mind in ways that just a few decades ago were unthinkable. As ideas from philosophy of mind begin to cross over into philosophy of religion, there is renewed interest in questions about the divine mind, about how it might relate to a human body, and about whether incarnation itself might be articulated with the conceptual tools offered by the current research developments in the philosophy of mind as well as in metaphysics.

The present volume brings together twelve new papers by key thinkers in the debate over the metaphysical possibility of the incarnation, to showcase and advance the new approaches to incarnation that contemporary philosophers of religion are developing today. (As with most treatments of the topic, they assume a Christian context for the doctrine of incarnation, though not necessarily Christian commitment.)

Versions of many of these papers were first presented at an international conference on the metaphysics of incarnation held at the University of Oxford in September 2009. That conference was part of a year-long research project on incarnation on which we collaborated in 2008–9 with funding from the Leverhulme Trust, whom we would like to take this opportunity to thank. We would also like to thank the Analysis Trust, the Aristotelian Society, the John Fell Fund, and the Mind Association for financing the conference.

Anna Marmodoro
Jonathan Hill

Contents

1. Introduction — 1
   Jonathan Hill

2. The humanity of God — 20
   Brian Leftow

3. Compositional christology without Nestorianism — 45
   Oliver D. Crisp

4. Should concretists part with mereological models of the incarnation? — 67
   Thomas P. Flint

5. Drawing on many traditions: an ecumenical kenotic christology — 88
   Thomas Senor

6. The metaphysics of kenosis — 114
   Stephen T. Davis

7. Hylomorphism and the incarnation — 134
   Michael C. Rea

8. The coherence of the Chalcedonian Definition of the incarnation — 153
   Richard Swinburne

9. The incarnation and unity of consciousness — 168
   Joseph Jedwab

10. Vehicle externalism and the metaphysics of the incarnation: a medieval contribution — 186
    Richard Cross

11. The metaphysics of the Extended Mind in ontological entanglements — 205
    Anna Marmodoro

12. Multiple incarnations and distributed persons — 228
    Robin Le Poidevin

References — 242

Index — 251

1

Introduction

Jonathan Hill

At the first ecumenical council of the Christian church, held at Nicaea in AD 325, the assembled bishops agreed on a document which would become known as the 'Symbol' of Nicaea. This brief statement of faith, a modified form of which would later become known as the 'Nicene Creed', said, among other things:

> We believe... in one Lord Jesus Christ, the Son of God, the only-begotten from the Father, that is from the substance of the Father, God from God, light from light, true God from true God... for us humans and for our salvation he came down and became incarnate, became human...[1]

The fathers of Nicaea had much to say about the Son's relation to the Father—but rather less about his relation to human beings. They found two words in the original Greek sufficient to assert that he 'became incarnate, became human' (*sarkothenta kai enanthropesanta*). That claim, that a divine being became human, is the doctrine of the incarnation. And the attempt to unpack these words and understand what they are really saying has been one of the perennial concerns of philosophical theologians ever since. What does the claim that the divine Son 'became human' amount to philosophically? What did that involve? How can we even make sense of the notion of a person who is both divine and human? Metaphysical theories of the incarnation address tough philosophical problems such as these. That is one reason why the debates between proponents of different theories have been so long-lasting—but also why these debates have been proven fruitful and remain worthwhile today.

Those who address these issues operate under certain constraints, which the vast majority of Christian theologians have agreed are important—although they have not agreed about how to express them or about which models

---

[1] In Tanner (1990: I 5).

respect them. First, Christ must be fully and genuinely divine. Second, he must be fully and genuinely human. Third, he must be genuinely a single person. If Christ had not met these conditions, he could not have been a true saviour. They are expressed in the christological 'Definition' laid down by the council of Chalcedon (AD 451) in the doctrine that Christ was a single person with two natures.[2] We may, then, take these constraints as basic to discussions of the metaphysics of incarnation. However, they pull in different directions. Historically, those who have sought to stress the true divinity and also the true humanity of Christ have found it hard to reconcile this with the affirmation that he was really a single person. Taken too far, this tendency may result in Nestorianism, the claim that Christ was two people, one human and one divine.[3] Conversely, those who have stressed the unity of Christ's person have faced difficulties in explaining how he could be both fully human and fully divine. Taken too far, this may result in Eutycheanism, the claim that Christ's divinity swamps his humanity.[4]

TWO PROBLEMS

Most philosophical treatments of the incarnation approach it as a problem—or set of problems—that needs to be resolved if the doctrine is to be rationally defensible. There are a number of such problems associated with incarnation, but the one that is usually taken to be the most pressing is what we might call the incoherence objection.

---

[2] Most discussion of the incarnation since, both medieval and modern, has used that Definition as a starting point. But even non-Chalcedonian theologians, who reject that Definition, have typically done so not because they reject the three constraints summarized above but because they consider that the Definition does not reflect them. For example, Monophysites such as Severus of Antioch (465–538) believed that the Definition's claim that Christ had two natures violated the principle of Christ's unity.

[3] Whether Nestorius himself—after whom the heresy is named—believed such a thing is a matter of debate; certainly he insisted that he did not. On Nestorius, see Wessel (2004) and Evans (2004b); for his own defence against the charge of dividing Christ, see Driver and Hodgson (1925). Nestorianism is sometimes defined as the recognition of two *subjects* within Christ (see, for example, Cross (2009: 452)). This is accurate as long as we mean *personal subjects*. Distinguishing more than one subject within Christ, in the sense of more than one property-bearer, may be orthodox if they are not distinct persons. After all, according to substance dualism, there is more than one subject in me (my mind and my body) in this sense, but they are not both persons; similarly, the human and the divine in Christ could be distinct subjects—and according to compositionalist theories, this is precisely what they are—without being distinct persons. On compositionalism, see below, pp. 12–14.

[4] Again, whether this is what Eutyches himself intended to say is uncertain. On Eutyches, see Frend (1972: 31–3) and Evans (2004b).

The incoherence objection

Divinity, we normally think, involves the possession of certain properties, such as omnipotence, omniscience, moral perfection, eternity, and immutability. Theologians have traditionally thought not only that God has these attributes, but that he has them necessarily: it is impossible for God not to have them, and any individual which does not have them is not God. They are properties that are essential to divinity. Human beings, meanwhile, have limited power and knowledge, are not morally perfect, are trapped within time, and are subject to change. There is good reason for thinking that at least some of these properties are essential to humanity—a being could not lack them and yet still be human. But these two lists of properties are inconsistent, in the sense that a single individual could not possibly instantiate all of them. A single individual cannot, for example, be both temporal and atemporal, or omniscient and yet also limited in knowledge. It seems, then, that a single individual cannot be both fully human and fully divine. But the doctrine of incarnation tells us that Christ *was* fully human and fully divine. That doctrine, then, seems to be incoherent.

Put this way, the problem is a logical or philosophical one, and it is of interest to philosophers beyond the relatively narrow question whether a certain Christian doctrine is coherent. In seeking to answer it, philosophical theologians are addressing not only how we think of God, but how we think of humanity as well. What properties are essential to humanity? What does being human actually mean?

The 'biblical Jesus' problem

There is also a related problem which is theologically rather than philosophically motivated. The New Testament, especially the Synoptic Gospels, presents Jesus as sometimes ignorant, sometimes powerless, and genuinely susceptible to temptation. That suggests that he lacked certain divine properties such as omniscience, omnipotence, and moral infallibility.[5] Considerations such as these have led many writers to see the ascription to Jesus of divine properties such as omniscience and omnipotence as problematic quite apart from any clash such properties may have with essential human properties. So we may say that the source of the incoherence objection is the limitations of *human nature in general* and its apparent inconsistency with the unlimited divine nature; but there is a further problem, which we may dub the 'biblical Jesus'

---

[5] Stephen Davis considers this in more detail in his paper in the present volume. See pp. 125–7.

problem, deriving from the limitations ascribed to *Jesus in particular* in the New Testament and elsewhere. When philosophical theologians offer strategies for explaining how Christ could be both human and divine, we should be careful to recognize which of these two problems they are addressing—for answers to one may not be effective as answers to the other.

LINGUISTIC VERSUS METAPHYSICAL SOLUTIONS

One issue facing philosophical theologians is that of language. When somebody makes a claim about how Christ is constituted, is she speaking ontologically, or only linguistically? Can we even distinguish between these? Take the Definition of Chalcedon itself. According to one interpretation, the bishops at Chalcedon, in articulating this Definition, were trying to describe what Christ was actually like. They were ascribing properties to him. So when they said that Christ is 'acknowledged in two natures which undergo no confusion, no change, no division, no separation',[6] they meant that Christ really exists in two things called 'natures' which have these properties: they were making an ontological assertion, one about how things actually are. And that raises the further question what these 'natures' are supposed to be, and in what way Christ exists 'in' them.

An alternative interpretation, however, holds that the bishops at Chalcedon intended to say no such thing. They were interested not in metaphysics but in religious language, and specifically in what sorts of statements about Christ were or were not permissible. When they made the statement just quoted, they were setting out rules for how one might use the word 'nature' in statements about Christ. As Sarah Coakley, an advocate of this interpretation, puts it, 'the "Definition" is *linguistically regulatory* rather than ontological in intent'.[7] It follows that trying to use the Definition as a sort of blueprint of Christ—as a description of what he is and how he is put together—is to misunderstand its purpose. It is more like an instruction manual for talking about Christ. The question what the Chalcedonian fathers 'meant' by words such as 'nature' doesn't really arise—all that matters is how they judged that these words should be *used*. And a single way of using incarnational language might be compatible with many different metaphysical models of the incarnation.

Similarly, some work on the incarnation has focused on whether, and how, certain linguistic formulations can be legitimate. But to do that is not,

[6] In Tanner (1990: I 86).   [7] Coakley (2002: 144).

necessarily, to offer a metaphysical *model* of the incarnation. We can illustrate this with two common ideas in modern philosophical theology: reduplication and relative identity.

Reduplication

'Reduplication', sometimes known as 'the *qua* move', is a very common idea in the literature on incarnation. It is a strategy intended to answer the incoherence objection, and it finds its roots in the Definition of Chalcedon itself. That Definition states that Christ is:

> ...begotten before the ages from the Father *as regards his divinity*, and in the last days the same for us and for our salvation from Mary, the virgin God-bearer, *as regards his humanity*...[8]

This 'as regards' (*kata*) suggests a way of qualifying the attribution of properties. Rather than simply saying that Christ has property X, we say that he has property X *as* M, where M stands for some category under which Christ falls. As it is sometimes expressed, he has X *qua* M. Similarly, he may have some other property Y *as* N, where N is another category under which he falls. It is not unlike a single individual having different properties—perhaps even contradictory ones—in virtue of playing different roles. For example, a judge hearing a murder case in court may be disinterested in the case *as* a judge who is impartial, even while she is very concerned about the case *as* a member of society. In the case of the statement quoted from Chalcedon, Christ is begotten before the ages *as* divine, and he is begotten within time *as* human. We can expand upon the idea to say, for example, that Christ is omniscient *as* God but has limited knowledge *as* human being, and so on for all of the other apparently contradictory properties. And this, supposedly, avoids the contradiction.

But what does this actually mean? An important advance in recent work on the incarnation has been the recognition that the reduplicative strategy, in itself, operates only at the linguistic level. Thomas Senor has pointed out that reduplicative statements can be interpreted in a number of ways: they may express quite different metaphysical models.[9] First, they could be understood as statements about *why* the subject has that property. Thus, to say that Christ is X *qua* M is to say simply that he is X because he is M, or in virtue of the fact

---

[8] In Tanner (1990: I 86), emphasis mine.
[9] Senor (2002: 229–31). See Cross (2009: 455–7) for still more possible interpretations of reduplicative statements.

that he falls under category M. But in that case the statement 'Christ is omniscient *qua* God' entails 'Christ is omniscient', and the statement 'Christ is not omniscient *qua* human' entails 'Christ is not omniscient'. On this interpretation, then, reduplicative statements will not resolve the apparent contradiction, since they entail statements that are explicitly inconsistent.[10]

Alternatively, reduplicative statements could be understood as modifying the subject of the sentence. So to say that Christ is X *qua* M, and Christ is Y *qua* N, is to say that Christ-*qua*-M is X while Christ-*qua*-N is Y. So we may attribute omniscience to Christ-*qua*-divine and the lack of omniscience to Christ-*qua*-human.[11] Such a strategy does avoid the contradiction, but it involves positing two different subjects in Christ. What is more, these subjects sound very like persons, since knowledge, power, and the other properties which are ascribed to these two subjects (limited in the case of one subject, unlimited in the case of the other) are the sort of properties that are typical of persons. But the belief that there is more than one person in Christ is Nestorianism.

A final alternative is that reduplicative statements could be understood as modifying not the subject but the predicate. So to say that Christ is X *qua* M, and Christ is Y *qua* N, is to say that Christ is X-*qua*-M and that he is also Y-*qua*-N. Here again the contradiction is avoided: omniscience and non-omniscience may be contradictory properties, but omniscience-*qua*-divine and non-omniscience-*qua*-human, it is held, are not. But these properties have an ad hoc feel to them. Moreover, it seems Christ is no longer omniscient *or* non-omniscient: he has instead the rather obscure properties of being omniscient-*qua*-divine and non-omniscient-*qua*-human.

Laying aside for the moment the problems associated with these different interpretations of the reduplicative strategy, the important point is that there *are* such different interpretations. The reduplicative strategy is, in itself, a strategy that operates at the level of language only. It is a way of avoiding ascribing explicitly inconsistent properties to Christ. It is not, in itself, a metaphysical strategy. It does not tell us *how* or *why* Christ avoids having inconsistent properties, or how this is compatible with his being fully divine and fully human. To do that, the defender of the reduplicative strategy must go beyond mere reduplication and into metaphysics, to show why the use of this language is legitimate.

---

[10] See also Morris (1986: 48–9).
[11] This approach is a common one among compositionalists. For more on this, see below, p. 18.

Relative identity

The notion of relative identity is a controversial one in modern metaphysics. According to classical ('absolute') notions of identity, identity statements are governed by the law of excluded middle. Two things are either identical or they are not. Proponents of relative identity, however, deny this. They argue that two things can be identical viewed in one way but non-identical viewed in another. That is, identity is 'sortal relative': it is possible for a and b to be the same F but not the same G.[12] As a result, the principle of the indiscernibility of identicals—according to which, if a and b are identical, then everything that is true of a is true of b, and vice versa—no longer holds. If this is so, then apparently incoherent theological claims may not be incoherent after all. For example, Peter Van Inwagen has argued that the doctrine of the Trinity involves no incoherence, since with the notion of relative identity we can say that the Father, Son, and Holy Spirit are the same God but different persons.[13] He has applied the same reasoning to the incarnation, suggesting that we can say that God the Son and Jesus of Nazareth are different beings but the same person. God the Son possesses the 'divine' properties that we wish to ascribe to Christ, and Jesus of Nazareth possesses the 'human' properties; since they are different beings, no contradiction between these sets of properties arises; but since they are the same person, no doctrinal problems arise either.[14]

The notion of relative identity is not a popular one among philosophers, and consequently this solution to the incoherence problem is not popular either. Once again, however, I suggest that the relative identity solution is not really a *metaphysical* model of the incarnation at all. Van Inwagen himself states that his aim is not 'to have penetrated the mystery of the Incarnation, but at most to have shown that that doctrine can be stated without formal contradiction'.[15] The defence involves showing that certain statements about Christ form a consistent set. It does not—in itself—involve showing what things would have to be true of Christ and the way he is constituted *for* those statements all to be true.

---

[12] The notion of relative identity has been defended by Peter Geach (1967–8: 3–11) and Nicholas Griffin (1977), and attacked by David Wiggins (1980: 15–44). For more, see Robin Le Poidevin's paper in this volume, pp. 234–5.
[13] See Van Inwagen (1988) and Swinburne (1994: 187–8).
[14] Van Inwagen (1994: 214–26).
[15] Van Inwagen (1994: 202).

TRANSFORMATIONALIST MODELS

Ever since the twelfth century, when Peter Lombard offered an analysis of what he regarded as the three major available models, philosophical theologians have tried to sort the available models by category and assess the strengths and weaknesses of each kind of approach.[16] One helpful way of doing so is to consider what proponents of the different models conceive 'becoming human' to involve. Philosophical theologians have given two main answers to this, and we can accordingly distinguish between two main groups of models of the incarnation.[17]

The first answer is straightforward: to *become human* means being *transformed into a human*. The Son is, to start with, a divine person, not a human one. At the incarnation, he is transformed into a human being—just as a caterpillar becomes a butterfly by being transformed into one. We may define 'transformation' in this context, roughly, as a process in which a single subject loses some properties (e.g. certain properties associated with being a caterpillar, such as being flightless) and acquires new properties (e.g. certain properties associated with being a butterfly, such as having the power of flight). An orthodox theologian will hold that the analogy is imperfect: when a caterpillar becomes a butterfly, it ceases to be a caterpillar, but when the Son becomes a human being, he does not cease to be a divine person. Nevertheless, the notion of transformation itself is similar; and defenders of this kind of model of the incarnation—which we may call the 'transformational' model—devote much effort to explaining what is involved in the transformation that becoming incarnate consists in.

Physicalist transformational models

Perhaps the paradigmatic transformational model is that of Trenton Merricks, who bases his model of the incarnation upon the physicalist claim that every human being is identical with his or her body. To become human, then, the Son needs simply to become a (living) human body.[18] So for Merricks, the

---

[16] For Lombard's discussion, see Rosemann (2004: 126–9).

[17] The major distinction I suggest here, between 'transformationalist' and 'relational' models, corresponds to the distinction that Anna Marmodoro and I have made between 'identity' and 'relational' models. See Marmodoro and Hill (2009).

[18] Merricks's reasoning also depends, in part, upon the premise that for the Son to become genuinely human he must bear the same relation to his body as we do to ours. Since we are identical to our bodies, the Son must also be identical to his; see Merricks (2007: 294). Brian

incarnation involves the incorporeal Son literally being transformed into a living human body.[19] While straightforward, Merricks's account has come under heavy fire, partly on the grounds that it is questionable whether the transformation of an incorporeal entity into a corporeal one is even conceivable.[20] The most extreme version of this kind of christology is that of Thomas Altizer, which became well known as part of the 'death of God' movement of the 1960s. According to Altizer, the incarnation involved God being transformed into a human being and losing all of his divine properties. Jesus consequently was a mere human, and no longer God, although he had the unusual property of having once been God. When he died, that was the end of the story, meaning that there once was a God, but now there is none.[21]

Dualist transformational models

An alternative kind of transformational model avoids some of the problems raised by the above account, by rejecting its physicalist premise. Defenders of this kind of model hold some form of substance dualism, according to which I am identical either with (a) my mind, or with (b) the combination of my mind and my body. For the Son to become human, then, means being transformed not into a human body but into a human mind, which is embodied *in* a human body. Effectively, the divine Son takes the place in Christ that would normally be taken by an ordinary human mind. On the first version of substance dualism just mentioned, the Son becomes identical with Christ's mind. On the second, the Son becomes identical with the combination of Christ's mind and his body. Models of this general kind appear to have been common in the fourth century, being most associated with Apollinarius of Laodicea, who was eventually condemned on the grounds that if Christ's

---

Leftow questions this premise in his paper in this volume. One may add that an orthodox Christian is surely committed to the view that the Son's relation to his body is not identical in every respect to the relation other humans bear to their body, since orthodoxy holds both that the Son existed before his body did and that other humans do not exist before their bodies do. If the Son's relation to his body can differ from ours in that respect without jeopardizing his true humanity, why not in other respects too? As noted below, compositionalists are committed to the claim that the Son's relation to not only his human body but also his human mind is not identical to the relation between us and our bodies and minds. See below, n. 24.

[19] See Merricks (2007: 294–9).
[20] One argument for this is that if something is incorporeal, it is *essentially* incorporeal, and if it is corporeal, it is *essentially* corporeal; it cannot change from one to the other while retaining its identity. See Anna Marmodoro's paper in this volume, pp. 213–16.
[21] See Altizer (1966: 69).

human soul was simply displaced by the Son, then he had no human soul and was thus not fully human.[22]

In modern times, a model similar to this, in which the divine Son animates a human body, is most associated with Richard Swinburne. He rejects the criticism of Apollinarianism by holding that, in Christ, the Son does not *replace* the human mind—the Son *is* a human mind, in virtue of (a) being related to a human body in the ordinary way, and (b) having a human stream of consciousness in addition to a divine one. Christ's true humanity is therefore not threatened.[23] On this view, incarnation is partly a matter of transformation (the Son *is changed into* a human mind), but it is also a matter of acquisition (the Son *acquires* a human body—he is not transformed into one), so we could see Swinburne's model as partly transformationalist and partly relational.

RELATIONAL MODELS

Models of the incarnation of the second major category explain incarnation *wholly* in terms of acquisition. For defenders of these models, *becoming human* doesn't mean being *transformed* into a human being at all; rather, it means entering into a certain kind of relationship with a human being—or, rather, with something that would have been a human being had it not been in such a relationship. What the Son acquires, on this model, is not simply a body (as on Swinburne's model), but a composite of body and mind.

We can put the difference between the two major kinds of model simply like this. There are many rival accounts of what it is to be a human being—physicalism, dualism, and so on. Suppose we ignore all these differences and say that an ordinary human being consists of X—where X may stand for a human body (for physicalists), a body–mind composite (for dualists), and so on for other accounts. Transformationalists hold that, in the incarnation, the Son *was transformed into* X; if he himself were not identical with X, then he could not really be said to be human, because *to be human is to be X*. Relationalists, by contrast, hold that, in the incarnation, the Son *became related to* X. On this view, ordinary humans are human in virtue of *being* X,

---

[22] For Apollinarius' texts, see Norris (1980: 103–11). For the prevalence of this kind of model in the fourth century, see Hanson (1985). I use the terms 'mind' and 'soul' interchangeably in this context, as is customary in discussions of this topic. Strictly speaking they are not synonymous, but it is generally assumed that, for reasons of simplicity, they may be treated as such in the present context.

[23] See Swinburne (1994: 192–200), as well as his paper in the present volume, pp. 153–67.

but it is not actually necessary to be X to count as human. It is sufficient to be related, in a sufficiently close way, to X. For example, suppose that X is a human body and a human soul, and that ordinary human beings are human because they consist of a human body and a human soul. A relationist might say that, to be human, it is sufficient to *have* a human body and a human soul. Being *identical with* a human body and soul is one way of having a human body and soul, but it is not the only way. When the Son became human, that meant that he acquired a human body and a human soul, to the extent that they were genuinely his, but he was not transformed into them.[24]

Concretism and abstractism

Defenders of relational models often speak in terms of the Son acquiring a *nature*. Such language takes 'nature' to mean a particular thing. On this conception, *my* human nature is distinct from *your* human nature.[25] However, an alternative definition of 'nature' exists, on which it is a set of essential properties. On this conception, a 'nature' is a universal, so *my* human nature is identical with *your* human nature. It is usual, in contemporary writing on the incarnation, to call the former understanding of 'nature' 'concretism', and the latter 'abstractism'.[26] The distinction between the two uses of the word 'nature' is also often taken to go hand in hand with the distinction between relational and transformationalist models. That is, defenders of relational models are typically concretists (they think that Christ acquired a second nature by entering into a relation with a concrete particular, because natures *are* concrete particulars), while defenders of transformational models are typically abstractists (they think that Christ acquired a second nature by

---

[24] Relationists are thus committed to the view that Christ is not related to his X in the same way that we are to ours, since he is not exhaustively composed of X, whereas we are. So on this view, being exhaustively composed of X is presumably a property of all *mere* humans, but it is not an essential human property.

[25] There are, furthermore, two ways in which 'nature' can be understood as a particular. The first is as a particular instance of a set of properties. For example, if I am 5'10 and you are also 5'10, then we can distinguish between *my* property of being 5'10 and *your* property of being 5'10. Particular properties of this kind are normally called 'tropes'. We could understand my human nature as a trope, or set of tropes, distinct from your human nature in this way. On this, see Cross (2009: 458–9). The second way in which 'nature' can be understood as a particular is as a *concrete individual*, something which instantiates a trope or set of tropes. On this view, my human nature is simply my X, and your human nature is simply your X. In discussions of the incarnation, when Christ's human nature is understood as a particular, it is usually this second way that is meant.

[26] The 'abstractist'/'concretist' distinction, as well as the associated terminology, was first suggested by Alvin Plantinga. See Plantinga (1999: 183–4), and also Leftow (2002: 277–9).

acquiring a set of essential properties, because natures *are* sets of essential properties). Thus, 'concretist' is sometimes used as a synonym for 'relational'.[27] Within a Chalcedonian context—where everyone accepts that Christ had two natures—this is legitimate. However, the existence of non-Chalcedonian christology means that it does not always hold. For example, someone might think that Christ became human by entering into a relation with a human X, but deny that that human X should be considered a 'nature'.[28]

Prophetic models

The most extreme relationist model is one where X is conceived as a quite distinct person from the Son. On this view Christ is not an integrated person at all, but just the divine Son and a human being operating closely with each other. The prophetic model, attributed to some ancient theologians, might fall into this category. On this model, Jesus was a human being who was inspired by God all the time: God spoke through him, as he also spoke through the Old Testament prophets. The only difference was that Jesus was in this relation to God permanently, while the prophets enjoyed it only at certain times.

Such a model holds that Jesus and the Son remain distinct beings—indeed, distinct persons—and as such it violates the constraint we saw earlier, that any viable christology needs to accommodate the claim that, in Christ, divinity and humanity are genuinely united.

Compositionalist models

A better kind of relational model is the kind often referred to as 'compositionalist'. On this view, the incarnate Christ is a genuine unity, but a composite one, just as the human body itself is genuinely a single thing, but with parts.[29] Different compositionalists offer different accounts of what, precisely, is a part of what in the case of Christ. On one version, Christ has two main parts, (a) the divine Son, and (b) the human Jesus. Jesus himself may be

---

[27] Thomas Flint uses it in this sense in his paper in the present volume.
[28] The Monophysite theologian Severus of Antioch held this view. On Severus, see Torrance (1988).
[29] It is important to note that although compositionalists generally speak of the 'parts' or 'components' of Christ, they do not necessarily mean this language literally. We may thus divide compositionalist models into 'mereological' models—which take the relation of divine and human to Christ to be literally that of parts to whole—and 'non-mereological' models, which do not. See Thomas Flint's comments in his paper in the present volume, pp. 52–6.

subdivided into a human body and a human soul or mind, in which case Christ has three parts—the Son, a human mind, and a human body. So when he becomes incarnate, the Son becomes a proper part of a greater whole, namely Christ.[30] Alternatively, some compositionalists prefer to think in terms not of the Son joining with the human mind and the human body *as parts of a larger whole*, but rather in terms of the Son acquiring the human mind and the human body *as parts of himself*. It is rather like if I put on weight. On Monday I consist of a certain quantity of matter.[31] By Friday, having enjoyed a number of generous dinners in the intervening time, I consist of that same quantity, plus some additional matter. But the person who exists on Friday is not some new composite person, made of me plus some fat. He is identical to *me*, the same person who existed on Monday; all that has happened is that that same person has now acquired some parts that he did not have before. In the same way, compositionalists who conceive of the incarnation in similar terms to growth hold that the Son is identical to the composite Christ, because on becoming incarnate the Son acquires parts rather than becoming part of a greater whole.[32]

Whatever version of the model they adopt, compositionalists who wish to remain orthodox will stress that Jesus—the human 'part' of Christ—is not, in himself, a person, even though he may have the full complement of parts or faculties that other people have. Perhaps he *would* have been a person if he had never become part of the composite Christ, but as it is, there is only one person in the composite Christ, and that is the Son, whether the Son is identified with the composite Christ or not.

Compositionalist models and relations

A question that quickly arises for any compositionalist model is this: if the Son can be legitimately said to be human in virtue of existing in a certain relation to a human X, what is this relation? Compositionalists have offered a

---

[30] In his paper in the present volume, Thomas Flint calls this model 'Model A': see pp. 79–82. In their papers, Brian Leftow and Oliver Crisp both defend it, the latter under the name of 'the Habitus model'.

[31] Or, if we reject physicalism, *my body* consists of a certain quantity of matter—and in what follows, substitute 'my body' for 'I'. The analogy is the same whatever relation we think holds between me and my body.

[32] This is the version of compositionalism which, in his paper in the present volume, Thomas Flint dubs 'Model T'. See below, pp. 71–2. Note, however, that some writers take 'compositionalism' to involve the claim that the Son is a proper part of Christ, which would imply Flint's 'Model A' and preclude 'Model T' as a version of compositionalism at all. See, for example, Thomas Senor's paper in the present volume, pp. 95–8.

number of answers. An ancient and popular analogy is that of body and soul in a normal human being. Just as I—according to substance dualism—consist of two distinct concrete entities, namely a body and a soul, and yet I am a single person, so too Christ consists of two distinct concrete entities, namely the Son and a human X, and yet is a single person. Even if we accept the analogy, though, it does not tell us very much unless we can spell out in more detail what it is about the relation between my soul and my body which makes it legitimate to call *me* a single person. One possible answer is that my body can be considered the instrument of my soul: I perform actions in the world *with* my body, and this is what makes it *my* body. Thomas Aquinas offers a similar analysis of the relation between the parts of Christ: the Son, during the incarnation, acts on the world *with* the human body and the human soul, and this is why they are *his* body and soul.[33] However, if I use an axe to chop wood, I do not thereby become an axe myself; if the Son bears a similar relation to a human X, that would not make him human either. Moreover, to be human involves, among other things, having agency. The third council of Constantinople (AD 680–1) recognized this when it decreed that Christ had a human will as well as a divine one, for otherwise he would not really be human. But if Christ's human body and soul are the instrument of his divine mind, it is hard to explain how they can be said to have any will or agency of their own. They constitute just a sort of puppet which the Son controls, and that brings us back to something like Apollinarianism, because although on this model there is a human mind distinct from the divine one, it is not a *complete* human mind.[34]

Two-mind models

Considerations such as these have traditionally led compositionalists to stress that Christ had two minds. When he became incarnate, the Son acquired not simply a human body, but a human mind as well, which remained distinct from his divine mind. Indeed, the reasoning that, without a distinct human mind, Christ could not have been truly human, has been especially prominent in recent philosophical theology, and has led some non-compositionalists, such as Thomas Morris and Richard Swinburne, to hold that Christ had either two minds or two streams of consciousness. However, some theologians have rejected the two-minds theory, on the grounds that it inevitably leads to Nestorianism. If Christ had two minds, he was simply two people.[35]

---

[33] See *Summa contra gentiles* IV, ch. 39, 9–12, in O'Neil (1975: 196–7).
[34] On this issue, see White (2008).
[35] For more on this objection, together with an analysis of the history of the two-minds doctrine, see Hanson (1984). See also Joseph Jedwab's paper in the present volume, pp. 178–80.

An important task of those who hold the two-mind theory, then, is to explain what the relation is between the two minds.[36] In particular, it must be shown how the two minds constitute only a single person, and not two distinct people sharing a body. Joseph Jedwab analyses this problem in his paper in the present volume.

STRENGTHS AND WEAKNESSES

At first glance, transformationalist models seem to have the edge over relational ones. The notion that becoming human involves being transformed into whatever X human beings consist of is more intuitive than the notion that it involves only entering into a relation with such an X. After all, a caterpillar that sits on the back of a butterfly does not thereby become a butterfly itself—in order to become a butterfly it must be transformed into one. Moreover, transformationalist models easily make sense of the Nicene claim that it was *the Son* who came to earth and was incarnate as Jesus. There is a strong Christian intuition that the human individual who walked in Galilee was identical with the divine Son, to the extent that someone could legitimately point to that human being and say 'Look, *here is* the Lamb of God!' (John 1: 36, NRSV, my italics).

Incarnation without change

So it is perhaps surprising to find that relational models—and, more precisely, compositionalist models—have been dominant, both in the history of Christian theology and among philosophical theologians today. There are a number of reasons for the dominance of compositionalism. One, which ancient and medieval theologians found especially compelling, is that compositionalist models explain how a divine person could become human without changing. Normally, for something to *become* anything involves change, the loss of some properties and the acquisition of others; but traditionally, Christian theologians have been committed to the notion that an essential property of God is his changelessness. Accordingly, some account had to be

---

[36] For a debate on the viability of some of the relations that have been proposed, see Bayne (2001), Sturch (2003), and Bayne (2003).

found which allowed the Son to become human and yet not change. Compositionalism provides such an account, since it explains the Son's becoming human in terms of entering into certain relations with a human body and soul. On at least some metaphysical accounts of the nature of relations, it is possible for at least some of one's relations to change without experiencing change *in oneself* (e.g., if Peter is taller than Paul, and Paul subsequently grows taller than Peter, Peter's relation to Paul changes without Peter himself really changing at all), and this, according to classical compositionalism, is what happened at the incarnation.[37]

Transformationalist models and the incoherence objection

A second reason why compositionalist accounts have been favoured, especially by more recent theologians, is that they offer a possible solution to the major problem we have already identified, the apparent incompatibility of divinity and humanity. Transformationalist models hold that there is only a single subject in Christ: the divine Son, who has become human. This one subject, then, must bear all the essential divine properties and also all the essential human ones, with the problems outlined above. Those who defend largely transformationalist models have adopted various strategies to address this. One, defended by Thomas Morris, is to argue that in fact there is (or may be) no contradiction between the essential divine properties and the essential human ones, because we simply do not know what the essential human properties are. It may be true, for example, that no mere human being has ever enjoyed unlimited power and knowledge, but it doesn't follow from that that no human being *could* have these properties—any more than the fact that no human being has ever been born on Mars means that anyone who, in the future, is born on Mars isn't human. So perhaps Christ could have all the essential divine properties of omnipotence, omniscience, and the rest, and lack what we think of as the human counterparts of limited power, limited knowledge, and so on, and yet still be fully human. He just wouldn't be *merely human*—but that is no more than orthodoxy requires.[38]

However, even if this takes care of the incoherence objection, it does not address the 'biblical Jesus' problem. As we have seen, many people find a problem with saying that Jesus was omniscient, omnipotent, and so on quite

---

[37] For example, Cyril of Alexandria, Nestorius' antagonist and a huge influence on subsequent Chalcedonian and Monophysite christology alike, suggests such an argument for compositionalism. See Russell (2000: 263, 268, 347).

[38] See Morris (1986: 66).

apart from any formal contradiction there may be between bearing these properties and being human. Some have therefore felt that even if Morris' strategy can overcome the incoherence problem, it does so at the price of making Christ unsympathetic and not *meaningfully* human.[39]

Other varieties of transformationalist models seek to overcome these problems by simply denying that Christ has all of the essential divine and human properties. There are two ways one could do this. The first is to say that Christ has all the divine properties, but lacks those human ones that conflict with them. However, not only does this not address the 'biblical Jesus' problem, it is Eutycheanism or even docetism (the heretical doctrine that Christ only appeared human).

Kenotic models

The second strategy is much more promising, which is to hold that Christ had all of the essential *human* properties, but not all of the essential divine ones. This is the 'kenotic' model of the incarnation, which has been popular ever since Gottfried Thomasius first explicitly formulated it in the nineteenth century.[40] On this model, the Son initially has all of the properties that are essential to divinity. Upon becoming incarnate, he acquires all of the properties that are essential to humanity, and in the process loses some of those that are essential to divinity. For example, he acquires the property of having limited knowledge, and in so doing loses the property of having unlimited knowledge. This strategy has proved popular because it addresses the 'biblical Jesus' problem as well as the incoherence objection. However, there is no single kenotic model of the incarnation. Although kenoticism may be a feature of transformationalist models,[41] it is also possible to construct a kenotic compositionalist model, as both Stephen Davis and Thomas Senor do—in different ways—in their papers in the present volume. On such a model, there are two subjects within Christ—the divine nature and the human one—but one of the conditions of becoming part of the composite Christ is that the divine Son loses certain of his properties, something that classical compositionalists deny.

But a common criticism of kenotic models is that they have difficulty explaining how the incarnate Christ can really count as divine if he lacks essential divine properties.[42] One possible answer is that although the Son

---

[39] See, for example, Thomas Senor's paper in the present volume, pp. 90–1.
[40] For Thomasius' presentation of the idea, see Welch (1965: 40–9). For more on kenosis, see Evans (2006b).
[41] Charles Gore, another important early kenoticist, offers what seems to be a transformationalist kenotic model. See Gore (1896: 157–62).
[42] For a detailed examination of the major objections to kenoticism, and some possible answers, see Forrest (2000).

loses (say) the property of *being omniscient*, he retains the property of *being omniscient unless restricted by being incarnate*, and it is the latter property, not the former, which is an essential divine property.[43] An alternative answer is to accept that the incarnate Christ does lack essential divine properties, but still counts as divine in a secondary sort of sense because he *was* divine—rather as former US presidents are still addressed as 'Mr President' despite no longer having the powers of office. A variation on this defence is to suggest that we are to think of divinity as a name that denotes, not as a kind. 'God', or perhaps 'the Son', does not mean a being who instantiates certain properties that are essential to divinity; rather, it names a particular individual. So the Son remains the Son, and remains God, no matter what properties he instantiates.

Compositionalist models and the incoherence objection

Compositionalist models, however, offer an alternative solution to the incoherence problem which some theologians have felt is easier to reconcile with orthodoxy. If there is a divine 'part' to Christ (the Son) and also a human 'part' (the X, e.g. a human body and a human mind), then we can attribute the divine properties to the former and the human ones to the latter. Since no single subject has both sets, there is no contradiction. Each set of properties can be attributed to Christ as a whole derivatively. Thus, Christ has perfect knowledge (because part of him, the Son, has perfect knowledge) and Christ also has imperfect knowledge (because part of him, Jesus, has imperfect knowledge), in the same way that a zebra is both black and white. This is how a compositionalist can make sense of the reduplicative attributions that we looked at earlier.[44]

Problems for compositionalists

But compositionalism faces problems too. On at least some versions, the Son is *not* identical with Christ—the Son is only a part of Christ. It appears to follow, then, that the person who walked and talked in Galilee was not the divine Son at all. He was only part of the Son; or, even worse, he was a part of the composite Christ, which also has the Son as another part, in which case

---

[43] See Morris (1986: 75).
[44] Eleonore Stump argues for this understanding of reduplicative attributions. See Stump (2003: 412–15).

Jesus wasn't the Son at all. The compositionalist must explain how John the Baptist could legitimately point to Jesus and identify him with the Son. An even more serious problem for compositionalism, and one which compositionalists have devoted much time to addressing, is that if Christ contains, in addition to the Son, an X (e.g. a human body and a human soul), and if in the normal run of things a human person just is an X, then it seems to follow that Christ contains, in addition to the Son, a human person. But that is Nestorianism, since it entails that Christ contained two persons, the Son and a distinct human being.

CONCLUSION

What I have sketched here is a bird's-eye view of the contours of debate concerning the metaphysics of the incarnation, setting out the major features on the map. The rest of the contributions to this volume offer more detailed surveys of some of these features. Brian Leftow, Oliver Crisp, and Thomas Flint all consider compositionalism and seek to defend it from some of the criticisms it has faced. Thomas Senor and Stephen Davis examine kenoticism, with the same goal. Michael Rea and Richard Swinburne offer broadly transformational models, the former using neo-Aristotelian metaphysics, the latter focusing on the question of Christ's divided mind. Joseph Jedwab takes up that question by considering what relation would hold between Christ's two consciousnesses, on a divided-mind model. Richard Cross looks at some of the relations that, in medieval philosophy, were held to obtain between the components of Christ on a compositionalist model. Anna Marmodoro proposes a new way of understanding these relations, using insights from a contemporary theory of the mind known as the Extended Mind hypothesis: high degrees of interdependence between the mind and its extensions onto external vehicles (and, by analogy, between God the Son and Jesus) give rise to ontological entanglements, with respect to which there is at present no theory of individuation which can tell us how many entities there are in the entanglement and what type of entity the entanglement is. And finally, Robin Le Poidevin considers a question facing all metaphysical models of the incarnation: is there any logical proscription upon a divine person's being incarnate more than once?

2

The humanity of God

Brian Leftow

One central claim of orthodox Christianity is that in Jesus of Nazareth, God became man. Chalcedonian orthodoxy has it that this involves one person, God the Son, having two natures, divine and human. If he does, one person has two properties, deity and humanity. But the incarnation also involves concrete objects: God the Son (GS), i.e. the second person of the Trinity, a human body (B), and (if there are such) a human soul (S). If God becomes man, these somehow become one thing. One question we can ask about the incarnation is what metaphysical account to give of their oneness. There are, I think, eight main options, if we keep the identity relation classical. They are that

1. GS = B,[1]
2. GS = S,[2]
3. GS = B+S,[3]
4. B constitutes but is not identical with GS,[4]
5. S constitutes but is not identical with GS,
6. B+S constitutes but is not identical with GS,
7. B+S became part of GS,[5] or
8. GS, B, and S came to compose one thing, but B+S did not become part of GS.

(1)–(3) are best understood as statements of cross-time identity:[6] there is one thing, GS, which at a particular point in its career became a physical object (B) or

---

[1] So Merricks (2007: 281–300).   [2] So Jedwab (2008).
[3] So Cross (2003: 306 n. 24).
[4] Michael Rea's paper in this volume gives a version of this, pp. 134–52.
[5] This is the view of Aquinas in at least some texts. For his evolving views, see Cross (2002: 52–64).
[6] As (1) and (3) involve intrinsic change in (GS), they require that GS is temporal, and so literal cross-time identity is appropriate. I am unclear whether one could so develop (2) as to be compatible with divine timelessness, but in fact everyone to whom I can confidently assign this view is a temporalist, and so would also accept that cross-time identity applies.

a body–soul composite (B+S). Just what the relation of constitution in (4)–(6) is has been controversial.⁷ On many accounts it is a close relative of identity.⁸ (7) and (8) do not say what the relations *are* in virtue of which these composition claims are true. Traditional christology is often content to leave these relations—those of hypostatic union—a mystery. If composition is restricted—i.e. if not every group of particulars exhaustively composes another particular—all we need say to explicate (7) and (8) is that there are some such relations. But if composition is universal—i.e. if every group of particulars exhaustively composes another particular—we must say more. For if composition is universal, GS, my left foot, and your nose exhaustively compose one thing, and if exhaustively composing one thing sufficed for an incarnation, GS would be incarnate in my left foot and your nose. So if composition is universal, (7) and (8) must add that only composition in virtue of hypostatic-union relations generates an incarnation.⁹

(1)–(8) sort into two broad classes. (1) says that in the incarnation, GS became a material object, (4) that GS became an object wholly constituted by matter. (3) and (7) say that GS became a partly material object, (6) that he became one partly constituted by matter. So we can call these materialist christologies. On (2), GS became a soul. On (5), GS became an object wholly constituted by a soul. On (8), I soon suggest, GS became relevantly like a soul. So we can call these dualist christologies.

To me, materialist christologies are non-starters. My intuitions say that (1) is flatly impossible. How could an immaterial thing become material? How could something relevantly like a soul became something relevantly like a stone? The answer seems to me, 'it couldn't'.¹⁰ But the rest do not differ significantly from (1) in the relevant respect: if it seems impossible that an

---

⁷ For the main alternatives, see Rea (1997). ⁸ See Rea (1997).

⁹ The relations of hypostatic union, whatever they are, are by definition whatever those relations are in virtue of which GS, B, and S compose one thing given restricted composition. In other words, given restricted composition, it is not an option that GS, B, and S compose something other than by hypostatic union. If composition is universal, then there are at least two (sets of?) relations in virtue of which GS, B, and S exhaustively compose one thing, bare mereological summation and hypostatic union.

¹⁰ Which is not to say that there are not metaphysical frameworks within which it seems to make sense (here I'm indebted to Hud Hudson). Suppose we assume eternalism (that all of time, past, present, and future, exists), four-dimensionalism (some objects are wholes composed *inter alia* of temporal parts), and universalism about composition. Then among other composites spread across time (and the realm of the timeless, if such there be) there will be many involving temporal parts (or the atemporal whole) of God the Son and temporal parts of various material objects, and some of these, one could hold, are truthmakers for talk of GS becoming material. But if we do not hold these three views, it is hard to believe that there are such things. I think that if the three views jointly generate them, that is reason not to conjoin those views.

immaterial thing become entirely material, it is no easier to see how one could become even partly material.

On the other hand, dualism comes in two main sorts, and the dualist christologies are most like what most will consider the less plausible sort. A view of human beings is dualist if it holds that the natural human endowment includes an immaterial particular, a soul. One sort of dualism holds that the bearer of the properties *being human* and *being a person* is the body-soul composite. Another sort, which we can call Platonist, holds that the bearer is the soul, the body being that by relation to which an immaterial person counts as human. On any orthodox view, Jesus' tokens of 'I' refer to GS. 'I' always refers to a person. Thus if GS remains immaterial in the incarnation, the referent is an immaterial person, as in Platonism. In the incarnation, the person GS becomes a human being. So if GS remains immaterial in the incarnation, this immaterial person must be the subject of the property of being human, again as in Platonism. Thus if Christians find materialist christology objectionable, they must cultivate a soft spot for Platonism. Even if they do not accept that Platonism is the truth about human beings who are not also incarnate deities, they must hold that as a theory about humans in general, Platonism is intelligible and at least somewhat credible—else they risk conceding that the incarnation is most like something unintelligible or non-credible.

Both broad metaphysical options for an orthodox christology are a bit unpalatable. But had it not actually happened, we would not have thought that God *could* become human, so it is not surprising if his doing so involves something we would not have thought true otherwise. As I've indicated, christological materialism does not seem possible to me, though my full reasons for this must await another occasion, and as Sherlock Holmes used to say, begin by eliminating the impossible. Then what is left, however unlikely, must be the truth. I have plumped for a version of (8) elsewhere.[11] On (8), while B and S are joined to GS, they do not become part of GS. GS does not come to consist of hands, feet, etc. Rather, GS has hands, feet, etc. grafted on. We usually think we consist entirely of human parts; GS consists of no human parts, but instead forms a whole with them. I claim that despite this apparent metaphysical difference, on (8), GS comes out fully human, and so (8) is orthodox. Some recent critics demur. Richard Cross, for instance, suggests that on my view, '[i]t is hard to see how the second person of the Trinity could be the subject of human attributes'.[12]

---

[11] Leftow (2002: 273–99).   [12] Cross (2009: 461–2).

Here I want to defend the claim that on (8), GS is fully human. I first suggest this by an analogous science-fiction story. I then offer a partial defence of the Platonist account of human beings. (8) can seem unorthodox in a different way, falling prey to the Nestorian heresy. I show that this does not follow. I next take up two abstract challenges to GS's humanity raised by Trenton Merricks. Finally, I deal with some specific, theologically important human attributes (8) lets GS have.

TRULY HUMAN?

On my account, the Word becomes flesh by having flesh grafted on. So here's a grafting story. Suppose that as some argue, personal identity follows identity of brainstem: I exist just if my brainstem exists, and wherever it goes, I am. Suppose too that there is no soul—we are purely material things. Suppose finally that my brain was grown in a vat. A brain so produced is a human brain; it might be an intrinsic duplicate of a human brain produced in the normal way. It may be or constitute a person if it supports a suitable psychology. On the brainstem account of personal identity we are now assuming, it is or constitutes a person if it contains a sufficiently developed brainstem. Because it includes *my* brainstem, *I* was produced as a brain in a vat.

A brain so produced is not on its own a human being. It is just a human body-part, as a hand produced on its own would be; so too a zygote is not a man, though it is not a body-part. In each case the reason is the same: too much of the human natural endowment has never been attached to or part of the thing.[13] The brain is biologically suited to be part of a human, but this does not make it a human being: so too, an engine sitting in a crate is structurally suited to be part of a car, but this does not make it a car. The brain is not biologically suited to grow into a human. Brains don't grow arms, legs, etc. Rather, the bodies they are normally part of do. There are in my case

---

[13] Perhaps there is symmetry here: perhaps if I begin as a brain I begin non-human, and trimming me down to a brain would make me cease to be human. If not, then temporal direction matters. That is, it is not simply lacking so much standard human equipment that entails not being a man: it matters whether one has ever had it. In this case, I submit, it is never having had or been attached to these parts that is incompatible with being a human being. If first I am a man, then I am trimmed down to just a brain, I remain a man—just one horribly disfigured. A regiment survives if even a single member makes it through a battle alive, but not if all that is left of it is one soldier's severed leg: sometimes a small part is enough to preserve identity under the original item's kind, as long as it is the right small part. Again, there are properties one can gain but not lose while one still exists (e.g. having been born in Brooklyn). Perhaps humanity is one of these.

no other bits to grow into the rest of a human. The brain's DNA is DNA that would have yielded a human in normal development circumstances, but this is not enough to make it a human being—again, a zygote is not yet a human being. A brain grown on its own from human DNA will not naturally be anything other than a brain.

So produced, then, I am at least initially a brain, not a man. I take it that the brain is a three-dimensional object persisting through time, not a 4D whole of temporal parts. The simplest assumption is that in the vat, I am identical with a brain, rather than being distinct from, constituted by, and spatially coincident with it. These assumptions are not wholly innocent in the present context; they help to make the example I develop more like (8) in relevant respects. But they have independent support and can fairly claim to be what common sense starts out wanting to say.

As the mad scientist grew my brain, he also impregnated a woman with genetically identical sperm, and so grew a human body. He removed what would have developed into a brain, though, substituting for its function in the developing fetus artificially. When both were sufficiently developed, he grafted fetal-brain me into the body. Once grafted into the body, I submit, I was no longer just a brain: I became a man. I had hands to grip with, feet to walk with, lungs to breathe with, and nerves and blood vessels that joined the brain seamlessly to the rest: everything true of humans beginning life in the normal way became true of me. I became a man because I became in the right way part of a composite containing what I had lacked of the full requisites for manhood. As I became a man in the woman's womb, spent the next (say) eight months there, and she gave me birth, she is my mother.

On (8), the Son is grafted onto B+S at conception. He thereby becomes in the right way part of a composite containing what he had lacked of the full requisites for manhood. So the Son is a man too, and Mary was his mother. This is my story about the Son's humanity in broad outline.

In the sci-fi case, I am a brain initially, but I become a man by embodiment. We may incline to say that the body's parts become my parts: I become a man, and so (we think) I consist of all the man's parts. So viewed, the case resembles (7) more than (8). But this is not the only way to look at it. If a male human is a brain, he consists of all the man's parts, but the man's parts do not include the parts of what embodies him. So if I am a brain, that I consist of all the man's parts does not entail that I consist of the entire composite. We might think that I become a man because (so to speak) my boundaries expand and come to include the whole composite—so that every part of the composite is part of me. This is a plausible thought, but again, this is not the only way to look at it. If a hand is grown separately and then attached to the rest of a human body, the body does not become part of the hand. Rather, the hand becomes part of the body. I begin as something grown separately and identical with a brain. If this makes me relevantly like a hand, then the body does not become part of me. In the sci-fi story, there are two ways to express what is initially true of me. We might say merely that I am initially a person composed of just the brain's parts. Say only this, and it seems natural that when the body is tacked on, I come to be a person composed of more than the brain's parts. I am a person, so a person's cross-temporal identity conditions are mine, and these do not rule out adding these further parts to what composes me. But we might instead say that what I am includes being a brain—that a brain's cross-temporal identity conditions are mine. If what I am includes being a brain, something becomes part of me just in case it becomes part of a brain. The rest of the body does not become part of the brain, any more than the rest of the body becomes part of the hand. Even if this is the right way to look at it, I submit that when the brain is put into the body, I become human as well as a brain. I am human, but the rest of my body is not part of me. It is instead that by composition with which I become human.

PLATONISM AND THE INCARNATION

Turn me into a soul rather than a brain, and my sci-fi case, viewed the second way, is an isomorph of Platonic dualism. I, the soul, am human, and my body is not part of me, but rather that by composition with which I become human. Platonists are sometimes explicit that it is the soul that bears the property of being human. Plantinga writes that 'I am a dualist: I believe that I and other (living) human beings are immaterial souls.'[14] Again, John Foster writes, 'Although the basic subjects involved in human mentality are wholly non-physical, each (is) intimately linked with a...biological organism...this link...enables the basic subject to qualify as human.'[15] For a person to be human is for it to have a full human natural endowment, which includes a human body. So it is for the Platonist. The Platonist simply has a surprising account of what having the body amounts to. On Platonism, the referent of 'I' is a soul. But it is a pre-analytic datum, not to be withdrawn as a result of metaphysical surprises, that I am a man, not just part of a man. Further, if I am a person, the whole composite including me is not a person. Persons do not have persons as parts. Still further, if I am a human, the whole composite

---

[14] Plantinga (1999: 186). My thanks to Joseph Jedwab for this reference.
[15] Foster (1991: 261–2). Again, my thanks to Joseph Jedwab.

including me is not another human. Humans do not have humans as parts either. Nor is my body on its own a human being. It is just a human body. If dualism is the truth about humans, nothing not including a soul counts as a human being.

On (8), B and S do not become parts of the Son, but still the Son is a man. The Son is not part of a man, but is a man due to other parts of the composite which are his manhood, his concrete human endowment, as a Platonic soul is not part of a human, but is human by being embodied in a body which completes a concrete human endowment. B and S are not parts of the Son, but his composition with them qualifies him as human, even as composition with a body qualifies a Platonist soul as human. If GS is the human, then the composite GS+B+S is not another human: again, humans do not have humans as parts. Nor is B+S on its own a human being, for reasons I develop below. Thomas Flint finds this a stretch:

> ...take an intelligent but theologically-untutored colleague...and ask what in the composite (GS+B+S) is a human being. The most likely response, I think, would be that (B+S) is the human...(the answer) we wouldn't expect...is that (B+S) isn't a human being, and neither is (GS+B+S), but (GS)—the part that's absolutely simple, entirely immaterial, utterly eternal—that and that alone is human.[16]

But so too, given an ordinary composite of soul and body, the untutored would not suppose that the soul is the human. If this is the right answer on Platonism, it is the right answer on (8). If it is intellectually respectable to be a Platonist despite this surprise, it is similarly respectable to hold (8).

Is Platonism respectable?

But *is* Platonism respectable? The claim that an immaterial soul is a human being is a bit hard to swallow. It says on its face that a human is not a material object. It seems to imply that humans lack spatial location, extension, parts and mass, are invisible and intangible, etc. But perhaps these things do not follow or are not the scandals they at first seem.

It is to begin with not clear that any Christian should think that humans are material objects. Christianity sits well with dualism, for Christianity believes in an afterlife, and if there is a soul to carry our identity forward into the afterlife, it is clear how we can survive to enjoy it. It is not as easy to see how materialism can carry our identity into the afterlife. On dualism, again,

---

[16] Comment delivered at 'Logos Workshop', 29 May 2009, University of Notre Dame.

humans are either immaterial or body-soul composites. But body-soul composites are not material objects. If something consists of some material parts and some sets, it is not a material object. If the set example is good, then as sets are immaterial, what consists of some material and some immaterial parts is not a material object. Something consisting of some matter and a soul is relevantly like a thing consisting of some matter and a set. It is at most partly material. So on either form of dualism, humans are not material objects. As our survival is more problematic if we are material objects, then, Christians should be favourably disposed to the claim that humans are not material objects. But if we are body-soul composites, there seems no answer to the question 'How much of us is the soul and how much the body?' If it has no answer, there is no fact of the matter about what proportion of us is material. If we are souls, then, we are zero percent material, but if we are body-soul composites, though we are partly material, no percentage is the percentage of us which is material. So what is true if we are only partly material is (at least to my ear) almost as odd as what is true if we are not material at all. Christians, then, do not have much reason to jib at the latter oddity.

Souls, space, and parts

Souls are immaterial, but not being composed of matter does not obviously entail lacking location and extension: colours are immaterial, but when I see the rose, I see redness, and there is nothing conceptually amiss if I infer from this that redness is where the rose is. It is a tenable view that the soul is located where the body is, or exists where each of its parts do (which gives it a sort of extension): Aquinas held both.[17] The dualist who believes we live in a spacetime universe would do well to hold something nearby. Souls have thoughts successively. So they are in time. If ours is a spacetime universe, whatever is in time is in space. So if ours is a spacetime universe, souls are in space. There seems no more reasonable place for a soul than in its body, and no place in its body seems better suited to this than the whole. Nor does being immaterial entail lacking parts: mathematics has parts including geometry and algebra, and books (which are types of which physical volumes are tokens) have chapters. We ordinarily take it that a human's parts include human body-parts, but this, frankly, is because we are unreflectively materialist; it is not a thought that obviously must be respected if one admits a soul.

---

[17] ST Ia 76, 8.

Visibility and tangibility

For a human to be visible is for him/her to have a visible body. Platonism can agree, *modulo* its account of how a human has a body. Swaddle the Invisible Man in spandex and you see *him*, not just the spandex. All it takes for the Invisible Man to become indirectly visible is that there be some matter, the spandex, with a particular set of causal relations to him: his outline expands the suit, and so we see his outline through the suit, and so we see *him* indirectly, through the suit. Why not, then, if we swaddle a soul in flesh? There could be causal relations to matter which enable us to see a soul indirectly, through its body. There is a good sense in which by observing vapour trails, we see indirectly particles which are not directly visible. For a Platonist, to have a body is *inter alia* for there to be a material object some of whose properties and movements are one's vapour trails. To see my body smile is to see *me* smile, whatever the causal story behind the smile. Can one see me smile but not see me? For Platonists, I suggest, men are visible, though indirectly so.

Now suppose that the Invisible Man is also intangible: that his body is a magnetic field. Alter the spandex suit so that its outlines are expanded by magnetic repulsion: it still seems intuitively that if I touch the suit, I touch the man, indirectly. I do not touch him directly, but his body resists my finger as I poke it into the suit, and so I feel it through the suit.

Mass and more

For humans to have a mass is for them to have bodies with masses. Again, Platonists can agree, *modulo* their account of what it is to have a body. On Platonism, a human has a mass without consisting of massy things. So parts of the account of mass that applies to things with massy parts can't apply. But other parts can. One thing true if humans have massy parts is that my mass is the minimum amount I must move in order wholly to change my physical location without divesting myself of body-parts. If I am a soul and located where my body is, I have a mass in this sense. So the Platonist has an account of what it is for a man to have a mass, which consists of part of what is true if humans consist of massy parts.

Thus a Platonist human can be located, extended, visible, tangible, and composite, and have a mass. A Platonist human has feet, and cannot easily get about the world without them. If my arm is chopped off, I lose a limb; a Platonist can agree, *modulo* the Platonic account of what it was to have that limb in the first place. We die if our bodies die, even if our souls survive death:

a Platonist can agree. If our hearts stop beating, we die: a Platonist can agree. A Platonist human has a brain, and it is entirely consistent for a Platonist to hold that humans cannot naturally think without their brains. So a Platonist can hold that humans need brains to think and hearts to avoid death. A human's life animates his/her body. A Platonist can agree. Aquinas wrote that 'the body participates in the soul's being'.[18] For Aquinas, for living things, to live is to be. So what Aquinas has in mind is this: the soul is intrinsically and primarily alive. The body is alive not intrinsically but by 'participating' in the soul's life. The life lived in the body is the soul's life. A Platonist can agree, adding that *of course* the life lived in the human body is primarily that of the person and human whose body it is. A Platonist human can be something that is not human without its body. It can even be something that depends on its body for every bit of the fullness of life humans normally enjoy—that without its bodily adjuncts is truncated, imperfect, even comatose. Thus the Platonist can embrace a wide range of truisms about human beings. The difference between the Platonist and other stories about humans comes down to this: for everyone, what make all these things true are parts of the concrete human endowment or human nature, parts of what makes the human being human. But for the Platonist, they are not also parts of the human.

One might have a different worry about Platonism: that if there is a soul, there is also a soul-body composite, and even if the soul is a legitimate candidate for being a person and a human, the composite is a better one. I agree. I am not a Platonist. But if what I've argued about Platonism is correct, I think the claim that a soul is a human being can be intellectually respectable, at least for Christians. So too then (8)'s claim that GS remains wholly immaterial, eternal, etc., and yet is a man.[19] One might reply, 'If the composite is a better candidate in the ordinary case, it's a better one for the incarnation'. But it would be better only if it were a *possible* candidate. Since the only person or human involved in the incarnation is GS, were the composite either, GS would be the composite, and so at least partly material. Again, this does not seem possible to me. One might then rejoin 'If ordinary human persons are composites, but GS is not, then GS is not human the way we are, and so the claim that in the incarnation GS became just what we are is false'. But it *is* false. GS did not become just what we are. GS is an incarnate deity, even if human, and we are not. The doctrine of the incarnation is that GS becomes fully human, not that he becomes exactly our sort of human. GS has the same human endowment we do. It makes him human one way; ours

---

[18] *QD de Anima* 1 *ad* 17.
[19] Of course, in GS's case, we do not have something that is imperfect and comatose without a body.

makes us human another way. *Per* my discussion of the truisms above, his having it implies for him what our having it implies for us, *modulo* such inescapable differences as that if what makes him human were annihilated he would continue to exist. I say a bit more about the difference between being human and being human just as we are below.

AN UNWELCOME ADDITION

One might wonder whether on (8), B and S compose a human or a person on their own. If B+S compose a human person, then since GS is then a different, divine person, there are two persons in the incarnate Christ. This would be the Nestorian heresy, the denial of the Chalcedonian Creed's claim that Christ's divine and human natures are 'united in one person and subsistence, not separated or divided into two persons'.[20] And it is not hard to see why this should be a heresy: if GS is one person and Jesus is another, different person, God did not become man in Jesus, but instead merely entered some sort of intimate association with a man.

Swinburne argues that in ordinary humans, the soul determines the identity of the person,[21] and so if Christ had a human soul, there would be two individuals, two persons, in the incarnation, which is the Nestorian heresy.[22] But even if we concede Swinburne's account of personal identity, it doesn't follow that S would determine the identity of someone other than GS. We can hold that S is precisely the human soul of Christ—i.e., that necessarily, whoever has it is incarnate second person, that it is naturally suited to provide that identity and no other. Then GS's identity is overdetermined—but why not? This move, incidentally, entails that GS did not become a 'body snatcher', preventing a person B+S would otherwise have constituted from coming to exist. If S is by its nature GS's human soul, there was no other individual to form: S could not exist unless GS were incarnate in a composite including it. Swinburne has objected that if the soul determines the person's identity, it should not be possible to be that person without having that soul, while on my suggestion, having S is not necessary for being GS: GS need not have become incarnate, and had he not, he would not have had S as his soul.[23] But this claim should not look obvious. Actually (let's say) I have a soul, which made me who I am. Why couldn't a numerically different soul have done the same job? It's

---

[20] 'The Definition of Faith of the Council of Chalcedon' in Percival (1994: 265).
[21] Swinburne (1994: 40–5, 193–4, 212–13).
[22] Swinburne (1994: 196–7).   [23] In conversation.

not obvious that theories of identity must say that properties (e.g. having soul S) sufficient to determine something's identity are also necessary for its having that identity. Here's one theory of identity: God has a complete concept of me, containing my essence and every contingent property I will ever have, and what made me myself was God's willing that that concept be instanced. If that's right, I don't see why God might not also have another complete concept, differing in some contingent attributes, such that had he willed to instance that, that would have made me myself, but with some contingent alterations. Here's another theory of identity: what makes me myself is not just my soul, A, but my soul plus having a certain genetic make-up. Actually sperm B and egg C met to jointly give me that make-up. So springing from the A and the initial matter of B and C made me myself: the property of having so originated is one having which suffices to determine my identity. But another sperm B* could have given me the same genetic make-up. So having the ABC property is not necessary to being me. Any example one gives here will depend on some theory of what determines persons' identity. All such theories are controversial. But if there is nothing obviously incoherent about my sample views, it is not obvious that a theory of identity must respect Swinburne's constraint, and the way is open to make the move I suggest about S. If we join this move to my foregoing argument, then I've contended that GS is a human person, B+S does not constitute GS, and B+S does not constitute a different human person than GS. These things jointly entail that B+S do not constitute a human person at all, and so avoid Nestorianism.[24]

Trenton Merricks raises the Nestorian question another way, writing that:

(B+S) is supposed to be intrinsically just like a complete human person. Indeed it would have been a human person had it not—perhaps per impossibile—been taken up by God the Son. But I have a hard time seeing how (B+S) fails to be a human person (as it must, lest this theory be Nestorian).[25]

Cross expresses related worries.[26]

One could, of course, just apply here the move just mooted in Swinburne's case. There are also other quick moves one can make. On (8), the Son is made human by composition with B+S. Plausibly HB. no human being can be made human by composition with another human.

---

[24] I owe this last move to William Wood.
[25] Merricks (2007: 282 n. 1). I note that if S is GS's human soul, as suggested in an earlier note, B+S do not compose either a human or a person on their own. If they composed either, the human or person they compose would be GS. But GS is the human person, on either (7) or (8), and there are not two of him. If S is GS's human soul, it is a human soul which (uniquely) is suited only to overdetermine the identity of a body–soul composite body and soul do not exhaust, not to determine the identity of a composite they do exhaust.
[26] Cross (2009: 461–2).

On (8), B+S is that by composition with which the Son is human. So (8) and (HB) rule out B+S' being a human being. Further, if B+S is a person, B+S is a human being. So (HB) and (8) give us that B+S is not a person. Again, FE. no full natural human endowment can belong to two persons.

(FE) allows for conjoined or overlapping twins: these aren't within the same full natural endowment, because they do not fully share brains, skulls, etc. Again, if two souls S and S* shared a body B, the full natural endowments would be S+B and S*+B, which aren't shared. Assuming that B+S belongs to B+S if B+S is a person, (FE) gives us that if B+S belongs to GS, B+S is not a person, and so not a human person.

Still, one person's *modus ponens* is another's *modus tollens*. If I have shown that (8), *B+S is a human person* and either (FE) or (HB) are inconsistent sets, some might therefore reject (8). So I must cast doubt on *B+S is a human person* in another way: and it would also be good not to have to rest all the weight here on the soul-of-GS manoeuvre. Note to begin then that Merricks's sole basis for suggesting that B+S is a human person is that B+S is an intrinsic duplicate of a possible human person. But this does not suffice for being a human person if being a human person is not an intrinsic property. Perhaps I have as a part an object, Minus, which is me minus the left hand I fortunately possess. Even if I do, we jib strongly at the claim that Minus is actually a human person: that human persons have large undetached parts who are also human persons. But Minus is an intrinsic duplicate of a human person—me, in a possible world in which I've lost my hand. So it does not seem to us that such duplication suffices for human personhood. Instead, it seems plausible that being a human person is what Sider calls a maximal property, one such that by the nature of the property F, large parts of Fs are not themselves Fs.[27] But if being a human person is maximal, it is extrinsic: whether Minus has it depends in part on how things are outside Minus. If there is such a thing as Minus, it suffices for Minus not to be a human person that Minus is conjoined with my left hand, to compose *me*. So if being a human person is maximal, being intrinsically just like one doesn't entail being one. But then it is not clear why we should infer from such duplication that B+S is a human person. Many things are intrinsic duplicates of possible Fs without being Fs: many properties are maximal.

Here is another way something could be intrinsically just like a human person, but fail to be one because of something extrinsic: suppose that far, far away, there is a parallel Earth every state of which at any time is a

---

[27] Sider (2001: 357–64).

physical duplicate of our own Earth's state at that time, save for anything corresponding to certain causal differences I will specify. There are laws guaranteeing these parallels; it is no accident that events on duplicate Earth parallel those on Earth to the extent they do. On duplicate Earth I have always had an atom-for-atom duplicate, Double, moving through its streets just as I move through streets here. Double moves as I move because I control it completely by telekinesis and 'active' telepathy (sending rather than receiving thoughts[28]).[29] If I think that Jones is a great pianist, an echo of that thought occurs in Double—because I think it. That is, the thought occurs in Double, but I am its sole ultimate source. If I decide to go to the concert, an echo of that decision occurs in Double, but I am its sole ultimate source. If Double then goes to the concert, that is because it was appropriately located to begin with, and its movements mirror mine, because I make my movements and am telekinetically linked to Double.

Double is my puppet. In one sense, Double lacks its own psychology. There are mental events in Double, but I cause them all. At each instant, Double's mental state mirrors mine, but the cross-temporal 'arrows' between them differ: past events in my mind and brain cause my present state, but past events in Double's don't cause Double's present state. Instead, present events in me cause its present state. This is compatible with mental–physical supervenience: wherever there is a mental event, there is the corresponding physical one. It may even let subvenient physical events account for the supervening mental ones: perhaps I physically cause Double's relevant physical events, always pre-empting the physical causes which would otherwise operate, and Double's physical events account for the presence of Double's mental ones. If events in Double give rise to mental dispositions, these dispositions parallel mine but are blocked from 'firing' as long as I exist. I pre-empt them; when the parallel disposition fires

---

[28] We have to suppose that my signals travel infinitely fast to make this work. So be it. This may not even be science fiction; some quantum phenomena make such signalling a viable hypothesis. But those unwilling to play along can suppose instead that if n is the amount of time it takes for a signal to get from me to Double, it is always the case that duplicate Earth at t+n duplicates Earth at t.

[29] If Double and I are physical duplicates, Double's physical states, duplicating mine, also include telepathic and telekinetic states fit to control some further duplicate, ad infinitum. It does not follow that there is a further duplicate for it to control. Double's states do not in turn control me if I control Double, of course. It follows that there is no intrinsic difference between Double and me in virtue of which it is I who control Double, rather than vice versa: this is fine, because our causal relations are not intrinsic to either of us, and it is a brute extrinsic causal fact that these run from me to Double, not Double to me. Nor then (for reasons which emerge) is there any intrinsic difference in our states at any time in virtue of which I am the person in the set-up and Double is not. But this is, of course, just what I'm arguing. It is compatible with this that there be differences in Double alone *over* time which play a role: on the story, part of the reason Double is not a person is the lack of causal relations between its earlier and later mental states.

in me, that rather than Double's disposition causes an event in Double. Further, in the situation as described, it is not all-things-considered physically possible that they do so, since (I am supposing) the connection between my mental life and events in Double is lawlike, given that I exist. One might therefore wonder whether Double really does have mental dispositions at all. For it is physically impossible that these states cause mental events: they could do so if I died and Double did not, but given the lawlike parallels between the planets, the laws guarantee that I die iff Double dies. However, it is metaphysically possible that the laws differ. Other laws could let Double survive me, and in this circumstance, these very states could cause mental events.

Let's consider Double's cognitive life in more detail. Any perceptual state in Double is caused by and so perceives objects in my environment, not Double's. Double consciously enjoys Double's perceptual states.[30] I do not. But my sensory and neural machinery cause them to occur, not Double's. Thus Double owns Double's conscious states and so do I. Still, though I do not enjoy Double's conscious states, its states are just echoes mine cause, with all the same content. Everything in Double's consciousness is also in mine. My occurrent perceptual judgments have echoes in Double. I cause the echo-judgments to occur; they are causal upshots of my perceptual mechanisms in the immediate past. Thus the echo-judgments are mine, not Double's, though they occur in Double. Any perceptual beliefs my perceptual states and judgments give rise to in me occur also in Double. They concern objects in my environment, not Double's. They are veridical if mine are. However, if they are beliefs as they occur in Double, they are my beliefs even there. To believe that P is to take it to be true that P. I do the taking, not Double, though in the case of the echo-belief the output representational state is stored in Double. But as stored in Double, perhaps these states don't count as beliefs, at least while I exist. Functional definitions of beliefs assign them *inter alia* a causal role in the production of behaviour. While I exist, Double's inner states can't play such a role; it is not physically possible that they function as states must be able to function to count as beliefs. I am simply unsure whether a metaphysical but not physical possibility of functioning as a belief suffices to render something a belief.

'I' tokens in Double's mind or mouth refer to me, not Double, since they are just echoes of my own. Thus Double cannot refer to itself or be self-conscious. Double's first-person beliefs are the echoes in Double of mine, and are true if mine are. In a sense, Double doesn't know who 'he' is, but I am in the process of arguing that the sense is this: there is no-one Double is—

---

[30] If these states are conscious in me, I take them to be conscious in Double as well. I aim to preserve the supervenience of the mental on the physical as far as possible in constructing this example, and consciousness is plausibly one supervenient mental quality.

Double is not a person—and so there is nothing of this sort to be known. Any state of knowing who he himself is that occurs in Double is a state of knowing who I am, and is veridical: it is just an echo of my knowing who I am. This does not subject Double to a kind of Cartesian deception. Cartesian deception involves having false beliefs. One must have beliefs to have false beliefs, and Double has none: perhaps nothing in him counts as a belief state, and if anything does, it is my belief, not his. Beliefs in Double are my states in Double, not Double's states.

Decisions and volitions belong to those who make them. Those make them who ultimately cause them to occur.[31] If I brainwash you into pulling the trigger at t, it is really I, not you, who have decided that you shall pull the trigger at t. Thus though decisions and volitions occur in Double, as events in Double's brain and (if there are souls) soul, they are mine, not Double's. In them *I* make use of Double's faculties. My intention to visit Rome is mine because I form it, it exists as a disposition in me, and I can bring it into play to regulate my behaviour. When I form such an intention, I also thereby cause the forming of an echo in Double. This exists as a disposition in Double, but Double cannot bring it into play to regulate its behaviour: it cannot 'fire' while I live. So the echo intention is as much mine as Double's, but even if it is Double's, Double cannot act intentionally. Rather, what appear to be Double's intentional acts are causal outputs of my own intentions. Double has the equipment to form and implement intentions and decisions. That equipment is used. But it is at my disposal, not Double's. It is used only as I use it. And perhaps it succeeds in producing intentions and decisions only if I die.

Double has never originated a decision or a thought.[32] Owing to my relation to Double, it has never been all-things-considered physically able to do so. It is not the case that Double is a person, but non-autonomous. Being a person requires at least the physical possibility of, for example, generating mental states, acting intentionally, or being self-conscious. These things are not physically possible to Double. Quite likely being a person requires being all-things-considered able to do these things: that is, being such that one can 'just do them', with no preparation needed save perhaps waking up, given that one is all-things-considered able to just wake up.[33] Double is able to be all-things-considered able

---

[31] If determinism is true, this needs severe qualification, but what emerges will serve my purposes just as well.

[32] If determinism is true, there is a sense in which none of us ever originate a thought or decision: it all goes back to the Big Bang. But *modulo* this we can still speak of ourselves as 'proximately' or 'as if' originating. A transform of my point will then apply.

[33] Someone in a reversible coma is a person, because he/she can 'just wake up'—which would be constituted by generating suitable mental states. Those in irreversible comas are no longer persons, on my account. If it occurs to you that Double is relevantly like someone in a coma,

to do all this. It has the right sort of brain, etc. But I keep it from Double's use, and so it is not all-things-considered able to do it. Being able to be all-things-considered able doesn't entail being able: I am able to be all-things-considered able to play the piano, since I can learn to do so, but I am not all-things-considered able, because I have not learned. A zygote is able to be all-things-considered able to generate mental states, etc., since it is able to develop into a person, but it is not all-things-considered able to do so and so is not a person, because it has not yet developed so. It is metaphysically possible that Double be just as it is, but I not exist, and perhaps if this were so, Double would be a person. But a mere metaphysical possibility of being a person does not suffice for actually being one: it is metaphysically possible that a zygote be a person, since it can grow into one. Double has the right sort of brain to generate mental states etc. But this doesn't suffice because it is compatible with being prevented from using the brain in the proper way. Given my effect on Double, it is relevantly as if Double lacked a cerebrum: Double has no use of it (though it consciously experiences what goes on in it) and the relevant parts of its operation are causally insulated from the rest of Double's body. Human bodies without cerebrums do not house persons. So because Double and I have always co-existed, I have always usurped his personhood: Double is not a person, solely because of his relations to me. (Double is conscious, but many things are conscious without managing to be persons.) The only person in the Double set-up is me.[34]

(8) permits the claim that Double's relation to me in some ways parallels B+S' to GS—and I do assert this. Note that if we accept (8) and model the causal relations between GS and B+S on the Double story, we do not wind up with too many thinkers. There is just one thinker: Double originates no thoughts, though it is a theatre for thoughts derived from elsewhere, and so too (say I) B+S. If B+S is like Double, B+S is no person either. Further, if something is a human being, it is a person if mature and undamaged. If this is correct, Double is not a human being either—nor then is B+S. Double is rather just the concrete natural endowment appropriate to a human being— and so is B+S. The Creed of the sixth Ecumenical Council has it that:

then still, Double is not all-things-considered able to wake up. Its 'coma' is irreversible: given the lawlike parallel between Double's planet and our own, I die iff Double dies. So it is not physically possible that Double survive me, and so not physically possible that Double awake.

[34] The Double story raises unsettling questions: could we be Doubles, all unknown? Do we know that our mental lives are our own, not someone else's in us? How can we, given that any basis we could have for believing this is itself something that could occur in the mind of a Double, or, coming from the other direction, what could there be that could occur in our minds but not a Double's, to give us grounds for rational belief that we are not Doubles? I see no easy answers, but this is just a new sort of sceptical scenario, and probably can be dealt with if other forms of scepticism can.

The humanity of God

In him are two natural wills and two natural operations indivisibly, inseparably, inconfusedly...and these two natural wills are not contrary the one to the other, but this human will follows and that not as resisting and reluctant, but rather as subject of his divine and omnipotent will...for as his flesh is called and is the flesh of God the Word, so also the natural will of his flesh is called and is the proper will of God the Word.[35]

The Double case has this feature. Double has all natural faculties of volition, decision, etc. These faculties operate as they naturally should, but only at my behest. The Creed continues that 'each nature wills and does the things proper to it'.[36] But the Council Fathers' rationale for this includes that whatever there is of passion in Christ, including passions of the will, must reside in his human nature.[37] They seem to have meant that some desires originate only in the human nature and are not ascribable to GS. The Double case does not allow for this. But it does not *specifically* address desires, and (I suspect) could be modified to let Double initiate its own desires: plenty of things are conscious and have desires without being humans or persons.

MERRICKS'S ABSTRACT ARGUMENT

Trenton Merricks offers an abstract challenge to GS's humanity on (8). On (8), GS acquires a human natural endowment, adding it to a pre-existing person to compose a larger unit consisting of a person and that by relation to which he is human. This is not so in our own case. So Merricks suggests that:

it is hard to see how 'taking up' an individual human nature makes God the Son human in the same way you and I are human; and if he is not human just as we are, I do not see how he could be fully human.[38]

A step at the end bears note: why think there is only one way of being fully human? Being fully human is meeting a certain standard; perhaps there is more than one way to meet it. In any case, 'makes God the Son human in the way we are' is ambiguous: it might refer to the way someone becomes human, or to the results of becoming human that way. It is not clear why we should think that *acquiring* humanity differently must make a difference to whether full humanity is acquired. If I begin life as a brain in a vat and thereafter have the rest of a human natural endowment grafted on, I acquire humanity differently than most, but I come out fully human. Nor, again, is it clear

---

[35] Percival (1994: 345). [36] Percival (1994: 346).
[37] Prosphonetus, in Percival (1994: 347). [38] Merricks (2007: 282 n. 1).

why not being identical to that human endowment should matter, as long as it is truly his and implies for him what ours implies for us, *modulo* differences inescapable on any account of the incarnation.

Merricks also raises a more concrete difficulty for (8). He frames his discussion in terms of the incarnation's posing a problem for dualist accounts of embodiment. However, if the two do not sit well together, Merricks's case transforms into a problem for dualist accounts of the incarnation. Merricks argues that if GS remains immaterial though incarnate, there is no account of the relation between GS and B in virtue of which GS is embodied only in B. Now this embodiment is an aspect of the hypostatic union as traditionally conceived, and as noted, traditional christology has been content to say that finally, this relation is a mystery—that we are not going to have a fully adequate account of it come what may. So this argument may not move traditional christologists. But analytic philosophers prefer to shed light where they can, and so might find this at least a *prima facie* strike against (2), (5), and (8).

Soul-to-body causation

On typical dualist accounts, a soul is embodied in a body due to causal relations between that soul and that body. Merricks parses one of these relations as a claim that the soul has direct control over that body.[39] He then reasons that as omnipotent, every divine person has direct control over every body. If this is correct and a typical dualist account of embodiment is true, every divine person is at least partly or to some degree embodied in every physical object.[40] Now Swinburne has at times simply accepted this;[41] he has also held that embodiment comes in degrees.[42] Anyone who accepts both claims need only find a way to say that the Son is more embodied in B than any divine person is in anything else—as we see shortly that Swinburne does—and he/she can still maintain that only in the GS–B case is the degree of embodiment *enough* to count as incarnation. Those less happy to accept universal divine embodiment can instead distinguish the way a non-incarnate divine person controls matter from the way an incarnate divine person might. I suggest elsewhere that if a divine person is not incarnate, he moves matter

---

[39] Merricks (2007: 284–5). he does not say just what he means by this, but his quotation of Swinburne suggests that it might not be far from the mark to cash this out in terms of being able to move parts of that body as basic actions, as Swinburne does.
[40] Merricks (2007: 285).
[41] For his twists and turns on this and some criticism, see Leftow (1997: 113–24).
[42] Swinburne (1993: 104–5).

only by intending that it move, and cannot move it in a basic act.⁴³ If a divine person is incarnate in a body, he can cause matter to move without intending it and in a basic act. I intend to raise my arm (a basic act) but not to contract my muscles, yet my intention causes my muscles to contract; so too GS, with B and nothing else, if he is incarnate in B. Merricks comments only that:

> this reply denies that God is a non-physical entity who causes physical events in the sense of 'cause' that non-physical souls cause physical events. And so, given this reply, the dualist loses her theism-based rejoinder to (the objection that) the physical and the non-physical cannot causally interact... Thus, insofar as the dualist thinks the theism-based rejoinder is a good one, she should reject this reply.⁴⁴

The 'theism-based rejoinder' was that the objection must be wrong, since God is non-physical and causes physical effects. But, of course, the dualist needn't endorse this rejoinder. More basically, even if God and souls interact with the physical in different ways, if God who is non-physical can affect the physical, appeal to him is a response to the objection as stated, which was that the non-physical simply cannot—in any way—affect the physical. Finally, even if God can't move matter as we do if non-incarnate, this doesn't suggest that he can't cause physical events 'in the same sense of "cause" that... souls cause physical events'. The sense of 'cause' is precisely the same. It is just that that sense is put to a different sort of use—in discussing non-basic rather than basic acts and intentional rather than unintentional acts. As this is all Merricks has to say against the suggestion that an incarnation might make a difference to the *way* a divine person controls some matter, I take this suggestion to stand. Thus a dualist account of the incarnation need not accept on grounds of soul-to-body causal relations that all divine persons are at least to some degree embodied in all matter.

Body-to-soul causal relations

On typical dualist accounts, a soul's embodiment in a body consists also in body-to-soul causal relations. Merricks cites Swinburne, who writes:

A person has a body if there is a chunk of matter through which he makes a difference to the world, and through which he acquires true beliefs about that world... men

---

⁴³ See Leftow (1997). Of course, he is able to be able to do this, since he is able to become incarnate. But being able to be able doesn't entail being able.

⁴⁴ Merricks (2007: 285 n. 8, 284). A quibble: Merricks begins this passage with the supposition that God's affecting matter as we do is impossible, after having quoted me saying 'In sum, God cannot... move matter by basic acts (again, with perhaps the exception of the incarnation).' I am in the piece he discusses precisely *not* claiming that God's moving matter as we do is impossible. I am claiming that a non-incarnate God's doing so is impossible.

have bodies because stimuli landing on their eyes or ears give them true beliefs about the world which they would not otherwise have... Our bodies are the vehicles of our knowledge and operation.[45]

Merricks then rejoins,

God has direct and immediate knowledge of everything in and around every body. And so insofar as having a body is having knowledge of what is in and around that body, each person of the Trinity has... every body.[46]

But Swinburne's claim is not that a soul has a body if it knows truths about what is in and around it. It is that an embodied soul has knowledge *through* its body, knowledge that *depends* on the body, knowledge for which the body is the *vehicle*. However hard these claims are to explicate, they try to get at something which is not captured even by talk of the body merely as causing knowledge in the soul; there is something intuitively right about them, and it is something Merricks's counterargument and its subsequent refinements ignore. A fairly natural first stab at explicating this extra something might be that as a soul's basic acts may consist partly in the motion of its body, and its body is just that which can be appropriately related to its basic acts, so some of a soul's cognitive states may consist partly in states of its body, and its body is just that which can be appropriately related to such cognitive states. Emotions have cognitive content—one is sad about something, for example, that the party is over. But having an emotion also plausibly consists at least partly in being in a particular sort of physical state. Perceptual states have cognitive content. But being in a perceptual state plausibly also consists at least partly in being in a particular sort of physical state. Perhaps GS has perceptual and affective states of this sort, B is the body implicated in them, and no other divine person has such perceptual and affective states: at least, nothing Merricks offers addresses anything like this suggestion.

I do not accept a standard dualist account of embodiment. My point is just that Merricks has not shown either that such accounts are untenable intrinsically or that they sit ill with belief in the incarnation. They are available to friends of (2), (5), or (8).

Basic embodiment

I myself think the embodiment relation is more fundamental than either cognitive or control relations and accounts for both the possibility (and

---

[45] Merricks (2007: 283), quoting Swinburne (1986: 146).
[46] Merricks (2007: 285).

limitations) of a soul's control and the composition of the relevant mental states. For if one asks why my cognitive or emotional states are implemented in these organs, not those, it seems explanatory to reply that this is because these are parts of my body and those are not. Again, if one asks why I can move this arm in a basic act but not that one, it seems a good answer to say, 'because this arm is part of my body and that is not'. But these are not good answers on a standard dualist account: if my being embodied *consists* in such facts, such facts cannot explain it. For they cannot jointly explain themselves, and one is not a plausible explanation of the other.

One account of embodiment as more fundamental is Aquinas'. For Thomas, the soul is the substantial form of the body. Its being embodied is its being related to the body as an essential property is. Its 'causation' is 'formal', not efficient; it constitutes the body a live human body rather than a mere collection of chemicals. I cannot do what is needed to explain these claims in a paper primarily about other things; I have offered accounts elsewhere.[47] But as something broadly on these lines would constitute my account of embodiment, I bring them in, because they may seem to open me to Merricks's arguments against dualists who take embodiment as unanalysable in terms of efficient causal relations.

I note, then, that on the Thomist account, *contra* Merricks, it is not the case that 'we do not know what the dualist means when she says that each of us "has a body"'.[48] We can say quite a lot about what embodiment involves, independent of issues of control and cognition. Merricks thinks it a difficulty that on a primitive-embodiment account 'it is possible for me to stand in all the seemingly relevant control and epistemic relations to a body without being (embodied in) it (and) I could be (embodied in) a body without being related to it by any control or epistemic relations'.[49] But both seem in fact to be possible. Someone in a permanent vegetative state has a body even if he/she no longer can control that body's motions or have cognitive or emotional states.[50] And the Double case above seems to involve or readily expand into my having the relevant causal relations to Double without being embodied in him, and seems to me to represent a genuine possibility.

---

[47] For texts and my detailed account of these claims as they occur in Thomas, see Leftow (2001: 120–38) and Leftow (2009: 395–416).

[48] Merricks (2007: 291).

[49] Merricks (2007: 291).

[50] 'Can' here at least expresses causal possibility. But it could express absolute, metaphysical possibility as well: perhaps the relevant causal laws no longer permit these things, and it is a tenable view that nomological necessity is just a species of metaphysical necessity.

TWO IMPORTANT HUMAN ATTRIBUTES

Thus the general, abstract issue of GS's humanity. Let's now consider a couple of important human properties.

Suffering and humanity

I think (8) lets us say that GS suffers. To begin, sometimes, within a composite object, properties automatically transfer from some to other parts of the composite. I put my left hand in the water. So my left hand is a proper part of something with a part in the water. Therefore my right is also a proper part of something with a part in the water. As the sun shines, photons constantly work their way from the sun's core outward. The sun's outer layers emit photons. Therefore it's also true that its core emits photons. We find this too in the incarnation. B+S needs food to remain biologically alive. If it goes without food long enough, it is no longer biologically alive. Just because GS is in the right way part of a composite including B+S, the Son too needs food to remain biologically alive (i.e. live, but with a life animating a body—the same sense in which Platonic souls can be biologically alive). For if B+S dies, the Son is no longer biologically alive—he is alive, but not biologically.

To be in the process of ceasing to be biologically alive is to suffer (in a causal sense) death. So the Son is liable to suffer death just because composed in the right way with B+S. Now consider having pain sensations. Pain sensations occur in B+S. So they occur in the composite the Son's inclusion in which makes him a man. This does not entail that he feels them. If brainstem me were grafted into the fetal body in such a way that I never felt sensations it is physically apt to be causing,[51] I would be a man, but a permanently anaesthetized man. It is compatible with (8) that the Son be like a permanently anaesthetized man. But (8) permits the addition that he is part of the composite in the right way to feel pain when B+S is appropriately affected. This is doubtless some sort of causal addition to (8). But (8) is not committed to the claim that composition explains everything. Causation may be part of the (8)-picture anyway: causal relations may be part of what makes an immaterial thing part of a composite with material parts. But even if this is true, causation is not the whole story. Part of it may be a non-causal embodiment relation. And composition remains an important part of it. GS

---

[51] E.g. its finger is burned, the burned area is physically apt to cause pain, but I do not feel the pain.

would not be a *man* feeling pain without it. Causal or other relations which did not provide composition would give us a spirit using a body and soul rather than a single thing composed of body, soul, and spirit. A spirit which merely uses a body and soul does not thereby become a man; a demon which possessed me would not thereby become human unless its causal relations with my body were sufficient for embodiment and were such as to render it and my body a human being composed of the two.

So (8) lets GS feel pain. Unlike the Double case, I suggest that B+S doesn't feel it: that only GS feels the incarnate Christ's sensations. This would not deny the nomic supervenience of the mental on the physical. That is satisfied only if every composite which has an appropriate physical property also has the proper psychological property. This is so in the incarnation; B is the part of the composite that has the physical property, and GS is the part that has the psychological one, much as on Platonic dualism, a body is the part with the physical and a soul the part with the psychological property. I'd say that primarily GS suffers,[52] the whole composite suffers in a derivative sense, and B+S does not suffer at all.

On having a mother

Much patristic controversy concerned whether Mary was GS's mother, or only the mother of B+S. So I finally consider whether (8) lets Mary be GS's mother. On (8), GS remains wholly immaterial. I've suggested that this is compatible with having a spatial location, and if GS has one while incarnate, he might have literally been in Mary's womb. But let's make things hard and take it that GS never had one. If so, GS was never enclosed by Mary's womb. Nor did GS pass through Mary's birth-canal. Thus one might wonder whether GS really does have a mother, on (8).[53] Well, just because GS is divine, not everything true of other humans and their mothers will apply in this case. Typically, mothers causally contribute to their offspring's ever existing, but GS preexisted Mary. Typically, one begins to exist in one's mother's womb; not so GS. Typically, one's mother contributes an egg which contributes half of one's genetic material; GS has no genetic material, save as a Platonic human does, and we have to be agnostic about the egg even in the case of the full composite, GS+B+S, because everything we know is compatible both with the claim that Jesus appeared in Mary's womb because God modified one of Mary's eggs and with the claim that Jesus (who *is* GS) appeared in Mary's

---

[52] This entails that GS is not impassible, but is compatible with GS's being immutable if it is compatible with GS's being atemporal—as I argued in Leftow (2002).
[53] So Cross (2009: 461), though not in these precise terms.

womb because God simply created a suitable zygote *ex nihilo* there. (Mary would then be GS's surrogate mother. But a surrogate mother is a mother.) Again, typically, all parts of a human are enclosed by its mother's womb and pass through her birth-canal. But if so much else that is true in ordinary human cases must be false for the incarnation, it's not clear why we should insist that this must hold here. Certainly there are coherent science-fiction scenarios in which it does not hold for some sorts of animal. Martians, we can suppose, are spatially scattered animals, consisting of a humanoid body and another bit controlled remotely by telepathy and telekinesis. They reproduce this way: when Mars and his wife Marta conceive the humanoid body, its own telepathic resources at once gather some matter and form it into the other bit, which is part of their offspring though in another location. If this is how it works, Mars Jr has some part not in Marta's womb almost from conception. It does not follow that Marta is not Junior's mother. If it is possible both that not all parts of an animal ever pass through its mother's birth-canal or exist in her womb, and that the woman nonetheless be that animal's mother, there is no bar in principle to a human being's having both a mother and an immaterial part never in the womb or the birth-canal.[54] I take it, then, that on (8), while GS is an unusual human being, he is as human as the rest of us.[55]

---

[54] Let me add one last rejoinder to Merricks. He writes:

It is odd that Leftow thinks that the incarnation is inconsistent with a normal human person's being identical with a body. For Leftow (2002) endorses a picture of the incarnation according to which the Son is not related to the body of Jesus like each of us is to our own bodies... Thus—given Leftow's view of the incarnation—an ordinary human person's being identical with a body wouldn't imply that the Son becomes identical with a body in the incarnation. Moreover, Leftow himself seems to identify a person in this life with her body, supplementing this with a Thomistic theory of the nature of living human bodies (2007: 296 n. 16).

The text he discusses claims that the thesis that all human persons just are their bodies is incompatible with the incarnation, because in the incarnation GS becomes a human person and GS cannot become a physical object. The text says nothing at all about the claim that all human persons other than incarnate deities—'normal human persons'—are identical with their bodies. Further, the article Merricks cites as Leftow (2002) is a historical piece offering a sympathetic, charitable account of Aquinas' views. It says nothing about my own. Finally, on my account, Thomas holds that a human is just a soul 'dusted' with prime matter—it is almost the case that there is nothing to a human but his/her soul. If this is correct, Thomas's view can't really be called a form of physicalism (as at Merricks (2007: 295)).

[55] My thanks to John Cottingham, Thomas Flint, Joseph Jedwab, Tim Mawson, Michael Rea, Richard Swinburne, William Wood, and audiences at Fordham University, St Louis University, and Notre Dame and Oxford conferences on the incarnation for comments.

3

Compositional christology without Nestorianism

Oliver D. Crisp

According to compositional christologists, in the incarnation the second person of the Trinity assumes a human nature, understood to be a concrete particular. The concrete human nature and divine nature of God the Son together compose Christ. That is, God Incarnate is a whole composed of the proper parts of God the Son and (the parts of) his human nature. According to many compositional christologists, this human nature comprises a human body and a human soul.[1] In which case, Jesus Christ consists of God the Son, and a human soul and a human body (i.e. a human nature), which together compose Christ. Elsewhere, I have called this sort of view a three-part account of the incarnation, where God the Son assumes a concrete particular at the first moment of incarnation comprising a human body + soul.[2] However, this is not the only live metaphysical option for those committed to a compositional account of the incarnation. One could hold to a two-part christology whilst maintaining that Christ's human nature is a concrete particular. One obvious way to make sense of this is to say that Christ is composed of God the Son and a human body capable of sustaining human mental life, where Christ's human body just is his human nature. Such an option might be attractive to those who maintain human beings are essentially material beings, but who think human natures are fundamentally concrete particulars of a certain sort. This need not entail Apollinarianism, provided some account can be given of Christ's human mental life consistent with the creedal claim that

---

[1] Unless otherwise stated, all references to 'human nature' are to concrete particulars of a sort, that is, to human body–soul composites, or what I have elsewhere labelled 'the concrete nature view'. See Crisp (2007: ch. 2).
[2] See Crisp (2007: ch. 2).

Christ possessed a human body and a 'reasonable' soul.³ There may well be other ways of carving up the number of parts in the incarnation alongside a commitment to Christ's human nature being a concrete particular, consistent with theological orthodoxy.⁴ But in what follows, I shall concern myself only with three-part, concrete (human) nature versions of compositional christology. Following in the steps of important patristic and medieval theologians, including St Thomas Aquinas and Duns Scotus, a number of recent philosophical theologians have articulated this view.⁵ But we will have to narrow the focus of our argument still further in order to make the analysis that follows manageable. Hence, this paper is concerned with one particular understanding of three-part compositional christology. I hope to tackle some of the other metaphysical options on another occasion.

Theologians usually dub the version of compositional christology that is the subject of what follows the *Habitus model*—about which, more in a moment. I shall outline this version of compositional christology and then set out five problems with it that have been raised in the recent literature, including the objection that the Habitus model implies Nestorianism, the heresy that Christ is composed of two persons. I shall then offer a partial defence of the Habitus model against these objections. I argue that, for the most part, the Habitus model is able to withstand these objections, although in the case of one of the objections some residual difficulties remain. In which case, if the argument given here is sound, the Habitus model offers an account of the metaphysics of the hypostatic union that is more robust than some

---

³ I have argued for this elsewhere in Crisp (2009: ch. 8). Apollinarianism is the heresy according to which Christ has a human body but fails to have a human 'reasonable soul'—a term culled from dogmatic statements such as that found in the Athanasian Creed, which states that Christ is 'perfect God and perfect man, of a reasonable soul and human flesh subsisting'. One could construe 'reasonable soul' as equivalent to 'human mind'. This appears to be consistent with at least some materialist accounts of human beings.

⁴ For instance, perhaps a mind–body dualist who is also an immaterial realist like Bishop Berkeley could claim that Christ's human nature, like all human natures, is an essentially immaterial entity: a human soul that acquires a certain bundle of properties that when collocated, constitute a human body. The immaterial realist might also claim human natures just are human souls and that human souls may or may not have an accidental relationship to a property bundle that constitutes a human body. In which case, what is non-negotiable in the incarnation is the assumption by God the Son of a human soul (i.e. a human nature). Possession of a human body (i.e. beginning to exemplify a certain property bundle that constitutes a particular human body) is not a necessary condition for being human. For a recent attempt to articulate a Berkeleyan account of the incarnation rather like this, see Hight and Bohannon (2010).

⁵ For discussion of the medieval school theologians, see Adams (1999), Adams (2006: ch. 6), and Cross (2002). Recent defenders of views similar to these medieval accounts include Thomas Flint, Alfred J. Freddoso, Brian Leftow, Eleonore Stump, and Peter van Inwagen.

recent authors suggest—although it may not offer a completely satisfactory model of the hypostatic union.[6]

THE HABITUS MODEL

According to the Habitus model of the incarnation, God the Son is not identical to Christ, though God the Son and Christ's human nature together compose Christ. Christ's human nature bears an accidental or contingent relation to God the Son. We might say that the human nature of Christ is the instrument of God the Son, in which he is 'embedded' from the first moment of incarnation and thereafter. An analogy often used to illustrate the Habitus model in medieval christology is that of a garment. The second person of the Trinity puts on human nature like a garment; he is 'clothed' by his human nature; but he is not identical to it. The analogy is, of course, limited, but may serve to illustrate something of the model we are concerned with.[7] In the recent literature it has been updated by Brian Leftow, who speaks of Christ's human nature as like a diver's drysuit. The suit is intimately connected to the body of the diver, enabling its wearer to manoeuvre and act in an alien environment without getting wet.[8]

This cameo of the model can be adapted by those who think God is in time, that is, temporalists, as well as by atemporalists or eternalists, who think that God is without time. For the temporalist it is true to say that at some particular time God the Son assumes human nature. For the temporalist who adopts the Habitus model, this means that at the moment of incarnation God the Son is embedded in a particular human nature ('his' human nature), to which he is intimately related at all times thereafter, unless he chooses to

---

[6] See also Brian Leftow's contribution to this volume for a further exploration of his version of the Habitus model.

[7] Compare St Thomas: 'Now the assumed nature is, as it were, a garment, *although this similitude does not fit at all points,* as has been said above (2, 6, ad 1)', ST 3. 3. 7, emphasis added. The history of this model is discussed in, amongst other places, Adams (1999), Cross (2002: ch. 1), Oberman (1963: ch. 8), and West (2007). One potential problem for the Habitus model that has dogged it in theological discussion is that if the human nature of Christ is really garment-like it looks like it is no thing (*non aliquid*). And this entails christological nihilism, the view according to which Christ's human nature is not a concrete entity as such. But, as we shall see, this need not follow if the Habitus model is expounded carefully enough. Pope Alexander III officially rejected the Habitus model for this reason in AD 1177. But if it is not an implication of the Habitus model, there may be reason to reconsider this papal rejection. See Oberman (1963: 252) for details.

[8] Leftow (2002: 292–3).

decouple himself from that human nature.⁹ The human nature thus assumed is rather like an environment suit for God the Son that enables him to act in the world among human beings. But advocates of the atemporal account of the divine nature can also appropriate the Habitus model. Then, God the Son eternally has the relevant accidental relation to his human nature, into which he is 'embedded'. His human nature, like the diver's drysuit, insulates him from the alien environment his human nature occupies, whilst allowing him to live and act in that environment. (The suit gets wet, of course, but the diver does not. Similarly, the human nature of Christ is in time, but his divine nature is not.)

Leftow is one contemporary author who has recently articulated what is effectively an atemporalist version of the Habitus model. Although he does not explicitly align his view with the model, his work draws on medieval accounts of the metaphysics of the incarnation, embracing the central tenets of Habitus christology as I have set them out. Thus Leftow:

> Perhaps the most formal, abstract thing one can say about the incarnation is this (following such as Aquinas): for the Son to become incarnate is at least for there to come to be a whole consisting of certain parts. Let 'the Son' name the Trinity's second person and 'Jesus Christ' name the whole consisting of the Son + B [the particular human body assumed by the Son] + S [the particular human soul/mind assumed by the Son]. Then, for the incarnation to take place is for Jesus Christ to come to be, by the joining of the Son, S and B.¹⁰

A little later, he adds, 'the Son is not identical with Jesus Christ. The Son is instead just part of Jesus Christ, the part which determines who Christ is.'¹¹ So it seems the Habitus model has at least one defender in the recent spate of literature on compositional christology.

Perhaps this is not so surprising. After all, there is much to commend the Habitus version of compositional christology. For one thing, if God the Son is not identical to Christ and bears only an accidental relation to his human nature, then it would appear that he is insulated from certain potentially metaphysically undesirable consequences of becoming incarnate. For instance, he need not undergo substantive change that might be theologically damaging, for example, being composed in part by, or becoming identical to, some parcel of matter.¹²

---

⁹ Orthodox christology presumes God the Son never decouples himself from his human nature. At the very least he is incarnate from the first moment of incarnation onwards, forevermore. Or, if God is atemporal, God the Son is eternally God Incarnate. In what follows, I shall take this for granted.
¹⁰ Leftow (2002: 287).   ¹¹ Leftow (2002: 290).
¹² This is theologically damaging if, like traditional Christian theists, one thinks that God is an essentially immaterial agent and God has all his attributes essentially. On this way of thinking, an essentially immaterial entity cannot be said to begin to have material parts.

What is more, for those who maintain that God is eternal and essentially metaphysically simple, having no distinct parts whatsoever (i.e. endorse the doctrine of divine simplicity), the Habitus model offers a way of making sense of the incarnation without identifying Christ's human nature with one of the persons of the Trinity. For an entity that is only accidentally related to a particular human nature may be shielded from any essential, intrinsic changes, such as 'growing' or 'expanding' to include a human nature as a proper part. At the very least, an entity that has this sort of relation to a human nature is not wholly or partially composed of the parts of that human nature. In which case, the Habitus model has the not inconsiderable advantage of preserving the metaphysical integrity of the divine and human nature of Christ in the hypostatic union.

PROBLEMS WITH THE HABITUS MODEL

But there are potentially significant drawbacks to the Habitus model too. Here are five of the most serious: one theological problem in two parts (or perhaps two closely related theological problems that share certain commonalities); and four metaphysical concerns.

We begin with the theological objection. The very fact that, on the Habitus model, God the Son is not identical to his human nature, raises the question of whether this is an unorthodox account of the incarnation. There are two related concerns here. The first comes from those who maintain that the catholic Creeds imply that God the Son is identical to Christ. For instance, the Chalcedonian 'Definition' of the person of Christ says, 'So, following the saintly fathers, we all with one voice teach the confession of *one and the same* Son, our Lord Jesus Christ... *one and the same* Christ, Son, Lord, only-begotten... *one and the same only-begotten* Son, God, Word, Lord Jesus Christ.'[13] If the phrase 'one and the same' is construed as an identity statement such that God the Son = Christ, then it looks like the Habitus model is in theological hot water. For it entails that God the Son is not identical to Christ. This we shall dub *the orthodoxy problem*.

The second theological concern is that the Habitus model implies Nestorianism. If God the Son is not identical to Christ, and Christ's human nature is composed of a human body–soul composite, or a body and soul rightly

---

[13] Tanner (1990: I 86), emphasis added.

related, what prevents this view from being Nestorian?[14] Human persons are composed of body–soul composites, or of a body and soul rightly related (on this way of thinking). One might be forgiven for thinking that when a human body and soul are present and rightly related, a human person is present. By insisting on a metaphysical cleavage between God the Son and the human nature of Christ (i.e. denying God the Son is identical to Christ or identical to his human nature), the Habitus model implies there are two entities present in the incarnation: one divine, the other human. Yet this appears to be straightforwardly Nestorian.[15] Christ's human nature seems to have all the concrete parts necessary for a human person—a human body and human soul rightly related. But then, what is it exactly that prevents the human nature of Christ from being a human person distinct from the second person of the Trinity? Call this *the Nestorianism problem*.

But there are also metaphysical difficulties for the advocate of the Habitus model in addition to the theological ones, the first of which is closely related to the foregoing objections. It looks like the Habitus model means God the Son is not human because God the Son is not identical to a human nature. Traditional, orthodox christology implies that at the incarnation God the Son *becomes* human in addition to being divine. If the Habitus model denies this, or entails the denial of this, then it is an unorthodox model of the incarnation. Let us designate this *the identity problem*.

A further metaphysical difficulty concerns what we shall refer to as *the insulation problem*.[16] It looks like the Habitus model insulates God the Son from having the properties his human nature does or performing the actions his human nature performs. In some cases this may not be a big drawback from the point of view of a defender of the Habitus model who is also a traditional Christian theist. God cannot suffer, so God the Son cannot suffer. Yet clearly, Christ suffers. So (the traditional Christian theist says) this must be parsed to mean 'Christ suffers in his human nature'. But even if we are willing to swallow this—via the deployment of reduplicative language, say[17]—do we want

---

[14] Recently, Richard Cross has made a similar claim with respect to Leftow's repristination of the Habitus model. Behind 'Leftow's impressive strategy' lies 'the danger of a Nestorian denial that the Son of God (as opposed to the whole of which it is a part) is human, or has human attributes, at all'. (2009: 462).

[15] Nestorianism is the heresy according to which God Incarnate is composed of two distinct persons; one human, the other divine. Scholarly study of a rediscovered copy of Nestorius' work, *The Bazaar of Heraclides*, has raised the question of whether Nestorius really was a Nestorian. But irrespective of whether Nestorius was a Nestorian, Nestorianism is formally heretical.

[16] I owe this objection to Thomas P. Flint's unpublished paper, 'A puzzle concerning the mereological model of the incarnation'.

[17] Reduplicative language as used in traditional christology is of the form S *qua* N is P. The idea is that by relegating particular attributes Christ has to one or other of his natures, one is

to concede that God the Son does *no action* that Christ is reported as doing in the canonical Gospels? Do we want to concede that he has *none* of the properties that Christ has? That seems like rather too much for an orthodox christologist to swallow.

Another concern with the Habitus model that follows upon the heels of the insulation problem is what I shall call *the no-person objection*.[18] We can frame it thus: *who* weeps over Lazarus in John 11: 35? Not God the Son, as has already been established. He is insulated from all that his human nature undergoes. He is incapable of suffering. But neither can Christ be said to be the subject weeping at Lazarus' grave, because Christ is not a person. Christ is just the mereological sum of God the Son and his human nature. And it certainly cannot be that Christ's human nature is a person on pain of Nestorianism. So Christ's human nature is also discounted from being the subject of the weeping reported in John 11: 35. But then it appears that no person is the subject of the weeping. And this is surely theologically intolerable.

A final obstacle for the Habitus theory is actually common to other theologically orthodox accounts of the incarnation, and is a particular concern for those versions of orthodox christology that presume Christ's human nature is a concrete particular. This is what we might call *the too-many-thinkers objection*. Trenton Merricks points out that the majority of substance dualists hold to the thesis, central to textbook Cartesianism, that human persons are identical with souls and only contingently related to a certain physical body, which is not a part of that human person. So, says Merricks, if one objects to this central claim of (textbook) Cartesianism, one is objecting to a central claim of the majority of substance dualists. Some substance dualists deny that human persons are identical with souls. Instead, they posit that human persons are soul–body composites. But, says Merricks, this raises a serious problem for this minority 'composite' version of dualism. For 'the dualist who denies that a person is identical with a soul must say that there are two objects with mental properties (a person and her soul) where normally we think there is one'.[19] This sort of problem has application to the Habitus model, and to other versions of compositional christology too. It looks like Christ's human soul is a thinking entity. In fact, if some version of substance dualism obtains, then in order to be fully human it is necessary that Christ

---

able to avoid the inference from 'S is N *qua* P' to 'S is N'. There are several ways in which this sort of language has been used in christology. Cross has a brief recapitulation of the issues in 'The incarnation'.

[18] This is also found in Flint's helpful paper, 'A puzzle concerning the mereological model of the incarnation'.

[19] See Merricks (2007: 282 n. 2).

possess a human soul. In which case, Christ has a human soul, which, *qua* soul, is a thinking substance. But God the Son is a thinking substance. In fact, he is the person who assumes human nature, including as one constituent of the human nature an additional thinking substance, the human soul of Christ. At this point it begins to look suspiciously like the compositional christologist has introduced too many thinkers into one person.[20] And this raises the question of Nestorianism once again.[21]

IN DEFENCE OF THE HABITUS MODEL

These are serious theological and metaphysical problems. What can be said in defence of the Habitus model? More than one might think at first glance. Let us consider responses to the objections in the order given above.

The orthodoxy problem

First, the theological worries. It does not seem at all obvious that the catholic Creeds require that God the Son is *identical* to Christ. When the excerpts from the Chalcedonian 'Definition' are read in their context, this becomes clearer. I give the whole 'Definition' below, highlighting the relevant phrases cited earlier:

So, following the saintly fathers, we all with one voice teach the confession of *one and the same Son,* our Lord Jesus Christ: the same perfect in divinity and perfect in humanity, the same truly God and truly man, of a rational soul and a body; consubstantial with the Father as regards his divinity, and the same consubstantial with us as regards his humanity; like us in all respects, except for sin; begotten before the ages from the Father as regards his divinity, and in the last days the same for us and for our salvation from Mary, the Virgin God-bearer, as regards his humanity; *one and the same Christ, Son, Lord, only-begotten,* acknowledged in two natures which undergo

---

[20] I presume that a human brain is, for the Cartesian, a sort of thinking mechanism, though it is not the subject of human thought—the soul is. If Merricks is right, then hylomorphists have an additional thinker to contend with in the incarnation over and above these two immaterial ones. But this is controversial. Stump for one appears not to take Thomist hylomorphism to have this consequence. She thinks of the human soul as similar to an Aristotelian form, or configurational state, that 'informs' or organizes the matter of the body such that, once configured, the two 'substances' (body and soul) form one distinct entity, a human. We shall return to this matter later.

[21] Another version of the too-many-thinkers objection is raised by Joseph Jedwab in his unpublished paper 'Against mereological christological concretism'.

no confusion, no change, no division, no separation; at no point was the difference between the natures taken away through the union, but rather the property of both natures is preserved and comes together into a single person and a single subsistent being; he is not parted or divided into two persons, but *is one and the same only-begotten Son, God, Word, Lord Jesus Christ*, just as the prophets taught from the beginning about him, and as the Lord Jesus Christ himself instructed us, and as the creed of the fathers has handed it down to us.[22]

The defender of the Habitus model can argue with some plausibility that, although the model is inconsistent with

1. Jesus Christ = God the Son,

it is commensurate with

2. The person who is Jesus Christ = God the Son.

As Leftow points out, the copula 'is' in (2) is not the 'is' of identity.[23] And, on the face of it, this appears to be commensurate with the statement given by the Fathers of Chalcedon.[24] Phrases that speak of 'one and the same Son, our Lord Jesus Christ', who is said to be 'but one and the same only-begotten, Son, God, Word, Jesus Christ' are not necessarily inconsistent with (2). 'One and the same Son, our Lord Jesus Christ' seems commensurate with 'there is exactly one person in Christ, namely God the Son'. 'One and the same only-begotten, Son, God, Word, Jesus Christ' may be similarly parsed as 'there is exactly one subject in the incarnation who is referred to in various ways. This subject is God the Son.' This need not imply that Christ and God the Son are identical—which is not to deny that the Chalcedonian 'Definition' is consistent with (1). In fact, it looks like the Chalcedonian 'Definition' is consistent with both (1) and (2). That is, this particular part of the symbol appears to be metaphysically underdetermined.

However, the Chalcedonian Definition is not the only Catholic symbol relevant to this objection. The Second Council of Constantinople in AD 553 issued a series of solemn anathemas in defence of the Chalcedonian settlement and against the Nestorianism of, amongst others, Theodore of Mopsuesta—by then deceased. Several of these anathemas are of relevance to the question of the nature of the hypostatic union. For instance, Anathema III says 'If anyone declares...that God the Word was...in him [Christ] in the way that one

---

[22] Tanner (1990: I 86–7).   [23] Leftow (2002: 294).

[24] This is moot, of course. But even Cross, who interprets the relevant statements of the Chalcedonian 'definition' in terms of identity between God the Son and Christ will only go as far as to say that Chalcedon *seems* to be affirming this. See Cross (2009: 452, 461). Later he acknowledges that his reading of Chalcedon 'is not universal amongst scholars' (2009: 472 n. 1).

might be in another, but that our lord Jesus Christ was not one and the same, the Word of God incarnate and made human . . . let him be anathema.'[25] At first glance, this does seem to fit better with (1) rather than (2). But the advocate of the Habitus model can agree that the only person 'in' Christ is identical with God the Son. In this sense the person 'in' Christ is 'one and the same' with God the Son, which is the important claim being made here. Similarly, the Habitus model is consistent with the notion that this person is 'the Word of God incarnate and made human'. Strictly speaking, God the Son is not Jesus Christ, of course. One could take the phrase 'one and the same, our Lord Jesus Christ' as equivalent to 'God the Son = Jesus Christ'. But it would be perverse to claim this was the only construal of this passage that made theological sense.

In fact, when one puts what is said in the third Anathema alongside some of the later comments of the Second Council of Constantinople, the picture that emerges is one that is consistent with the Habitus model. (It may even offer some support to the model.) Take, for instance, Anathema VII. It speaks of the hypostatic union as a union 'in which neither the nature of the Word has changed into the nature of human flesh, nor the nature of human flesh changed into that of the Word (each remained what it was by nature, even after the union, as this had been made in respect of subsistence)'.[26] This is echoed in Anathema VIII: 'In saying that it was in respect of subsistence that the only-begotten God the Word was united, we are not alleging that there was a confusion made of each, of the natures into one another, but rather that each of the two remained what it was, and in this way we understand that the Word was united to human flesh.'[27] In both of these passages a similar claim is made about the hypostatic union. This is that the two natures united in Christ are not changed through being united in Christ. Each nature 'remained what it is by nature', even when the personal union had taken place. This, I suggest, is a significant dogmatic statement. Suppose we construe 'change' here to mean 'fundamental, or essential change'. Some changes occur in the hypostatic union, such as the human nature of Christ beginning to exist, or acquiring the property 'being a human nature in personal union with a divine person'. But perhaps fundamental change, that is, change that would alter the nature of a thing, does not—perhaps cannot—occur at the incarnation. (It certainly cannot occur in the divine nature if God is essentially immutable.) Then, given what Anathemas VII and VIII state, whatever else happens in the hypostatic union the divine nature of Christ cannot be fundamentally, or essentially, changed by it, or as a consequence of it.

---

[25] Tanner (1990: I 114).   [26] Tanner (1990: I 117).   [27] Tanner (1990: I 118).

I take it that the divine nature is essentially a metaphysical simple. By that I mean the divine nature is not composed of more fundamental parts. It is, in this limited respect, metaphysically primitive. This claim is distinct from the traditional doctrine of divine simplicity, according to which the divine nature is not just a metaphysical simple, but is an entity that has no parts *whatsoever*. The paradigm of the sort of immaterial metaphysical simple I have in mind is the soul. It is an immaterial entity that is not composed of more fundamental parts.[28] It cannot be divided or partitioned as my body can because it is essentially a simple, though (I presume) it has distinct properties. In these respects souls are different from bodies, which are composed of more fundamental parts, can be partitioned or divided in virtue of having proper parts, and are not metaphysically primitive. Now, plausibly, the divine nature is analogous to a soul in being essentially a metaphysical simple. God the Son has the divine nature (he is a divine person). So God the Son is a metaphysical simple.[29] Now, recall the words of Anathemas VII and VIII cited above. The hypostatic union of Christ's human and divine natures cannot fundamentally change the natures thus united through, or as a consequence of, the act of union. So Christ's divine nature, being essentially a simple, cannot begin to be composite at the first moment of incarnation by, say, 'expanding' to include a concrete human nature as a proper part or parts—for this would constitute a fundamental change to the divine nature of God the Son. This is consistent with the Habitus model, according to which God the Son does not fundamentally change at the first moment of incarnation. The relation he has to his human nature is an accidental one, the human nature he assumes being like an instrument in which he is embedded.[30]

The claim that God the Son is a metaphysical simple is a traditional one. The Habitus model is able to accommodate this claim along the lines required by Anathemas VII and VIII. When the earlier are set beside the later anathemas, the overall picture of the hypostatic union that emerges is, I suggest, consistent with the Habitus model. But it seems to be consistent with other

---

[28] Compare Chisholm (1991).

[29] This is ambiguous between the claim that (a) each divine person in the Godhead is a metaphysical simple, and (b) the divine essence is a metaphysical simple. I am sympathetic to the latter, although I will not offer an argument for this here.

[30] Granted, this may not be the only way one could construe the metaphysics of the hypostatic union in keeping with the Anathemas of the Second Council of Constantinople. But I am not concerned with other ways of construing the metaphysics of the incarnation here. Nevertheless, here is an example of one sort of alternative view consistent with the Anathemas of the Second Council of Constantinople: if one allows that human nature is fundamentally a property rather than a concrete particular, exemplifying this property need not entail a fundamental change in the person who begins to exemplify it, if, say, it is an accidental property of the one who possesses it.

accounts of the incarnation too. That is, it appears that the Anathemas of the Second Council of Constantinople, like the relevant dogmatic claims of the Chalcedonian 'Definition', are metaphysically underdetermined since both symbols appear to be consistent with the Habitus model as well as the stronger metaphysical claims made by those christologists who think God the Son is identical to his human nature. But that is all to the good. It means that there is no reason to think the Habitus model falls foul of Catholic orthodoxy—as expressed in the Chalcedonian 'Definition' and the Anathemas of the Second Council of Constantinople. And it also offers some indication as to why the orthodoxy of the Habitus model has been mistakenly called into question. The two Catholic symbols we have considered appear to be consistent with more than one metaphysical account of the incarnation.

The Nestorianism problem

But what of the second theological objection, that the Habitus model yields Nestorianism? In the recent literature, Thomas Senor has made this claim. He says that 'the tradition holds that Jesus Christ was a human person—although not *only* a human person'. So the problem for the compositional christologist, as he sees it, is 'that if the human body and mind of Jesus Christ compose a person *on their own*, then it looks as though we have fallen into the heresy of Nestorianism'.[31] Later, when dealing with the question of whether God the Son is identical to God Incarnate, he responds 'The tradition clearly teaches "yes": Jesus Christ and God the Son are identical; "they" are the same person. And herein is a significant problem for the CA [Compositional Account]: it must, in the end, deny this.'[32] The reason being that the compositional account that he is considering states God the Son is only a proper part of the individual who is Christ. In which case, God the Son and Christ are not identical—which we have already noted are key claims for the Habitus model.[33] On this basis he reasons that the non-identity of God the Son and Christ, 'brings with it one or the other of two unwelcome consequences: either there are two persons in the incarnation or the composite Christ is not a person'.[34]

We will deal with the second horn of this dilemma when considering the no-person objection. What of the first horn, to wit, that the compositional

---

[31] Senor (2007: 53).   [32] Senor (2007: 55).

[33] Like Stump and Leftow, Senor does not use the theological terms given to the different versions of compositional christology he discusses. But he has in view Leftow's account, which is basically a version of the Habitus model.

[34] Senor (2007: 55).

account implies Nestorianism just in case it avoids the no-person objection? There are several things to say by way of response to this. First of all, Senor's reasoning is predicated on a theological misunderstanding. By his lights, the tradition teaches that Christ is a human *person*. To get Nestorianism, he tells us, something more than the affirmation that Christ is a human person is required. This is supplied by the notion that the human nature of Christ composes a human person *distinct from God the Son*. But this is not quite right. Orthodox christology presumes that there can be only one person 'in' Christ, that is, the second person of the Trinity. Once one concedes that Christ 'contains', is (partly) composed by, or even, is identical to, a human person, it is already too late to claim to be within the bounds of orthodoxy. For then, either Christ is fully, but merely human—in which case, he is identical to a human person distinct from God the Son, as many non-incarnational christologists have claimed, or, Christ 'contains' or is composed of both a divine person and a human person and Nestorianism follows.

In the case of non-incarnational christology, Christ is fully but merely human. He is not God incarnate. So he is a human person.[35] In fact, on medieval accounts of the incarnation a human nature unassumed by a divine person inevitably becomes a fundamental substance, or supposit, independent of the divine nature, forming a human person. Exactly how that occurs need not detain us here.[36] And, in any case, many modern theologians opt for the view that Christ is not God incarnate but a mere human person for reasons other than the rejection of medieval metaphysics.[37] What is important for our purposes is that the sort of non-incarnational account of Christ in view here means that Christ is fully and merely a human person. And if Christ is fully and merely human, then he is identical to a human person and Nestorianism does not obtain. Hence, Senor is right to think that claiming Christ is a human person is not sufficient to imply Nestorianism. However,

---

[35] Historically, most non-incarnational christologists I know of begin with the idea that Jesus of Nazareth *must* be a human person, and that classical christology is predicated on a serious theological mistake. This is what the position of classical liberal theology amounts to in the work of theologians like Albrecht Ritschl. And this sort of view has been very influential in modern theological revisionist accounts of christology, especially non-incarnational accounts like that proffered by John Hick (1993).

[36] There was a lively debate about this in medieval school theology and several theories were advanced to explain this. For discussion see Cross (2002).

[37] For many modern theologians this is tied up with a rejection of classical christology with its emphasis on what is often called 'the Christ of faith' and a turn to the so-called 'historical Jesus' that is 'recovered' through historical biblical criticism. I have challenged this false dichotomy in Crisp (2007: ch. 6).

this can only obtain where one denies Christ is God incarnate. But this is hardly the result Senor wants, given his advocacy of traditional, Chalcedonian christology.

We turn to the second possibility, which is that Christ is a human person as well as a divine person. It should be clear from the foregoing that nothing needs to be added to this claim in order to furnish us with Nestorianism. From what he says in his essay (and his other articles on the subject), it is evident that Senor is no friend of non-incarnational christology. In which case, by his own reckoning, his position presumes the very Nestorianism he accuses compositional christologists of embracing. To put it another way, if, as Senor states, the tradition does hold that Christ is a human person in addition to being a divine person (which it emphatically does not), then any model of the incarnation that implies or entails that Christ is a human person in addition to being a divine person turns out to be orthodox after all. But, according to Senor, compositional christology implies that Christ is a human person in addition to being a divine person, and this is unorthodox because Nestorian. So, compositional christology is unorthodox if it is orthodox and orthodox if it is unorthodox, on the terms set out by Senor. The result is a *reductio ad absurdum* of Senor's objection.

Evidently, something has gone seriously awry here. But some readers may think this response to Senor rather unfair. It is very easy when dealing with the metaphysics of the incarnation to make a mistake of the sort Senor does. Let us give him the benefit of the doubt and assume that what he meant to say was that the tradition teaches that Christ is *a divine person with a human nature*. By contrast, the Habitus model implies Christ is a divine person and a human person, somehow united. What will the defender of the Habitus model say to that? The obvious response involves attempting to block the inference from human nature to human personhood. One could claim that the logic of the Habitus model is that there are not two persons in Christ because his human nature is subsumed into a larger whole. Or, his human nature fails to be a person distinct from God the Son in virtue of being part of a larger composite that includes God the Son.[38] Another way to block the nature–person inference is to argue that no proper part of a person constitutes a person, on analogy with the claim that no proper part of a member of a natural kind constitutes a member of the same natural kind. This is the line Leftow takes, utilizing the famous 1001 cats example of Peter Geach.[39]

The analogy goes like this. Consider Tibbles, a *felis domesticus*, or domestic cat. His being a cat makes him a member of the biological family, *felidae*. We

---

[38] This is Stump's suggestion (2002: 58, 59).
[39] See Geach (1980: 215), cited in Leftow (2002: 281 n. 22).

might say that the *felid* Tibbles is an instance of the natural kind *felidae*.⁴⁰ But Tibbles has numerous proper parts, including the part that is composed of all of Tibble's parts minus one hair. Call this Tibbles-Minus. Question: does Tibbles-Minus compose another cat numerically distinct from Tibbles? It certainly looks like it. But if that is the case, then apparently the removal of two of Tibbles' hairs will generate a third cat, and so on, until, it seems we have at least 1001 cats—presuming Tibbles is not a follicly challenged felid and has at least 1001 hairs. But it seems bizarre to think that there are at least 1001 cats sitting on the mat, composed of proper parts of Tibbles. How do we resist this conclusion? By claiming that no proper part of a member of a given natural kind constitutes another member of the same natural kind. That is, no proper part of Tibbles, such as Tibbles-Minus, constitutes a member of the kind, *felidae*. There is only one felid on the mat, and that is Tibbles.

Leftow enjoins us to apply this reasoning to the incarnation in the following way:

> given a set of parts composing at time t a member of a natural kind (e.g., cat), no subset of that set composes at t a member of the same natural kind. Well, then: persons are a natural kind. So if at t S [the human soul], B [the human body] and the Son compose a person, no subset of {S, B, and the Son} does so.⁴¹

This looks plausible. And it offers the friend of the Habitus model a way of resisting the accusation of Nestorianism. God the Son is the only person present in Christ. His human nature never composes a human person distinct from God the Son because (a) no person can have a person as a proper part (from Leftow's adaptation of the 1001 cats manoeuvre, above), and (b) at no time does the human nature of Christ exist apart from God the Son, the divine person who assumes it at the first moment of its existence. So the human nature is never in a position to form a supposit distinct from God the Son, which, on the medieval way of thinking, is a necessary condition for the instantiation of personhood—presuming the Boethian definition of person as an 'individual substance [i.e. fundamental substance] of a rational nature'.⁴²

Senor thinks this is a serious theological difficulty for the Habitus model Leftow offers. He comments, 'GS [God the Son] cannot be a proper part of JC [Jesus Christ] if JC is also a person. Thus, if GS is a person (and surely that is nonnegotiable) then either JC is not a person or GS isn't a part of JC.'⁴³ But we have already seen that it is simply creedal orthodoxy to maintain that the only

---

⁴⁰ All that is important here is that 'cat' maps onto a particular natural kind. I am not making the broader claim that all biological families have a one-to-one correspondence with natural kinds.
⁴¹ Leftow (2002: 282). ⁴² See Thomas, *Summa Theologiae* 1.29.1.
⁴³ Senor (2007: 56).

person present 'in' Jesus Christ is God the Son. Jesus Christ cannot be a person distinct from God the Son on pain of Nestorianism. So it is difficult to see what this aspect of Senor's objection amounts to, apart from the assertion that the version of compositional christology he has in his sights (a version of the Habitus model, as it happens) is unorthodox because it cannot agree to the claim that Christ is a person. But, as I have tried to show, on the terms Senor sets out this implies Nestorianism. So this is hardly an objection to the Habitus model. However, quite apart from Senor's theological infelicities, the Habitus model is consistent with the statement that the person who is Jesus Christ is God the Son. There is no unambiguous creedal testimony from either the Chalcedonian 'Definition' or the Anathemas of the Second Council of Constantinople that requires more than this. The upshot of this is that Senor's response to Leftow's use of Geach's 1001 cats is not successful in showing that the Habitus model is unorthodox, or that it implies Nestorianism.

The identity problem

The identity problem is that according to the Habitus model God the Son is not human because he is not identical to a human nature. Traditional, orthodox christology implies that at the incarnation God the Son *becomes* human in addition to being divine. If the Habitus model denies this, or entails the denial of this, then (so the objection goes) it is unorthodox. But in order to make good on this claim, one would have to concede that there is sound theological reason to think that God the Son becoming human entails God the Son becoming identical to a particular human nature. But why concede this? Orthodox christologists are agreed that the relation God the Son bears to his human nature is a contingent one: he is not required to assume human nature; there is no necessity for him to assume human nature; in becoming human he freely assumes a human nature. In one sense, the assumption of human nature means God the Son does 'become human': he 'becomes' the divine person who is Jesus Christ. But for the atemporalist this boils down to the claim that God the Son is eternally the divine person who is Jesus Christ. No temporal 'becoming' occurs here. (Matters are more complicated for the temporalist. But I shall ignore this complication, since, like Leftow, I am interested in the atemporal view of the matter.) Clearly, this does not imply that God the Son is identical to his human nature, as we have already seen. There is no creedal pressure to assume 'becoming' here implies some identity between God the Son and his human nature. So I conclude that the Habitus model is not required to embrace the idea that God the Son is identical to a particular human nature.

The insulation problem

The Habitus model appears to insulate God the Son from having the properties his human nature does, or performing the actions his human nature performs because he is not identical to his human nature. The most difficult version of this problem arises for atemporalist advocates of the Habitus model, like Leftow. As already mentioned, divine immutability and impassibility are constituents of traditional, classical Christian theism and of the views of those theologians who have deployed this sort of thinking about Theology Proper in their accounts of the incarnation. So this is not a new problem. The claim that the divine nature of Christ must be shielded from human emotion, as well as other sorts of change, such as property changes, is the sort of problem common to any account of the incarnation that is committed to the atemporalist picture according to which God does not change in any substantial way. It is not a problem peculiar to the Habitus model of the incarnation. This much we can say *ad hominem*. But, of course, this does nothing to alleviate the difficulty posed. The real issue here is whether God the Son is so insulated from the actions and mental states of his human nature that although Christ suffers, weeps, performs physical acts, and so on, God the Son does not. His human nature does these things, he does not.

But consider a rather different way of thinking about this matter according to which God the Son acts in the incarnation through his human nature rather like one might use a tool to perform a particular task. In a similar way, Professor Stephen Hawking talks, but he uses an electronic box to do it.[44] When we speak to Professor Hawking, we are really speaking to a human–box composite, a joint system that produces the words we hear. If we ask who speaks when we hear these words the answer is in one sense the box, but in a more fundamental sense, Professor Hawking. The sounds issue from the electronic box. But it is the Professor who speaks through the medium of the box. He is the one who programmes it to make the sounds he intends to convey as speech. Something similar obtains with respect to the incarnation, according to the Habitus model. God the Son is present in the world through his human nature. He uses his human nature rather like Professor Hawking's electronic box, as an instrument that enables him to perform certain sorts of task. If we ask the question, who weeps at Lazarus' grave in John 11 or eats broiled fish on the beach after the resurrection in John 21, the answer is also similar to the Professor Hawking example. In one sense the human nature of Christ does these things. It is what we might call the proximate cause of the weeping and so forth. But the ultimate cause is surely God the Son. He acts

---

[44] I owe this example to Brian Leftow.

through his human nature, in order to bring about Christ's weeping at Lazarus' grave and eating broiled fish. When we deal with Christ weeping or eating, or performing some other human action we are faced with a human–divine composite, a 'joint system' that produces the human acts we see.

This looks like it implies causal overdetermination—Christ's human nature and his divine nature cause a given action like weeping at Lazarus' grave? But this need not follow if, say, the divine person *moves* the human nature to bring about the action in question. Richard Cross worries that this means that the Trinity moves Christ's human nature to bring about the actions of the human Christ because of the so-called Trinitarian Law: *opera trinitatis ad extra sunt indivisa* (the external acts of the Trinity are indivisible).[45] If all the external acts of God are Trinitarian acts, then if God the Son moves his human nature to eat broiled fish, the Trinity moves Christ's human nature to eat broiled fish. But I do not see why this is a special problem for the version of the Habitus model I am concerned with. The Trinitarian Law applies to all the external acts of God. The Trinity upholds and sustains Christ's human nature at every moment it persists through time. The Trinity concurs with every mundane act the human Christ brings about just as the Trinity concurs with every mundane act I bring about—given a doctrine of God's general concurrence with the mundane actions of creatures. As it is usually understood, the Trinitarian Law still provides metaphysical room, so to speak, for external acts of the Trinity that terminate on particular divine persons, such as the incarnation. We say that God the Son assumes human nature. But really, this is a Trinitarian act that terminates on one divine person in particular, God the Son. Similarly, God the Son moves his human nature to eat broiled fish. This is a Trinitarian act in one sense, but it terminates upon the person of God the Son in particular, since it is *his* human nature (i.e. the human nature he assumes—it is not assumed into the divine essence) that is in view.

Is this sufficient? It does mean God the Son *simpliciter* does not weep or eat broiled fish. But then, what is so strange about that? God the Son is an essentially immaterial being. He is incapable of weeping or eating. But his human nature is capable of these tasks. In the same way, as a consequence of his physical condition Professor Hawking is incapable of making the sounds of audible human speech. But his electronic box is capable of performing this task. Of course, there are limits to the analogy with Professor Hawking. I take

---

[45] Cross (2002: ch. 10). Cross, following Scotus, thinks a better way to make sense of the action of God the Son 'in' or 'through' his human nature is to say that the human nature causes the human acts of Christ (weeping, eating, etc.) but that these acts are predicated of God the Son via the *communicatio idiomatum* (communication of attributes), which, as we have already noted, involves predicating the attributes (actions, etc.) of the individual natures of Christ to the person 'in' Christ, namely, God the Son.

it that the personal union brought about by the incarnation is much more intimate than that between Hawking and his electronic speech apparatus. For one thing, God the Son seems able to bring about basic actions in his human nature, such as Christ's weeping at Lazarus' grave, whereas Hawking is not able to do this with his electronic apparatus, which has to be programmed manually. This is not necessarily inconsistent with the point being made here about God the Son's insulation from the properties and acts of his human nature. For, to change the analogy for a moment, the Cartesian can say 'my soul brought about the raising of my arm'. But no one would think this implies that the soul of the Cartesian has an arm. I conclude that although God the Son is insulated from the changes his human nature undergoes, this does not necessarily constitute a problem for the Habitus model.

The no-person objection

Granted that God the Son is insulated from physical or emotional changes that his human nature experiences, we can ask the further question, if Christ weeps over Lazarus *who* is the subject of this action? Not God the Son, as has already been established. He is insulated from all that his human nature undergoes. He is incapable of suffering. Not Christ, because Christ is not a person on the Habitus model. Christ is just the mereological sum of God the Son and his human nature. Nor can it be that Christ's human nature is a person on pain of Nestorianism. So Christ's human nature is also discounted from being the subject of the weeping reported in John 11: 35. But then it appears that no person is the subject of the weeping.

What are we to say to this? Perhaps the doctrine of the communication of attributes may be of some use at this juncture. Elsewhere I have defined this as follows:

Communicatio idiomatum: The attribution of the properties of each of the natures of Christ to the person of Christ, such that the theanthropic [i.e. God-Mannish] person of Christ is treated as having divine and human attributes at one and the same time, yet without predicating attributes of one nature that properly belong to the other nature in the hypostatic union, without transference of properties between the natures and without confusing or commingling the two natures of Christ or the generation of a *tertium quid* [third sort of thing].[46]

This version of the communication of attributes blocks the inference from 'S is N according to his F nature' to 'S is N'. The human nature of Christ

---

[46] Crisp (2007: 7–8).

weeps. God the Son does not, indeed, cannot, if he is essentially impassible. Yet God the Son is said to be the person who weeps according to his human nature. The property 'being the entity that weeps at Lazarus' grave' belongs to the human nature of Christ. But the property 'being the person who weeps at the grave of Lazarus' belongs to God the Son. In virtue of the hypostatic union, the property in question is attributed to God the Son via the communication of attributes. But can we run this in the opposite direction? That is, can we say S is the person who does N, when strictly speaking it is the nature F possessed by S that has or does N? Let us return to our earlier example of Christ's weeping in John 11. According to orthodoxy, Christ is one divine person who assumes a human nature in addition to his divine nature. The two natures must not be confused or fundamentally changed through, or as a consequence of, the event of hypostatic union. So if we ask whom it is that is weeping at Lazarus' grave, the answer—according to orthodoxy—must be the person 'in' Christ. There can be only one person in Christ (again, according to orthodoxy). So it is God the Son that weeps. But God the Son cannot weep, on account of being an essentially immaterial being that is immutable and impassible. Well then, we are left with saying this: the human nature of Christ weeps. The divine person who possesses this human nature is the one that moves his human nature to weep. He does not weep 'in' his divine nature, but only 'in' his human nature. Granted, on this way of thinking, one cannot say 'the divine person weeps' if this means 'the divine person *simpliciter* weeps'. But if we mean by this 'the divine person moves his human nature to weep' or even just 'the divine person weeps in his human nature', then we can affirm it.[47] This, I think, is one of the least satisfactory parts of the Habitus model. And it is here that the defender of the Habitus model has to take considerable care so as not to fall into the trap of conflating that which is ascribed to the person with that which applies only to one of the natures of Christ.

The too-many-thinkers objection

Assuming Christ has a human body and human soul (or human body–soul composite), Christ's human brain is a thinking substance. Christ's human soul

---

[47] There are ways of finessing this application of the communcation of attributes. For instance, with the concept of synecdoche—that is, ascribing to the person 'in' Christ the property that is had by only a part of Christ, his human, or his divine, nature. Or, as Marilyn Adams has recently suggested, by emphasizing the fact that Christ's human nature is not essential to God the Son. Then, applied to the Habitus model, God the Son has the attributes of deity *simpliciter*, but has human attributes only in a qualified way. See Adams (2006: 135–6).

is a thinking substance. God the Son is a thinking substance. But this adds up to too many thinking substances for only one subject of the incarnation.

But consider again the textbook Cartesianism, mentioned earlier. According to the Cartesian, humans are identical with their souls, which are 'plugged into' or 'interface with' a human brain at the pineal gland. It looks like both the human soul and the human brain on the Cartesian account are thinking entities. So textbook Cartesianism appears to have an analogous too-many-thinkers problem. But perhaps not: the Cartesian could reason that the human soul is a thinking substance that uses the human brain with which it is 'attached' to act in the corporeal world. The brain, then, is something like an instrument of the soul. (Recall the Professor Hawking example, used earlier.) Expand this to include the incarnation. Then God the Son assumes a human nature, including a human soul 'attached' to a human body. According to this textbook Cartesian story, normally when a human body and human soul are rightly configured the human person present (i.e. the human soul) uses its brain to think and perform actions through its body in the physical world. But in the case of the Habitus model, this does not occur because, although the natural endowment of a human person is present (a human soul, which in this case is 'attached' to a human body), this fails to form a fundamental substance, a supposit. The second person of the Trinity is the fundamental substance in the incarnation. He is the person who assumes his human nature. And he uses both the human body (including the human brain) and the human soul of Christ as his instrument. Now there is no need to think that there are too many thinkers. Although there are three thinking substances present in the incarnation, there is only one subject, God the Son, who acts upon, or through, his human nature—the human nature in which, so the Habitus model states, God the Son is embedded post-incarnation.

Of course, this is only a model. It may be that some other version of substance dualism better approximates to the truth of the matter (perhaps one where the relationship between body and soul is much more intimate and more carefully drawn, such as that offered by Richard Swinburne in his modified Cartesian account in *The Evolution of the Soul*[48]). Be that as it may, it seems to me that the too-many-thinkers objection need not have purchase if the advocate of the Habitus model makes clear that the incarnation involves God the Son using his human nature as his instrument, much as the human soul of a human person normally uses its brain in a manner similar to an instrument. Adding an additional 'thinker' in the person of God the Son need not make matters more difficult, if something like the medieval

---

[48] Swinburne (1986).

metaphysical story of the assumption of human nature by the Son is co-opted by the defender of the Habitus model, including the commitment to two ranges of consciousness in the incarnation, one essential to the divine person, and another accidentally related to him via his assumption of human nature.

CONCLUSION

I have argued that the Habitus model of the incarnation, as one version of a three-part compositional christology, is consistent with the dogmas of Chalcedon and the Second Council of Constantinople. It does not entail Nestorianism. And it has the resources with which to withstand the versions of the identity objection, the insulation problem, and the too-many-thinkers objection proffered here. It is possible to use the communication of attributes to help make some sense of the no-person objection. But this, I concede, is a tricky area in the metaphysics of the hypostatic union in which more work needs to be done. The objective throughout this paper has been merely to defend central tenets of the Habitus model, rather than to endorse the model. I have not suggested that the Habitus model is the *right* way to conceive of the metaphysics of the hypostatic union. But if the argument offered here is successful, a number of intellectual impediments to the model will have been removed or (in the case of the no-person objection) significantly reduced.[49]

---

[49] Thanks are due to Gavin D'Costa and Paul Helm for comments on the paper, Brian Leftow for comments on the Habitus model, Richard Cross, Tom Flint, and Joseph Jedwab for providing me with copies of the essays mentioned in the footnotes. Versions of the paper have been read at the Center for Philosophy of Religion Research Seminar at the University of Notre Dame and the Theology Reading Group at the University of Bristol in 2009. I am grateful to those present on these different occasions for their helpful comments.

4

Should concretists part with mereological models of the incarnation?

Thomas P. Flint

Concretism, as I shall use the term, is the claim that, in becoming incarnate, the Son of God took upon himself or assumed a concrete created individual that, had it existed on its own (i.e., unassumed), would have qualified as a full human person.[1] Though some might differ with this assessment, I think it's fair to say that concretism has historically been the dominant position among Christians endeavouring to understand the incarnation.[2] In recent christological discussions, the dominance of concretism has become less evident. I think this shift is unfortunate, since concretism has much to be said in its favour, and alternatives seem to enmesh us in even greater quandaries.

Still, what *kind* of concretism one should endorse (assuming one endorses it at all) is a difficult question. Concretists have frequently suggested that mereological models—models focusing on parts and wholes—can augment our understanding of the incarnation. But such models, when examined carefully, can appear to engender more problems than they solve.

Before examining these problems, I will need to do (all too quickly) a number of things. First, I will offer a few of the numerous reasons for

---

[1] Two points should be noted here. First, my account of concretism should not be taken as asserting that, to be a concretist, one needs to believe that the created individual assumed by the Son *could* have existed on its own; some (though by no means all) concretists would think that the 'had it existed on its own' clause is introducing a counterpossible. Second, the name 'concretism' stems from Plantinga (1999).

[2] Concretism's roots can clearly be identified quite early in the history of christological speculation; see, e.g., G. W. H. Lampe's discussion of Irenaeus in Cunliffe-Jones (1978: 42–50). For an interesting overview of the historical background, see the Introduction in Cross (2002). I should also note that, in calling concretism the dominant position, I don't mean to suggest that non-concretist views have not had able defenders, or that all of those alternatives were ruled out by the great christological councils or by subsequent church pronouncements.

endorsing concretism. Second, two desiderata for a fully developed concretism will be introduced. Next, I will explain why mereological models of the incarnation, insofar as they appear to satisfy those desiderata, are naturally alluring to one with concretist sympathies. Only then will I turn to the central aims of this essay: explicating the problems associated with mereological models, suggesting senses in which those models should (and shouldn't) be embraced, examining what alternatives to mereological models might be available to the concretist, and highlighting the strengths and weaknesses of those alternatives. Finally, I will venture some conclusions concerning what position regarding models of concretism is most worthy of our support.

One final preliminary. I shall be presupposing the common medieval picture of human beings as created human bodies informed by created human souls. Given this presupposition, concretism implies that the incarnation involved the Son of God's assuming such a concrete, created body–soul composite. For the sake of clarity, I'll refer to this body–soul composite by the acronym CHN, for Christ's human nature. The term 'nature', then, as I'm using it, refers to a concrete individual. Finally, I note in passing my belief that the precise make-up of CHN—a body–soul composite, a body alone, a soul alone, whatever—is not of much relevance for the ensuing discussion.

REASONS FOR CONCRETISM

Why be a concretist? Addressing that question in sufficient depth would require an essay of its own. I will limit myself here to identifying and very briefly discussing what I see as three solid reasons to prefer concretism.

First, as already noted, concretism has been the dominant view throughout most of the history of Christian thought. For those of us who view tradition as a solid, albeit defeasible, guide to belief, concretism seems to be the default position.[3]

Second, concretism seems ideally suited to allowing us to defend a fully orthodox christological stance, one which endorses the full panoply of human and divine attributes possessed by the incarnate Son. Christ was divine and thus omnipotent; he was also a human being with limited

---

[3] In speaking of the tradition being defeasible, I am, of course, referring only to the tradition propounded by mainline Christian philosophers and theologians, not to the tradition formalized in official Church teaching.

powers. Being God, he was omniscient; being a human who grew in knowledge, he was, at least at times, ignorant of certain things. Because of his divinity, some (though not all) would say, he was eternal, immutable, and impassible; because of his humanity, we should still say that he was temporally limited, changeable, and subject to suffering. With both the divine Son and the created CHN in our ontological toolbox, we have the means plausibly to understand how such seemingly incompatible claims can turn out to be true, for the divine properties are naturally seen as latching directly onto the divine person, while the human properties pretty clearly are immediately ascribable to CHN and only indirectly ascribable to the Son. Admittedly, we haven't yet told a story as to *precisely* how contradiction is avoided, but the presence of the concrete individual CHN allows us to see ways (including, as we'll soon see, mereological ways) in which such a story might be told, ways that don't seem as readily available if we reject concretism. For if there *aren't* two distinct concrete individuals (one fully and directly human, the other fully and directly divine) united in the incarnation, then how do we avoid saying that there was only *one* individual who was *both* omniscient and limited in knowledge, *both* eternal and temporal, and so on?

Finally, concretism makes it much easier to take seriously the claim that Christ was 'a man like us in all things but sin'.[4] In particular, it makes it much easier to see Jesus as a man who freely resisted genuine temptation, given that CHN can be viewed as an agent with morally significant freedom, even though the Son himself cannot be seen as anything other than essentially perfect in all respects.[5] Building such freedom into a non-concretist christology seems much more challenging, unless one is willing to abandon the traditional view that the incarnation in no way affected the Son's divine attributes (including essential moral perfection). If we need to choose between concretism and kenoticism, concretism seems preferable.

Needless to say, opponents of concretism would argue that none of these or any other argument in favour of concretism is decisive. But assuming that these and/or other considerations are sufficient to warrant the adoption of concretism, or at least to make concretism a live contender for a Christian's support, let us proceed to consider what an adequate concretist theory needs to do.

---

[4] The words here, which appear in Eucharistic Prayer IV of the Roman Missal, come originally (I believe) from the Third Council of Constantinople, which in turn was paraphrasing Chalcedon. All are based on Hebrews 4: 15.
[5] See Flint (2001) and Flint (2004).

DESIDERATA FOR CONCRETISM

Concretism is often, and understandably, seen as flirting with the heresy known as Nestorianism, which claims (roughly) that the Son became incarnate by assuming a complete and independent human person; thus, the incarnation involves a relationship between two distinct persons, one solely divine and one solely human. Orthodoxy requires us to reject this duality of persons. Only one person, the Son of God, is present in the incarnation, and that one person is truly divine and truly human.

It's easy to see why concretism might appear to savour of Nestorianism. For it's plausible to assume that CHN, as a body–soul composite that thinks and feels and acts, must be a person. If concretism is to remain orthodox, then this plausible line of reasoning needs to be severed. And so, the first desideratum for concretism is that it offer an account of the incarnation that renders it reasonable to deny the personhood of CHN.

The second desideratum has more to do with the Son than with CHN. As I have already suggested, no understanding of the incarnation could rank as acceptable if it didn't warrant our ascribing to the Son the full array of characteristically *human* properties that the Church, through both its conciliar pronouncements and its liturgical practice, has affirmed. We need to be able to say that the Son became man; that he was born of the Virgin Mary (who can thus properly be called the Mother of God); that he 'increased in wisdom' (Luke 2: 52); that he freely suffered and died for us; that he rose from the dead; and so on. Such properties—becoming human, being born, learning some things and being ignorant of others, suffering, dying, and the rest—do not prima facie seem to be ones that a God of Anselmian perfection could even possibly possess. So concretism will be worthy of our support only if it can help render plausible the claim that, by assuming CHN, the Son truly can be said to exhibit these various human properties.

Let us state these two desiderata in parallel fashion. If concretism is truly to augment our understanding of the incarnation, it needs to offer an explication of the relation between the Son and CHN that allows us to say:

(α) that CHN *lacks* something (being a person) it seems *prima facie* he should *have*

and

(β) that the Son *has* something (human properties) it seems *prima facie* he should *lack*.

The better a concretist picture does in satisfying (α) and (β), the stronger that picture would seem to be.

THE ATTRACTION OF MEREOLOGY: MODEL T

One way for a concretist to try to satisfy (α) and (β) is to think of the incarnation as a case of a substance's gaining a part. The Son, one might think, exists prior to becoming incarnate as a simple divine being. In becoming human, the Son or Word of God (whom I'll label W) takes on CHN as a part. This assumption results in a Son who combines both his original divine substance (D) and his created human nature (CHN), which we are supposing to be itself a complex individual composed of a human body (B) and an immaterial human soul (S).

I call this attempt to explicate the doctrine of the incarnation *Model T*, after St Thomas, who suggests in places that this might be the best picture we can offer of the ontological structure of the incarnation.[6]

Before proceeding, a word about what I'm labelling D seems in order, for Trinitarian concerns could quickly complicate matters here. For if the Son, *qua* divine person, were (absent the incarnation) simply *identical* with the divine substance, then mustn't we say the same of the Father and the Holy Spirit, each of whom is consubstantial with him? And if we *do* say the same about them, how can we maintain the crucial Christian claim that the three persons are distinct? Obviously, the Trinity is not, and cannot become, my principal concern in this essay. *Perhaps* our worry can be assuaged, though, if we view D as standing for the divine substance *plus* whatever properties or characteristics (e.g., being generated by the Father) distinguish the Son from the other two divine persons. In making this suggestion, of course, I'm not offering a full-fledged theory of the Trinity, since I'm not saying precisely *what* the divine substance is, or just *which* additional properties (or relations or characteristics) need to be brought in, or exactly *how* those additional properties are related to or united with the divine substance. My hope is that understanding D in this admittedly rather sketchy way (as *the divine-substance-plus-whatever*, as I'll say henceforth) is sufficient for us to proceed without first solving all Trinitarian puzzles.

---

[6] See, for example, *Summa Theologica* III, 16, 8, and III, 16, 6, ad 1. See also Freddoso (1983: 305–8) and Cross (2002: ch. 2).

As we'll soon see, Model T is not the only mereological model available to the concretist. And it must be admitted that this model would surely strike some classical theists (e.g., those wishing to uphold such traditional divine attributes as simplicity and immutability) as *prima facie* unattractive. Still, Model T clearly offers us certain advantages, especially those of clarity and familiarity; after all, most of us think we encounter cases of substances gaining parts on a fairly regular basis. But these rather generic benefits pale in comparison to the specific christological payoff that Model T seems to provide. For if Model T is embraced, our two desiderata seem to be satisfied.

Take first (α), the claim that CHN doesn't by itself qualify as a person distinct from the Son. On Model T, CHN is a proper part of a substance (the Son) who qualifies as a person. Now, it seems somewhat plausible to say that no substance has a distinct substance as a part. And it seems even more plausible to say that no person has a distinct person as a part. These two metaphysical principles are ones that many would be inclined to defend regardless of their theological beliefs. And, of course, if either is defensible, then the claim that CHN is not a person seems solid, given Model T.

What, then, of (β), the thesis that human properties are properly ascribable to the Son? Model T seems promising here too. For we often say that properties immediately ascribable to a part are indirectly ascribable to the whole, even if other parts lack that property. The horse has crossed the finish line because his nose (though not his tail) has crossed the finish line; the apple is red because its skin (though not its core) is red; and so on.[7] Thus, on Model T, it seems we might well be able to say that the Son indirectly learns and suffers and dies because CHN, his proper part, directly learns and suffers and dies.

PROBLEMS WITH MODEL T

Model T seems to say that the incarnation can be understood straightforwardly as a case of a substance gaining a part. But there is a standard objection to mereological increase, an objection sometimes called the growing argument, that is difficult to handle for mundane cases of substances gaining parts, and, as I see it, even harder to handle in the case of Model T.[8] The objection comes in both a temporal and a modal version, the former dealing

---

[7] The apple is borrowed from Leftow (2002: 273–9), who in turn appears to have inherited it from Freddoso (1983: 306). The pedigree of the horse is murkier.

[8] For a discussion of the early history of this argument, see Sedley (1982). For a more systematic treatment of the problem and of possible solutions, see Olson (2006).

with substances gaining parts as we move from one time to another, the latter with analogous growth as we move from one possible world to another. For our purposes, it will be simpler to focus on the modal version.[9] There are a number of ways in which the puzzle might be presented, but the following relatively uncomplicated version should do for our purposes.

The incarnation has almost always been seen as a contingent event. The Son of God became incarnate in our world, but it was not necessary that he do so; there are worlds in which no incarnation takes place. Suppose we let N stand for some no-incarnation world, and Y for a world (such as ours) in which the Son assumes a human nature. Since one and the same Son, W, exists in each of these worlds, it follows that:

(1) W in Y = W in N.

Model T asserts that, in worlds such as Y where B and S (the created body and soul) are on the scene, they combine with D (the divine-substance-plus-whatever) to compose the Son. But in worlds such as N, where B and S don't exist, or at least aren't assumed by the Son, there *are* no parts to compose the Son other than the divine-substance-plus-whatever. In such worlds, then, it seems that the Son must be simply identical with D. So:

(2) W in N = D in N.

Now, that divine-substance-plus-whatever is itself a necessary being; it exists whether or not the Son becomes incarnate. Hence, it follows that:

(3) D in N = D in Y.

But from (1) through (3), it appears to follow that:

(4) W in Y = D in Y.

But (4) is clearly lethal to Model T. For that model insists that the incarnate Son is a composite being, one who is not identical with D, but rather has D as a proper part. If our argument holds up, then, Model T is untenable.

Well, *does* the argument hold up? Clearly, it does if the three premises are accepted and the standard notion of identity, one which warrants transitivity, is upheld. To counter the argument, then, we need to find reason to reject a premise or to abandon standard identity. Let's consider, again with scandalous celerity, the available alternatives.

Can we plausibly deny the validity of the argument by denying the transitivity of identity? Fans of relative identity would say that we can, for identity,

---

[9] For the temporal version of the incarnational puzzle, see the excellent discussion in Le Poidevin (2009).

they say, is relative to kinds. (4) would follow from (1) through (3) only if the same kind were involved in each of these three identity claims. But some might think that it's not evident that this is the case. (1), they might say, is claiming that W in Y and W in N are the same *person*, whereas (3) is suggesting that D in Y and D in N are the same *substance-plus-whatever*. Hence, (4) simply doesn't follow from (1) through (3).

Though this is, in some respects, an attractive response, its flaws seem to outnumber its merits. Even many of those attracted to relative identity would probably wonder whether *person* and *substance-plus-whatever* are sufficiently distinct kind-concepts to block the conclusion from following. More centrally, though, I suspect that relatively few proponents of Model T could rest easy if their defence of the model *required* their embracing relative identity. The arguments here are complex, but my guess is that the vast majority of Model T advocates would prefer to find firmer ground from which to defend it.

If we grant that the argument is valid, we can avoid the conclusion only if we can justifiably impugn one of the premises. But can we? Let's consider them one at a time.

The first premise asserts that the Son who exists in worlds where he becomes incarnate is identical with the Son who exists in worlds where he doesn't. This seems like a safe enough claim. I suppose that some philosophers might have qualms about it—for example, those who agree with David Lewis that all of us individuals are world-bound, and only counterparts who are more or less like us exist in other possible worlds. Building a plausible Christian position on such a metaphysical base, however, would be challenging, and I presume that few Christians would feel drawn toward even attempting to do so.

How about (2), the claim that, in incarnation-less worlds, the Son is identical to D, the divine-substance-plus-whatever? So long as we're thinking of D as concrete rather than abstract, this claim too might seem safe enough; after all, if he never takes on a human nature, what more could there have been to the Son other than his divine-substance-plus-whatever? Yet there are at least three ways of responding to the general growing argument that, applied to our incarnational variant, would lead to a rejection of (2).

First, some respond to the growing argument by embracing the possibility of distinct but spatially coincident objects. The lump of clay that composes the statue of Sophocles at t exists in exactly the same location as the statue at t, but (say coincidence theorists) is nevertheless a distinct material object, for the lump has properties the statue lacks—e.g., the lump can be formed into a ball without being destroyed, whereas the statue can't. Applying this response to our current puzzle is a bit tricky, since the notion of coincidence usually assumed is that of *spatial* coincidence, and neither the Son nor the divine-substance-plus-whatever is typically thought of as having any spatial dimension or location, at least not absent the incarnation. Still, the advocate of coincident objects might be willing to stretch the position sufficiently to apply it to our puzzle; and if she did, the result would probably be a rejection of (2). The Son and the divine substance, she might say, are (so to speak) metaphysically coincident in N, but from this we cannot infer that the two are identical.

Appealing to distinct but mereologically coincident objects to solve the generic growing argument is a controversial move on its own.[10] Thinking that this approach allows us to save Model T seems even more contentious. It's puzzling to think that the statue, though coincident with the lump of clay, is nonetheless a distinct material object. It's much harder to understand how the Son, in a world where no incarnation occurs, could be coincident with a concrete substance-plus-whatever distinct from himself. Is this substance-plus-whatever supposed to be a person? If not, why not? Is *it* omniscient, omnipotent, and wholly good? If not, how could it qualify as a *divine* substance-plus-whatever? On the other hand, if it *is* omniscient, omnipotent, and so on, have we not added to the Trinity a *fourth* entity that exhibits these perfections? These and many other questions arise when we try to transform the coincident objects approach to save Model T. So this solution, too, seems problematic.

Somewhat more promising is a second way of justifying the rejection of (2), that offered by advocates of numerical sameness without identity.[11] The growing argument and other puzzles regarding constitution are genuine problems only if we assume that sameness entails identity—i.e., only if we assume that, for example, if a statue is made of a lump of clay, the statue and the lump can be the same material object only if they're identical. Now, as we've already seen, it seems clear to many that the two aren't identical, since their modal properties differ. But it doesn't follow that the two aren't the same material object. For the statue can be seen as what Aristotle would call an accidental unity—something that comes into existence when a substance (in our case, the clay) contingently exemplifies a property (here, the complex formal property that renders the clay a statue of Sophocles). And accidental unities, though not identical with their 'parent' substances, are counted as the same material objects. The statue and the lump of clay, then, are distinct and coinciding entities, but one and the same material object.

This Aristotelian position (as I'll call it for purposes of simplicity) is developed in far greater detail than my brief summary can capture. To my

---

[10] For a nice summary of some of the problems, see Olson (2006: 407–9).
[11] See Rea (1998a); Brower and Rea (2005); and Rea (2009).

mind at least, it seems clearly superior to the distinct-but-coincident-objects approach, since on this view we needn't say that, with the statue and the clay, we have two separate but precisely overlapping material objects. True, there is still something hard to swallow here; distinct yet coincident *material objects* are expelled, but distinct yet coincident *entities* (accidental unities and their parent substances) rush in to take their places. And there are other puzzling elements to the view.[12] Still, as solutions to the growing argument go, the Aristotelian position is clearly one that's worth taking seriously.

But how well does this position handle the growing argument as applied to Model T? If it is to help here at all, it seems it will have to be by motivating a rejection of premise (2). And it seems clear how (2) could be attacked by an Aristotelian defender of Model T. (2) says that, in N, a world with no incarnation, W is identical with D—the Son of God is identical with the divine-substance-plus-whatever. But on the Aristotelian view, this seems false, for the two have different modal properties if Model T is correct: W can have D as a proper part (as it does in Y), while D, of course, cannot. So (2) is mistaken; W and D are not identical. They are, of course, the *same* in N, but sameness does not equal identity.

There are reasons, though, to wonder about the adequacy of this solution. On the Aristotelian view, the statue and the clay, though the same material object, are still distinct. Consider W and D in N; they're the same *what* but distinct *whats*? Presumably they're the same person—if not, obvious troubles ensue—but how exactly to categorize the distinction? Are they distinct accidental unities? Presumably not; presumably there's no possible world where the unity that is D fails to exist, and so it's not an *accidental* unity at all. Are they distinct essential unities? This might seem more promising, for the divine-substance-plus-whatever seems to fit comfortably into this category. But then, what essential unity is W in N? It can't be the divine-substance-plus-whatever, for then it would be not merely the *same* as D, but *identical* with it, and the justification for denying (2) would collapse. But it's hard to see what *other* essential unity it could be. So there are problems about how the Aristotelian can plausibly distinguish W and D in N. Here too, then, we have a rather questionable means of discrediting (2).

A third justification for rejecting (2) is based on the claim that, whenever an object gains a part (temporally or modally), a new object, composed of the

---

[12] Some problems with the Aristotelian position are fairly basic. Not everyone will agree that there even *are* such *things* as accidental unities. We find it convenient at times, such critics might say, to *speak* as if there were such *things* as statues (in addition to lumps of clay) or fists (in addition to hands), but practical convenience should not be confused with ontological commitment. Applying the Aristotelian position to the doctrine of the Trinity has also drawn criticism. See Craig (2005) and Hasker (forthcoming).

original object's original parts, comes into being. Take our statue of Sophocles, and imagine the sculptor in some other world deciding at the last minute to add a bit of clay weighing one pound. In the actual world, let us assume, the statue weighs 99 pounds. And the very same statue exists in that alternate world in which the sculptor makes the last-minute adjustment, though it weighs 100 pounds there. But the pre-addition parts, so the argument goes, continue to exist and also form an object in that alternate world. What object? Well, it can't be the statue, for *that* object, we have assumed, includes that extra bit of clay in the alternate world. So the object formed by the original clay in the alternate world must be a *new* 99-pound object, one that came into being in the alternate world only when that extra bit of clay was added, one that doesn't even exist in the actual world.

If this approach, which Eric Olson tendentiously calls 'the way of funny persistence conditions',[13] were embraced, rejecting (2) would be warranted. For if adding a part brings into being a new object formed by the original parts, then adding CHN to the Son brings D into being. And if D exists only if the Son becomes incarnate, then D isn't identical with the Son, or with anything at all, in worlds where no incarnation occurs.

The way of funny persistence conditions, though, faces serious problems, both as an answer to the generic growing argument and as grounds for rejecting (2). Let me mention just one. Take the statue example again. Isn't it rather odd to think that, by adding a pound of clay to something weighing 99 pounds, the sculptor could bring into existence something new—something that wouldn't exist if he didn't add that pound of clay—something weighing, still, 99 pounds? And isn't it even odder to think that the Son's divine-substance-plus-whatever could properly be seen as, in effect, a *creature*, as something that comes into being as an ontological side-effect of the Son's becoming incarnate?

It seems, then, that none of our purported ways of discrediting (2) is easy to swallow. Since I know of no other means of impugning (2), we need to conclude, I think, that the advocate of Model T may well find it difficult to reject (2). And this means that the tenability of Model T may end up depending upon (3), the claim that D in N is identical with D in Y. Unless that premise can be shown to be suspect, Model T looks like a lemon.

One means of discrediting (3) is apparent: that of adopting what (again, following Olson) we can call the way of sparse ontology.[14] Sparse ontologists deny that just *any* two parts of a thing together compose a distinct, larger thing. Consider again our statue of Sophocles immediately before the sculptor, in that

---

[13] Olson (2006: 406).   [14] Olson (2006: 404–6).

alternate possible world, adds that last lump of clay. The various lumps that were slapped together to make the statue in our world continue to exist individually in the alternate worlds where the additional lump is added. But do they continue to form a single distinct object in those worlds? Sparse ontologists say no. There simply is no such thing as the-statue-minus-the-final-lump in the alternate world. But then, in the case of the incarnation, there is, in worlds where the Son assumes CHN, no such thing as D. The *components* of D continue to exist individually, but they no longer constitute an object. And this means that (3) is false.

As a response to the generic growing argument, sparse ontology may well be our least implausible alternative. As a solution to our incarnational puzzle, though, it raises enough additional questions to make one wonder whether we can rest happy with it. For sparse ontology seems to require that the Son, in worlds without an incarnation, is composed of distinct parts, parts that continue to exist (though they fail to compose anything) in worlds where the Son assumes CHN. But what component parts could the non-incarnate Son have? Even if there is a theologically tenable answer to this question, one might wonder what has become of the Son's divine-substance-plus-whatever once we adopt the sparse ontologist's solution. If there is no such thing as D in worlds where the Son assumes a human nature, then D turns out to be not only contingently a *person*, but contingently a *unity*. And if D just *is* the divine-substance-plus-whatever of the Son, then the incarnate Son *has* no divine-substance-plus-whatever in those worlds. These are claims few Model T-ers would presumably be eager to endorse.

Sparse ontologists might not be without responses here. For their view seems to require that D be thought of, not in the rather schematic, unexplicated fashion I have thus far irenically favoured, but explicitly as a *composite object*, with the divine substance and the Son's distinguishing characteristic (e.g., that of *being generated*) as its components. Hence, sparse ontologists might contend, even though D *itself* doesn't exist in incarnation worlds such as Y, its components, including the divine substance, do survive. I must confess that this type of response is in many ways rather attractive. Still, thinking of the Son and the other members of the Trinity as essentially composite in the way this solution requires (thinking of the characteristics that distinguish them from one another as literally *parts* of each person) and thinking of the divine-substance-plus-whatever as a contingent unity seem to me rather unappealing, all things considered.

I believe we've now pretty much exhausted the standard responses to the growing argument. While some of those responses, when applied to our incarnational version of the argument, are more attractive than others, none of them offers us a clearly and fully defensible means of countering that argument as applied to Model T. What this suggests to me is that we have some reason to doubt Model T's claim to offer us an accurate picture of what takes place in the incarnation. If Model T has survived the challenge posed by our puzzle at all, it's more as a road-weary clunker than as the sleek, smooth-running model it initially appeared to be.

Now, some concretists would respond at this point that what our discussions really have shown is only that Model T is confused, not that a mereological approach to the incarnation is misguided. What we need to do is not to abandon such an approach, but to trade up from Model T. What we need is a *different*, philosophically coherent mereological model of the incarnation.

A MEREOLOGICAL ALTERNATIVE TO MODEL T

And there is another model available. It's a model that has attracted prominent proponents, both medieval (e.g., Scotus) and modern (e.g., Leftow).[15] On this model, the Son unites himself to CHN in the incarnation. But the composite thus formed is not the Son. The Son remains simply one part of the composite entity that results from his assuming a human nature. That composite entity, which (following Scotus and Leftow) we can call Christ, is a contingent thing, composed of another contingent entity (CHN) and of a necessary one (the Son). Since this model is one inspired by Scotus, it would be appropriate to call it Model S, thereby contrasting it nicely with the more Thomistic Model T. But since I'm already using S to refer to part of CHN, we can both avoid possible typographical confusion and serendipitously salute automotive history if we instead label it Model A.

There is much to be said on behalf of Model A. It allows us to view Christ as having two distinct natures, thereby escaping monophysitism. It permits us both to deny that CHN is himself a separate person from the Son (hence eluding Nestorianism) and to maintain, if we wish, that though CHN and Christ are temporal entities, the Son is himself timeless and unchanging.[16]

---

[15] For Scotus, see Cross (2002: 128–33). For Leftow, see (2002: 287–91), and his paper in this volume. Eleonore Stump also appears (though less explicitly than Scotus and Leftow) to endorse this alternative. See Stump (2002: 206–9).

[16] For a careful discussion of how this model might help to dismantle arguments for the incoherence of a timeless incarnate God, see Leftow (2002: 292–9). Note, though, that denying the personhood of CHN on mereological grounds seems somewhat harder on Model A than on Model T, since the 'no proper part of a person is itself a person' principle doesn't, on Model A,

Finally, the puzzle that afflicts Model T has no potency against Model A. For on our new model, (4) can be accepted without dissent or apology. The Son and his divine-substance-plus-whatever simply *are* identical whether or not the incarnation occurs. The coming into existence of CHN changes not who the Son is but only what things are related to him and (hence) what composites the Son is a part of. So (4) is just fine, and our supposed puzzle no puzzle at all given Model A. Indeed, the very fact that there even *seemed* to be a puzzle can now be seen as the price we paid for endorsing a confused mereological model.

Model A, then, has much going for it. At times, I am inclined to buy it. But, thus far at least, I've not been able to sign on the dotted line. My hesitation to embrace Model A is based not on philosophical worries but on theological ones. The advocates of Model A are right, I think, in suggesting that it is free of the metaphysical puzzle that troubles Model T. But I'm not convinced that Model A allows us to say and to believe the sorts of things we as Christians want to say and believe about the incarnation.

Recall Leftow's example of the apple. If the skin of the apple is red, it's appropriate to say that the apple—the whole of which the skin is a proper part—is red. But it would be odd indeed to say that if (and because) the skin is red, the core is red. The core may be part of a whole that is red, but the core itself just can't sensibly be called red. Transferral of properties from part to whole makes sense (at least, it often makes sense), but such transferral from one part to another part generally doesn't make sense.

Similar points hold with regard to Model A. If Christ is composed of W and CHN, and if CHN suffers, then it's fine to say that Christ suffers. But there's no evident mereological argument for saying that W suffers. And if W just *is*, as Model A maintains, the Son, then there's no mereological justification for saying that the Son of God suffers. With *this* property (that of suffering), many advocates of Model A might welcome this result; after all, they might say, don't we *want* the divine component of Christ to be insulated from suffering? The problem, though, is that Model A seems to insulate the Son from *all* of the actions and properties of Jesus. The Son didn't suffer. He also never changed water into wine, never wrote in the sand, never wept at the tomb of Lazarus. He wasn't tempted in the garden. He didn't freely accept death on a cross. He didn't die for our sins. To be sure, *Christ* did all these things; but the *Son* did none of them. CHN was born of the Virgin Mary. Perhaps, then, we can say that Christ was born of the Virgin. But the Son

---

entail CHN's non-personhood unless we say that Christ is a person. And as we'll soon see, there are reasons to doubt that Model A is most plausibly developed in this direction.

clearly wasn't. Mary was the mother of Christ, but not the mother of the Son. And so she was not the mother of God.[17]

I don't see how an orthodox Christian can rest happy with these implications. And there are others equally or even more troubling. The Gospel of John tells us that the Word became flesh. This is usually taken to mean that the Son became a human being. But *did* the Son become a man on Model A? Was the Son a man at all? CHN was, it would seem, a human being, and so perhaps, by extension from part to whole, was Christ.[18] So the Son was part of something that was a man. Does this make the Son a human being? It's not clear that it does. Again, the core of the apple is part of something red, but the core itself is not red. So the Son is not a human being. The Son is not a man. The Word did not become flesh because the Word is not flesh. Has not Model A so insulated the Son from humanity as to call into question the very meaning of incarnation?

One more point. The Son on Model A is part of Christ. Is Christ, strictly speaking, a person? If we say yes, then, since Christ is distinct from the Son, we have two distinct persons in the incarnation and all the unsavoury Nestorian ramifications that follow.[19] But if we say no, as most proponents of Model A appear to say,[20] then it seems there simply is no person to whom the activities of Jesus of Nazareth can be ascribed. CHN walked into the temple and threw out the moneychangers. Who did these things? Who is the *person* acting here? CHN? No; he's not a person. Christ? No; we've assumed he's not a person either. The Son? No. True, he's a person, and a part of Christ; and Christ is the whole to whom the actions can be ascribed. But it's hard to see how any of this makes CHN's actions the actions of the Son. Again, the apple core just isn't red. So, if Model A is accepted, it seems that, when CHN upended the moneychangers' tables, what we have is an action which

---

[17] Note also that using the word 'Christ' to name the composite of the Son and CHN seems to lead to rather strained readings of several conciliar proclamations. For example, Chalcedon speaks of the second person of the Trinity as 'one and the same only-begotten Son, God, Word, Lord Jesus Christ'. This surely appears to be a string of appositives, all referring to the same person. But the Model A-er cannot read the council's words in this straightforward way, since 'Christ', for them, names a composite object that has the Son as a proper part.

[18] The claim that CHN was a human being is denied by Leftow; see (2002: 278–9). But his denial appears to be based on the assumption that anything that is a human being is a person, an assumption that I see no reason to accept. (Neither, I think, did Aquinas; see, e.g., *Summa contra gentiles* IV, 35 and 37.) After all, what kind of being *is* CHN if not a human one?

[19] One might attempt to avoid Nestorianism by saying that the Son is a person in an immediate sense, while Christ borrows personhood from the Son, and thus is a person in an indirect sense. But is personhood the type of attribute that can properly be 'loaned' from part to whole? And would this position truly remain orthodox?

[20] See Cross (2002: 130–2) for a discussion of Scotus's position here. See also Leftow (2002: 294).

ultimately belongs to no person whatsoever. And this too, it seems to me, is very hard to swallow.[21]

It goes without saying that the advocates of Model A would not be mute in the face of such criticisms.[22] And perhaps it could be shown that my theological concerns are baseless. But I have my doubts. The problems with Model A *appear* to be fundamental and significant. In moving from Model T to Model A, it's far from clear that one is better off.

PARTING WITH MEREOLOGICAL ACCOUNTS?

So neither of our mereological models, taken seriously and at face value, seems to deliver what it promised. Now, I think it would be premature to conclude that the models are of no value, for it could well be that the problems I have raised can be handled effectively. But suppose they can't be handled effectively. Even then, rejecting the models outright might not be the wisest course. Most of those who have forwarded Model T have done so with a degree of hesitation that is sometimes ignored in discussions of the view.[23] Model T, they have suggested, offers an illuminating model of the incarnation, but it's not an accurate metaphysical description; it's the best we can do, but liable to lead us into error if taken flat-footedly. The divine-substance-plus-whatever and CHN are rather *like* distinct parts of a composite Son who has become incarnate by adding a human part to his divinity. Still, the mereological talk here is metaphorical; Model T is *only* a model, not an honest-to-God blueprint of what happened in the incarnation.

This type of hesitancy has not, in general, been as evident among advocates of Model A. The Son and CHN, they seem to be saying, *really are* parts of the

---

[21] In his paper in this volume (pp. 45–66), Oliver Crisp argues that, even on Model A, we might be able to call CHN's actions the Son's actions if we think of the Son as *causing* CHN to think and act as he does. Though this is a possibility worth exploring, I doubt that this picture of a fully determined CHN will ultimately prove attractive. Furthermore, the part–whole relationships *affirmed* by Model A seem paradoxically insignificant if this attempt to *defend* Model A is correct. If the *causal* relationship between the Son and CHN is what's doing all the work, does it matter whether or not the two are related *mereologically*?

[22] See, for example, Cross (2002: ch. 8), where he attempts to explicate how christological predication would work on the Scotist picture. I cannot enter here into the details of this intriguing discussion, but I can register my grave doubts that Cross offers the advocate of Model A any convincing means of dealing with the theological objections lodged above.

[23] See Freddoso (1983: 305 n. 16), and Flint (2001: 5). Note also Aquinas's claim, in *De unione Verbi incarnati* 2, that 'the human nature in Christ' subsists 'not properly as a part in a whole, but through an ineffable assumption'.

composite Christ. But, of course, there's no reason that Model A-ers *couldn't* adopt the hesitant approach of their Model T brethren.

Let's ingeniously call these two approaches to mereological pictures the *metaphorical* and the *literal* positions. What our examination of our two models suggests, I think, is the preferability of the metaphorical to the literal. Taking a mereological account to offer more than just a helpful model of the incarnation simply opens the door to far too many unsavoury philosophical and theological conundrums. The more we think about mereological models, the more the metaphorical stand seems appropriate.

Is there a cost associated with moving toward the metaphorical? Recall (α) and (β), our two desiderata for a concretist christology. The motivation behind developing a mereological picture such as Model T in the first place was that it would allow us to satisfy these desiderata. If CHN *really is* a part of the Son, then we seem justified in saying both that CHN lacks the independence necessary to qualify as a person and that the Son can borrow human properties from his human part. But if we've abandoned a literal reading of the model, have we really made any progress in satisfying (α) and (β)? If CHN *isn't really* a part of the Son, then mustn't CHN be seen as a person? And mustn't CHN's human properties be seen as belonging *only* to CHN, not to the Son?

There may well be a price to be paid for going metaphorical, but I do wonder if the cost is as high as the previous paragraph suggests. If CHN is literally a part of the Son, let's suppose, CHN *isn't* a person. But it hardly follows that if CHN is only rather *like* a part of the Son, CHN *is* a person. Perhaps one of the ways in which CHN is like a part is that his relationship to the Son precludes his own personhood. Taking Model T metaphorically implies that not *all* the distinctive part–whole relations between CHN and the Son hold, but it hardly entails that *none* of them do. So the price of abandoning a literal reading of Model T may be less exorbitant than some have suggested.

ALTERNATIVES TO MEREOLOGICAL PICTURES

Still, the failures of the mereological models we have examined should make one wonder if concretists are wise to take the whole/part relationship as the sole, or even the best, building block for an illuminating picture of what happened when the Son became incarnate. A number of interesting alternatives are indeed available and have been much discussed. Let me mention two: taking CHN as akin to the clothes that a man wears, or to the instruments he uses to accomplish certain purposes.[24] These analogies are worthy of far more attention than I can give them here. Each seems successful in satisfying at least our second desideratum for an adequate concretist picture. For properties of clothing or instruments are indeed readily transferred to their users. It makes sense to say that I cut the lawn even if I used a mower to sever the blades of grass; and most of us would agree that the baseball hit the batter even if it struck his uniform rather than his skin. But these analogies do a much poorer job with our first desideratum—illustrating how CHN could lack the property of being a person, a property it seems *prima facie* he should have, and lack it because of his relationship to another person. After all, when are we tempted to think of a uniform *itself* as a baseball player, a temptation overcome only when we recognize that it's being worn by a genuine player? How often are we inclined to view a hammer as *itself* a carpenter, an inclination that dissolves only when we notice the actual carpenter using it? Clothing and instruments just seem categorically far more distant from those who wear or use them than CHN seems from persons. Hence, it seems to me, neither of these models throws much light on how a concretist can avoid Nestorianism.

A couple of less-discussed models might also be worthy of consideration. First, the concept of *condensation* might offer us a helpful picture. Consider the relationship between, say, a philosophical essay and the rather complete handout the author distributes when delivering the paper orally. It's easy enough to imagine the handout's being sufficiently different from the paper that no one would see it as a *part* of the paper; the relationship between the two isn't a simple mereological one. Still, the handout could easily be extensive enough that, if one saw *only* the handout, one might be inclined to say that it was *itself* a philosophical essay, albeit one sorely in need of stylistic fine-tuning and substantive augmentation. Only when one recognizes its status as a condensation of the *actual* paper would one come to view it as something other than an essay itself. It *could*, one might think, have stood on its own; absent the relation of condensation, we might well ascribe the lofty status of essayhood to the piece exactly as it is. Given that relation, however, we don't.

Second, one might offer a picture of the incarnation built on the notion of *ownership*. Consider the difference between a division of a company and a wholly owned subsidiary. A division, as its name suggests, is properly thought of as a part of the larger, whole corporation. But things are different with a

---

[24] Cross offers a nice introduction to the so-called *habitus* (clothing) metaphor (2002: 30–2). G. P. Fisher argues that the instrumental model first appeared very early in the patristic period. See Cunliffe-Jones (1978: 32–3). Though either of these models *could* be given a mereological interpretation, that's not the most natural way to take them. Does anyone outside of philosophy departments and lunatic asylums really think that I and my clothes are literally proper parts of a larger, anthrosartorial whole?

subsidiary. Though owned by company C, subsidiary S is its own legal entity, not a part of C; the two are closely related, but non-mereologically. Note that, though subsidiary S might well be given a large degree of autonomy by company C, there's no question that C is ultimately in control; it can change S's leadership, its policies, its divisions, and so on, pretty much at will. Note also that, even if S does in fact do things more or less on *its* own, it would be natural for C to claim those actions as *its* own, in an indirect sense. Suppose that C acquired S in part because it knew of S's plans to expand its operations into China. If these plans proceed as intended, unencumbered by the acquisition, it would be natural for C's board of directors to say, 'Well, we're finally moving into China!' when reviewing S's activities at its next board meeting. Note that S might lack nothing that it needs to be a company on its own. Only because it's a possession of another corporate entity does it lack the status of being a company. The parallels to the incarnation are, I trust, evident.

Modelling the incarnation on either of these notions—condensation or ownership—could, of course, proceed in a number of different ways. Many things can be viewed as condensations of others; think of a quick sketch which an artist makes of a complex drawing, or the pared-down version of a play entered in a theatre competition. The same, of course, holds for ownership. Companies own subsidiaries, but similar relationships hold (or at least did hold in less enlightened times) between countries and their colonies, slaveholders and their slaves, parents and their children, and so on. Exploring the varieties within these two types might well prove illuminating.

I don't mean to suggest that either of these approaches offers us an ideal picture of the incarnation; each presents us with its own infelicities. Thinking of CHN as some type of condensation of the Son might help with (α): no condensation of a person, we might think, is itself a person, even though it would have been had it existed on its own. But condensational pictures help somewhat less with regard to (β). What property *that it doesn't have on its own* would we be inclined to ascribe to an essay because its outline has that property? Perhaps there are some, but it's not easy to think of many, or at least of many interesting ones; generally, transferral of properties from condensed to uncondensed doesn't seem as plausible as transferral from part to whole.[25] Furthermore, to me at least, condensational models simply don't have the right feel; CHN, as a flesh and blood, created human being,

---

[25] I don't mean to say that there are *no* such properties. For example, a condensation of an essay may be *comprehensible to us* in a way that the essay itself, on its own, wouldn't be. Understanding the condensation in this manner may well entail that we have at least a degree of understanding of the uncondensed itself. I'm grateful to John Hare for bringing this point to my attention.

doesn't seem much like a whittled-down version of the Son. Ownership models seem more promising in many respects. They give a more convincing means of satisfying (β) than condensational models do (company C really *has* moved into China because subsidiary S has), and the 'doesn't feel right' objection cuts much less ice here. But, of course, ownership models rely on notions of ownership that we haven't even tried to analyse, and that at least appear inappropriately conventional rather than natural; one might well wonder whether the relation between the Son and CHN doesn't need to have more non-subjective ontological oomph than the notion of ownership can provide.

CONCLUSION

So there are indeed challenges that remain even if we augment mereological models with alternatives. Yet it seems clear to me that it would be wise for concretists to devote more of their energy to thinking about such alternatives, and this for a number of reasons.

First, it's not obvious that the difficulties accompanying, say, ownership models are any *worse* than those that we've seen accompany Model A and Model T. Until such models were developed with greater care and depth, any conclusions concerning their relative merits would seem premature.

Second, it's surely conceivable that our best picture of the incarnation will come from mixing some of these models together. James Madison, in *Federalist* 39, argues that the governmental arrangement proposed in the new US Constitution follows a national model in certain respects, but a federal model in others; only by combining *both* models, he suggests, do we come to an adequate picture of what the framers had forged. Maybe something similar is true with the incarnation. Maybe any attempt to shoehorn the incarnation into a *single* well-known model is bound to fail, while combining some of these models will provide us with greater insight. Admittedly, I don't quite see how this is likely to work in the case of the incarnation, but, again, viewing such combinatorial attempts as doomed to failure seems out of order.

Finally, and perhaps most important, paying attention to some of these alternatives might free all of us from the misconception of thinking that concretism stands or falls with mereological approaches. It doesn't. The arguments in favour of concretism are independent of the mereological models, and their soundness doesn't depend upon those models. The weaknesses of literal mereological models, and the problems that beset the alternatives we have briefly examined, *may* suggest that concretists should say, with Aquinas, that the relation between the Son and CHN really is *sui generis*—that all attempts simply to subsume it under more familiar relationships will fail. But even if this is so, it gives us, I think, no reason whatsoever to abandon concretism.[26]

---

[26] Earlier versions of this paper were presented at an APA Central Division session, at the University of Texas at San Antonio, and at the University of Notre Dame. I am grateful for the many comments I received at these sessions. Special thanks are due to Michael Almeida, Oliver Crisp, John Hare, David Hunt, Joseph Jedwab, Dean Kowalski, Brian Leftow, Alvin Plantinga, and Michael Rea.

5

Drawing on many traditions: an ecumenical kenotic christology

Thomas Senor

INTRODUCTION

The traditional Christian doctrine of the incarnation is profound and yet deeply confounding. On the one hand, it stirs the heart and has great spiritual and emotional value. The claim that the Creator-God, the omnipotent source of all that is, cares enough about humanity to take on our nature and endure the brutality that characterizes the Passion of Christ is profoundly moving. Furthermore, it allows the Christian to have confidence that God not only has propositional knowledge of what we experience and of our difficulties and hardships, but that God is able to empathize with us too. In short, the doctrine of the incarnation brings God to us and puts God in our shoes in a way that no non-incarnational theology ever could. Yet while the doctrine of the God-man certainly stirs the soul, it just as surely confounds the mind, and in many ways and along a host of different dimensions. For example, in claiming that Jesus Christ is both 'fully God' and 'fully human' the Christian is claiming that God the Son has (or at least had) a pair of natures. Yet one might have thought a nature is that which makes one what one is. If that is right, how is it possible for a single individual to have multiple natures? Second, even if it is possible for an individual to have more than one nature, how is it possible for the nature of God and the nature of humanity to be exemplified in a single individual? Even if some natures are somehow compossible, why should we think that the infinite divine nature would be compatible in a single individual with the puny, metaphysically wispy nature of humanity? Ideally, these and other similar questions should be answered by a good account of the metaphysics of the incarnation.

An ecumenical kenotic christology

In developing a philosophically satisfying christology, one will have to make a decision at the very beginning: is consistency with the ecumenical creeds and the decrees of the early councils a condition of adequacy on one's account of the incarnation? If so, there are very clear constraints on what one's christology will look like. If not, what kinds of constraints *will* be acknowledged? Now one might be tempted to think that either you develop your theory of the incarnation within the constraints of the tradition or anything goes. I don't think that is right, however. For instance, one might hold that consistency with scripture is all that matters. If, given the right interpretation of scripture in light of the contemporary biblical scholarship, one constructs an account of the nature of Christ that best explains the scriptural data but that doesn't comport particularly well with, say, the Nicene Creed, one will certainly have been operating under serious constraints, even if they are not as onerous as they are on one who accepts the creeds and councils. It's actually an interesting question, it seems to me, what one should do if one sincerely believed that the scriptural and, for want of a better term 'traditional' view of the nature of Christ were to diverge. Obviously, different branches of the Christian church, if they are to follow their own rules, are going to be committed to different conclusions. Be all of that as it may, I intend to sketch an incarnational view with the goal of conforming to both scripture and the creeds and councils.

So conformity with the tradition is a constraint on our philosophical theorizing about the incarnation. But stated that way, we don't get much help. For we need to know what that commits us to if we are to know our boundaries. So here is a list of what I think are desiderata of a successful metaphysics of the incarnation, traditionally construed:

1. It must entail that Jesus Christ and God the Son are identical.
2. It must entail that God the Son has whatever properties are essential for divinity even during his earthly ministry.
3. It must entail that Jesus Christ has all the properties that are essential for humanity.
4. It must not emaciate either the divinity or the humanity of God incarnate.
5. While providing an account that helps resolve logical difficulties in the doctrine, it must not remove all of the mystery from the incarnation.

While points (1)–(3) are straightforward, the fourth and fifth points could use a little explaining. Let's take them in order. In the first paragraph of this essay, I noted that the doctrine of the incarnation is both intellectually confounding and deeply moving. An attempt to give a theory or model of the metaphysics of God incarnate is primarily aimed at making the doctrine less confounding. But it should not do this at the expense of emptying it of its emotive force because, or so it seems to me, its emotive effect is tightly linked to its spiritual and perhaps even soteriological effect. So, for instance, an account which resolved the logical difficulties but which entailed that Jesus Christ never suffered pain or felt abandoned should be rejected for failing to satisfy desideratum (4). Alternatively, a theory that entailed that Jesus' divinity was, to all intents and purposes, ersatz divinity should similarly be rejected. With regard to (5), any account that would try to explain everything of significance in the incarnation in such a way as to completely remove a sense of mystery is surely too simplistic and fails to keep in mind the enormous cognitive and ontological gulf that separates humanity from the divine.

I'm not claiming that the five points above are exhaustive of the desiderata for an account or model of the metaphysics of the incarnation. But, if one wants one's view to be in conformity with the scriptures, creeds, and councils, and to be spiritually satisfying, one's account had better play by these rules.

In what follows, I will sketch three approaches to understanding the nature of the incarnation that can be found in the contemporary philosophical theological literature. These are (1) Thomas Morris's two-minds theory, (2) the compositional account one finds in Aquinas and recently expanded and defended independently by Eleonore Stump and Brian Leftow, and (3) the kenotic view as one finds it in the writings of Ronald Feenstra, Stephen Davis, and C. Stephen Evans. After evaluating each position, I will argue that a broadly kenotic christology that incorporates insights from the two-minds view and the compositional account is the best prospect for a metaphysics of the incarnation that satisfies the five desiderata. Because there is so much to be done in this paper, both my presentations of the positions and my objections to them will have to be somewhat brief. Similarly, at the essay's end what I will give will be a sketch of an account. So while I hope that there will be some level of cogency and convincingness to what I argue, I do not pretend to be presenting anything that looks like a knock-down argument against any of these positions or a particularly strong argument for the position I favour.

MORRIS'S TWO-MINDS VIEW

In his ground-breaking work *The Logic of God Incarnate*,[1] Thomas V. Morris defends an account of the incarnation that appears to satisfy our desiderata. There are two main moves that Morris makes: first, he marks the distinction between being 'fully human' and being 'merely human' and claims that there is no reason in principle why a divine person couldn't be fully human even

---

[1] Morris (1986).

though that person could not be merely human. Second, Morris argues that establishing that, in principle, human and divine natures are compatible is necessary but insufficient for providing a suitable account of the incarnation. Basically, the reason for this is that such an account might not satisfy our fourth desideratum: Jesus might be technically human but if he experiences the world only as God, then he is not 'like us in all ways except sin'—or for that matter very much like us at all. So in an effort to give us a more typically human Jesus, Morris develops the two-minds view, according to which Jesus Christ had two minds—one human and the other divine. Let's now look at each component a little more carefully.

Natural kinds and 'full' and 'mere' humanity

The primary problem that drives Morris's account of the incarnation is the objection that the doctrine can't possibly be true since it involves ascribing logically incompatible properties to Jesus Christ. Following Morris, let's call this the 'Incoherence Objection'. The idea is that if Jesus is God, then he must have whatever characteristics are essential to divinity. Such properties include omnipotence, omniscience, omnipresence, etc. But, the objector continues, it is a necessary truth that no human being can have any of those properties since by definition (or, better, by nature) humans are limited in power, knowledge, and spatial location. So if he is both divine and human, then Jesus has a long string of pairs of incompatible properties (or at least properties and their logical complements).

According to Morris, the first counter-move that the Christian should make is to inquire about the epistemic status of the claims about what is necessary for being human. Why should she think that it is a necessary truth that no human being be, for example, omnipotent? The response is that this just falls out of either the definition of the term 'humanity' or the content of the concept. That is, we might think of humanity as being something like a nominal essence. This will be a collection of properties that we use when we classify objects in ordinary life. Just as the nominal essence of gold will be those properties we commonly associate with gold, so the nominal essence of humanity consists of those properties we typically associate with being human. The point is that nominal essences are known *a priori*. One reflects on one's concept and what one finds embedded there is an essential part of it. So when we reflect on our concept of humanity, we can see that having various limitations of finitude are crucial components of the concept.

Morris argues that this is the wrong way to think about the nature of humanity. Instead, we should treat it along the lines of a 'real essence' or what has come to be called a 'natural kind essence'. Consider the often-used example of tigers. If we stick with cluster concepts or nominal essences we define them as large, striped, carnivorous quadrupeds that are typically black and yellow. While some such list of properties is generally fine for picking out tigers when one goes to the zoo, it clearly does not get at the essence of tigerhood. For a tiger can lose one or more of its legs, its taste for meat, and even its stripes without ceasing to be a tiger. To be a tiger is to be a member of a certain zoological type and such types are individuated at the genetic level. So even though in ordinary life we use certain epistemically available markers to pick out something as a tiger, such markers do not get at the essence of the natural kind. There are, of course, some kinds (speaking a bit more loosely here) that are *a priori* known. For example, to be a bachelor is to be a member of a (non-natural) kind and the method for finding out what is necessary and sufficient for bachelorhood is *a priori* reflection on the concept. Concepts that are *a priori* knowable along these lines are known as 'cluster concepts'. They just consist in clusters of other concepts that compose them.

Once we've distinguished between natural kind concepts and cluster concepts, the relevant question is into which classification does humanity fall? The answer should be apparent: the concept of 'human being' is a lot more like that of 'tiger' than that of 'bachelor'. So we should figure that what it is to be human is to be a certain zoological type (perhaps with an additional, immaterial part; I don't mean to be begging questions against dualism). But if humanity is a natural kind, then a determination of its essence is not to be done via conceptual analysis or *a priori* reflection of any kind, but by *a posteriori* investigation (and perhaps metaphysical theory development). In short, there is no good reason to think that 'not being omnipotent' will just fall out of 'is human' because almost *nothing* just falls out of a natural kind concept. Once this point is made, we can see that there is significant flexibility in what the Christian might say about the nature of humanity and there is in principle no reason why she can't deny that a human must be contingent, limited in knowledge and power, etc.

Morris next introduces his distinction between mere and full humanity. To be merely human is to be fully human and also not a member of a higher ontological type; to be fully human is simply to have all of the qualities necessary for humanity. The Christian, then, can say that there is no *a priori* or even *a posteriori* reason for thinking that nothing that is human could possess any of the omni-properties. Of course, if God the Son is identical to Jesus Christ, then Jesus can't be said to be merely human, but that doesn't rule out his full humanity. So the first part of Morris's response to the incoherence objection is to deny that being human requires lacking the omni-properties on the ground that kind essences aren't known via *a priori* reflection.

Two minds

As mentioned earlier, Morris has foreseen a potentially crippling objection to his account.

> But this appears to leave us with a person who was Jesus of Nazareth and was omniscient, omnipotent, omnipresent, and necessarily existent. Of course, we ordinary human beings exemplify the logical complements of each of these attributes of deity ... Such properties as being restricted in knowledge, limited in power, localized in presence, and contingent in existence will be held to be at most essential for being merely human. But this can appear to be a near *reductio* for the strategy. Can a fully human being be omnipotent, omniscient, and the rest? Did Jesus have these properties? The New Testament portrays him as at times tired, hungry, and as lacking knowledge of certain things. And surely no amount of modal manipulation of human nature can render it possible that this man was also incorporeal, immutable, and impassible. At this point, the initially promising strategy for blocking the incoherence charge can appear to break down.[2]

Indeed. But Morris has a solution, a way of allowing him to continue to hold the claim that Jesus had all of the essential attributes of God without taking away from his experience as a human being. The answer, according to Morris, is to posit two minds in the incarnate God—one is the omniscient divine mind that is from eternity and is the seat of the omni-properties had by Jesus Christ. The other mind is the earthly mind which came into existence around 3 BCE and grew in knowledge and wisdom in much the same way that the average human person's mind developed in first-century Palestine. The two-minds view is supposed to help with the objection in the above quotation because it was the human mind that was primarily operative in the earthly life of Jesus. Morris postulates that there was an asymmetrical accessing relationship between the minds: the divine mind had complete access to the thoughts, experiences, beliefs, etc., of the human mind but the human mind had limited access to the divine mind. In fact, the human mind could only know of the divine mind what the divine mind revealed to it. So the mind that was conscious in the earthly life of God incarnate was the finite mind that was taken on with the human nature. For the most part, then, the experience of Christ was like the experience of those around him. How much the human mind knew about its relationship with the divine mind is an issue that different two-minds theorists may disagree about, and is to be decided on (as far as possible) in light of the scriptural record.

---

[2] Morris (1986: 72–3).

There is one further refinement that needs mentioning. Morris notes that were he to end his account here he'd have a major problem: for the asymmetrical accessing relation that the earthly mind of Jesus has to the mind of God the Son is also had by each of us with the mind of God the Son. The Son has complete access to our mental life and we have whatever access to his he allows us to have. So wherein is the uniqueness of Christ? Morris's answer is that unlike us, the causal and cognitive powers of the earthly mind are none other than the cognitive and causal powers of God the Son. But the rest of us have independent cognitive and causal powers. Our mental powers are brought about by God but they are numerically distinct; the powers of Jesus just are the powers of God the Son.

Evaluation of Morris's view

While this overview is admittedly sketchy, it does provide enough of the motivation and detail of the theory to allow for at least a *prima facie* evaluation. The first thing to notice is that it seems to do very well regarding the five desiderata. It insists on the identification of God the Son and Jesus Christ and entails that this divine person has all the kind, essential properties of divinity and humanity. The two-minds component of the theory allows a plausible case to be made for claiming that the conscious life of Jesus was very different from the consciousness of God the Son, even though the latter was in some sense in the background. Furthermore, it is clear that a fair bit of mystery remains. In particular, the matter of what it would be like for a single person to have two fully conscious minds is beyond the ability of human beings to enter into empathetically.

For some readers, the mystery that remains is rather too much. For, it has been contended, persons necessarily have single minds. Even if there are periods of mental fracture where streams of consciousness come apart, what unites the minds into a single person is their causal history and, perhaps, their being grounded in the same physical organ. Split personalities can then be regarded as one person in a way that two minds that are not grounded in the same underlying stuff and which can never be integrated with each other cannot. Worse still, John Hick has argued convincingly that Morris's view faces a dilemma: either the two minds each has its own set of causal and cognitive powers or they don't.[3] If they do, then Morris doesn't have an answer to the objection that the relationship between the mind of God the Son and Jesus of Nazareth is precisely the same relation that the mind of God the Son bears to every other person. However, if each doesn't have distinct

---

[3] Hick (1989).

cognitive and causal powers, then Morris's theory apparently collapses into monothelitism, a heresy condemned at the Third Council of Constantinople (the Sixth Ecumenical Council) which was summoned in 680 CE. The monothelites believed that while there are two natures in the incarnation (hence they believed they could accept the teaching of Chalcedon) there was but a single will. When Morris claims that the cognitive and causal powers of God the Son are numerically the same as the powers of the earthly mind of Christ, he apparently means at least that the two minds share a will. Hick maintains that Morris must have been thinking that a 'mind' is not much more than a set of beliefs, and thus that Morris's view is overly intellectualistic. Now I agree with Hick in thinking that Morris must be assuming that minds are individuated strictly by sets of mental states (Humean bundles, it would seem). But what's wrong with the position is not that it is overly intellectualistic. For among the states in that bundle will presumably be conative states too; emotions will be part of the package. The problem is that such a method of individuation leaves out an essential characteristic of minds: their causal powers—cognitive, conative, and emotive powers. If each distinct mind requires its own set of powers (and that is very plausible), then the two-minds view will require two wills and Morris will lose his answer to the uniqueness question.

Before leaving our discussion of Morris, I'd like to make one further point. Although Morris's view is generally distinguished by its invoking of two minds, I can't see how any theorist who wants to obey the rules laid down by the creeds and councils can avoid positing a pair of minds in some fashion or other. For the claim that there was a single mind was held by Apollinaris and denounced as heresy by Pope Damasus in the Council of Rome 381 CE. As I understand it, Apollinaris held that incarnation consists of Son of God's taking the place of the human rational soul in the body of Jesus that contained only an animal human soul; Jesus was literally God made *flesh* rather than God made *man*. So if we are to be true to our desiderata, we will have to posit a view in which two distinct minds (or rational souls) come to inhabit or at least be uniquely associated with a particular human body. It is a terrific irony that Morris's two-minds account fails in that it does not posit two minds.

THE COMPOSITIONAL ACCOUNT OF THE INCARNATION

One perspective that actually does posit two distinct minds is the compositional account of the incarnation. In the past few years, this Aquinas-inspired position has been championed by such philosophical luminaries as Eleonore

Stump and Brian Leftow.[4] According to the compositional account, Jesus Christ is metaphysically compositional. That is, Jesus Christ is quite literally composed of God the Son together with a body and rational soul (or human mind). Since God the Son is spirit and essentially a divine mind, and a human mind is also predicated of Jesus Christ, the view entails that there are two minds.

One clear motivation for this position is that it is seen as a way of dealing with the incoherence problem that Morris was attempting to solve. The properties that we take to be the limitation properties are properties not of the one incarnate person, but rather of the human parts of the person. Leftow says explicitly that we should read sentences like 'Christ died *qua* human but not *qua* divine' mereologically. That is, it is asserting that Christ had a part that died (the human mind and body—or at least the human body) and a part that didn't (God the Son). So for any of the problematic properties we can say at least that the one property is had by the divine part and the other is had by the human part. Stump and Leftow split company regarding what to say about what properties the one incarnate person had. Stump says that when a whole has a part that has a property, then the whole has that property 'to some degree'. But there is no contradiction in saying that a composite object has property P to some degree and lacks property P to some degree. So for example, someone who had very strong arms and very weak legs would be *strong to a degree* and *not strong to a degree* (and the same goes, of course for weakness). Leftow demurs here and claims only that some properties had by parts accrue to their wholes and some do not. We will have to decide, he says, on a case-by-case basis. So, for example, Leftow suggests that the omnipotence of God the Son transfers to the composite whole; similarly, the property of being created as instantiated by the human body and soul will likely transfer to the whole, while the property of being uncreated had by the divine part will not.

My outline of the compositional account can be briefer than my sketch of Morris's view because it is in a way, less complicated. Once one understands its mereological nature, one sees, at least roughly, how the compositional account will answer standard coherence objections.

That's not to say that the view doesn't have its share of difficulties. Notice that any of the objections to Morris's two-minds view to the effect that multiple minds entail multiple persons will apply to the compositional account. Although the emphasis isn't on the duality of minds here, the fact is that the account posits a distinctly human mind (or rational soul) and a

---

[4] Stump (2002) and Leftow (2002).

divine mind. As far as I can tell, neither Stump nor Leftow has a view about how these minds relate to each other. But since their position is that Jesus Christ is the mereological sum of God the Son, the human mind, and the body that the Son takes on, they at least have a theory that explains why you and I aren't also God incarnate: our human bodies and minds compose a human person that is ontologically distinct from either the person of God the Son or Jesus Christ. In short, Christ has one crucial part that we lack: God the Son. But as I pointed out at the end of the last section, it appears that no view that doesn't posit two distinct minds in God incarnate will satisfy the general 'creeds and councils' condition of adequacy on accounts of the incarnation. So the fact that the compositional account both entails two minds and also explains the uniqueness of the two-minded incarnation it posits should be seen as a theoretic strength rather than a weakness.

Be that as it may, the compositional account is problematic. In fact, I think it suffers from multiple debilitating problems. First, it fails to satisfy the identity desideratum. For if God the Son is a proper part of the composite object that is Jesus Christ, then God the Son is not identical with Jesus Christ since no part can be identical to the whole of which it is a proper part. So Jesus and the Son are numerically distinct entities. Worse still, the view, taken in light of the councils and creeds, entails that Jesus Christ is not a person. Here's why. Nestorianism was rejected at the First Council of Ephesus in 431 CE for denying the hypostatic union and claiming that a distinct person was associated with each nature in the incarnation. The Council declared that although the incarnation involves complete human and divine natures, they are joined in a single person. But if there is a single person in the incarnation, and God the Son is not identical with Jesus Christ, then one of them isn't a person. But surely God the Son, the Second Person of the Trinity, is a person. Therefore, Jesus Christ is not.

The lesson here is that when the creeds speak of the Son's taking on human nature, they should not be understood to be making a mereological claim. The Son does not become a part of a non-personal whole. Rather, the Son bears a relation to human nature which allows him to be numerically one and the same as the human person Jesus Christ. Furthermore, it is very unclear to what extent the compositional account really helps with the incoherence objection. For the tradition insists that there be a single subject of predication in the incarnation. So even if we are to attribute the limitation properties to Christ's human part and the omni-properties to his divine part, we still have to have something to say about the single subject of predication that is the person of God incarnate. Saying that he has the divine properties *in a respect* and the human properties *in a respect* just doesn't answer the question of what properties to attribute to the single person. As Leftow says, we will have to decide the matter on a case-by-case basis; but if that is so, then it is unclear how the compositional account is offering anything like a substantive or systematic response to the incoherence objection.

Nevertheless, there is something suggestive about what the compositional account has to say about the charge of incoherence. For example, consider the following instance of the problem: one can be human only if one is created; one can be divine only if one is not created. Nothing can be created and not created, so therefore nothing can be divine and human. As we've seen, the compositional account will try to answer the objection mereologically: Jesus Christ has a human part that is created and a divine part that is uncreated. Some properties of proper parts accrue to the whole and some do not. In this case on the compositional account, one can plausibly argue that since the composite Christ consists of two significant created parts, the whole takes on the property of being created rather than uncreated (even while it contains the uncreated part of God the Son).[5]

ADOPTING INSIGHTS FROM THE COMPOSITIONAL ACCOUNT

While I believe we've seen ample reason to reject the compositional account, and hence the adequacy of any defensive manoeuvre that depends upon it, there is something one can say that is in the near neighbourhood and that is promising. One can maintain that in taking on human nature, God the Son came to bear a relation to the acquired human mind and body that allowed some of the properties of that mind and body to become properties of his without claiming that the mind and body were parts of his.

To see this, consider the following example. Robert is an actor who will begin a role in six months in which he will play the part of a man who weighs eight hundred pounds. To get into the character properly, Robert is fitted with a costume that will give him the realistic appearance and the manoeuvrability of a man who, at six feet tall, weighs eight hundred pounds. Furthermore, when Robert is in costume he in fact weighs eight hundred pounds—or, more exactly, the combined weight of Robert and his costume is eight hundred pounds. Let's further suppose that he will not remove the suit until he has finished playing this part in nine months' time. Consider, then, the following claims about Robert when he is many months into his character:

---

[5] I subject the compositional account to a more rigorous attack in Senor (2007).

1. Robert weighs eight hundred pounds.
2. Robert can move only laboriously.
3. Robert gets winded just walking down the hall to go to the bathroom.
4. Robert feels ashamed when he goes out in public.

Let's stipulate that before putting on his present costume, none of these claims is true. Robert is a man who, at one hundred-eighty pounds is in good shape, is light on his feet, and takes deserved pride in his appearance. But now that he's been in character for quite a while, it would be wrong or at very least misleading to continue to flatly deny the truth of (1)–(4). The sober metaphysical truth is that the costume is not part of him; instead he is embedded in it in such a way that it is through his character (and the costume) that he experiences the world and even, to a degree, himself. So while he doesn't literally weigh eight hundred pounds, that is what the scale will read anytime he steps on it, and he feels the way an eight-hundred-pound man feels—both with respect to his wind as he walks, the speed at which he is able to move, and even the way he knows he is perceived by other people. Getting back to our list, then, while (1) is strictly speaking false, (2)–(4) are true. And Robert has the attributed properties in virtue of them being embedded in a costume that is not literally part of him.

I believe it will be useful to make a distinction between a couple of different ways of having properties. Some properties a thing has strictly in virtue of its parts—both proper and improper. Robert has the properties of being human, of being intelligent, and of being male in virtue of the parts that compose him. However, while in costume Robert also has the properties of being slow-moving and not fitting into a standard chair. These are properties he has not in virtue of his parts but in virtue of the suit into which he is embedded. Even so, it seems to me, they are genuinely properties he currently possesses since it is straightforwardly true that he can't now fit into a chair or walk quickly. Let's call properties that stem directly from one's parts 'direct properties'. In contrast, properties that one has only because one is embedded in a particular circumstance will be termed 'derivative properties'. So my being able to type, walk, and read are direct properties of mine; my ability to be in St Louis tomorrow or fix my toilet are derivative since I have those properties only in virtue of being embedded in a circumstance in which there is (relatively) high-speed travel and toilet-fixing tools.

Let's complicate matters a bit. Suppose that what is essential to Robert is that he have the DNA he has. Suppose further (and unrealistically) that anyone with that DNA will always be thin and, barring injury and while in youth, swift (henceforth, I'll assume the qualifier 'barring injury and while in youth' without stating it). Put in the terminology I have here explicated, it is essential to Robert that he have the intrinsic properties of being thin and swift. But now here's an incoherence objection to Robert's current predicament: Nothing can be Robert that doesn't have Robert's DNA. Nothing can have Robert's DNA and not be thin and swift. However, no one who wears the fat suit can be either thin or swift. But it is impossible for anyone to be both 'thin and swift' and 'neither thin nor swift'. So therefore it is impossible for Robert to wear the fat suit.

Something has gone wrong, since it is surely possible for Robert to be embedded in the fat suit and when he is to be neither swift nor able to fit into a chair. The problem occurs early on in our assumption that anything with Robert's DNA would be swift and able to fit into a standard chair. What the DNA can be expected to do is to guarantee that in his youth and apart from injury, Robert will have the direct property of being swift and thin *provided that he is embedded in a circumstance that renders that possible.* Now I'd very much like to have something enlightening to say about what being embedded in a circumstance comes to, but I'm afraid that I do not. What is crucial for our purposes, though, is that being embedded doesn't change one intrinsically even if it does alter one's properties. Being in the suit makes Robert now unable to fit into a chair or move swiftly. Yet (and this is the big point) *he* hasn't changed in any intrinsic way. (Notice that if his acting role required him to gain six hundred and twenty pounds instead of wearing a suit of that weight *he* would have changed substantially in a way that he hasn't changed by putting on the suit.) So while we have to give up the claim that given his DNA, Robert is necessarily swift and thin, we can continue to hold that his DNA is essential to him and that his parts necessitate that he be intrinsically swift and thin even if his circumstances prevent him from being this, all things considered.

Let's consider again (1), i.e., the claim that Robert weighs eight hundred pounds. Because the suit isn't a part of Robert and one's weight is purely a function of the collective weight of one's proper parts, (1) is false. Even so, Robert has a pretty good idea of what it is like to be an eight-hundred pound man. That is, although Robert isn't even derivatively eight hundred pounds, his experience of the world, while in costume, is very much like that of a person who weighs that much. Let's call properties like this—that is, properties that a person doesn't literally have but which the person's experience is as though he had—ersatz properties.

Assuming a story like Robert's makes sense, we can make an analogous claim about the incarnation. Some properties had by the human mind and body of Christ are had by the Son and some aren't. So being created will not be even an ersatz property of the Son since it is a property of the human mind and body that is not come to be had by the Son, and isn't really even part of the way the incarnate Son experiences the world (he experiences human limitations but there is nothing particularly experiential about the property of being created). However, arguably, being spatial will be a property that the Son will now have derivatively—that is, in virtue of the relationship he bears to the spatial human body (and perhaps mind). Being limited in knowledge and power might also be plausibly thought to be derivative attributes of the incarnate God. Even though he would not have them were he not tethered to the human body and mind, given that his experience of the world during the incarnation was severely mediated by that body and mind, we can plausibly claim that he was so limited during his earthly ministry.

I'm getting ahead of myself. For as we will see, I think that a broadly kenotic perspective can make the most sense of these kinds of insights and it is to that position that we will turn after taking stock.

ADOPTING INSIGHTS FROM THE TWO-MINDS VIEW AND MOTIVATING KENOTICISM

Over against both the two-minds view and the compositional account, the kenotic view attempts to do its explicatory work in a somewhat different fashion. The emphasis in the first two approaches is additive; the focus is on God the Son's assuming or taking on humanity. Taken neat, this seems to cause problems with coherence. And even assuming the omnipotent, omniscient, omnipresent Son can add a human nature to his being, in what sense is the resultant person a genuine human being? The claim that the Son took on human nature needs to be paired with the view that in doing so the Son surrendered or gave up or at least qualified divine characteristics he previously had.[6] Whether in the end this helps or not (and I think it does), I believe that it is a significant motivation for contemporary kenotic theories to which we will turn presently.[7] For the moment, though, let's take stock of what I've argued (or at least claimed) so far.

I've argued above that although Morris's two-minds theory is flawed, his point that humanity should be seen as a natural kind and hence that the concept of 'humanity' is a natural kind concept is very important for making

---

[6] Although I'm using expressly temporal language, I don't mean to beg any questions here about divine atemporality. Perhaps the timelessness advocate can translate these claims into terms of logical or modal order.

[7] I'm not suggesting that kenoticism has historically been motivated primarily by the metaphysical issues which are the focus of this paper but only that one sees its use here as a motivation to take the view seriously.

headway on a coherent account of the incarnation. For as long as the concept is thought of as a cluster concept or nominal essence, then it will consist of the set of qualities that we standardly employ when we think about humans and pick them out amongst other things. We will then naturally think that being limited in knowledge and power, created, mortal, and perhaps even morally flawed are all essential to our humanity. However, if humans are natural kinds, then the essence of what it is to be human is to be found not in armchair conceptual analysis but in biology: to be human is to have the human genome. But it doesn't fall out of the natural kind concept of humanity that nothing could be human and yet unlimited in power.

As Morris himself recognizes, it won't do to simply make what we might think of as the anti-kenotic move and insist that, for any inconsistent pair of properties that one is tempted to attribute to Jesus Christ one should attribute the divine property at the cost of the human property. For even if that were a way of resolving the incoherence objection, it would give us an account that would fail to satisfy our desiderata since it would effectively gut the humanity claim of all content. We saw when we discussed the compositional account that even though it is a mistake to think that the human body, human mind, and God the Son literally compose Jesus Christ, there is a way of plausibly arguing that the properties had by the Son in virtue of taking on humanity accrue to the Son at least as ersatz properties and perhaps even as derivative properties. So while we might say that some of the alleged inconsistent properties are in no good respect both attributed to the incarnate Son because the limitation property turns out not to be essential for being human, we can say that each member of some other pairs are had by the incarnate Son (even if one of the properties is only derivative, or even ersatz).

So while I think that both Morris's two-minds view and the compositional account have fundamental flaws that keep either from being generally adequate theories of the incarnation, there are important insights offered by each and which should be incorporated into a metaphysical account of the incarnation. In what follows, I will sketch a role that the kenotic view can play which, in addition to the aforementioned insights, seems to me to provide a theory that manages to both provide a solid answer to the incoherence charge and satisfy our desiderata.

THE KENOTIC PERSPECTIVE

Kenoticism is something of a newcomer in christological theory. Originating in Germany in the nineteenth century in the work of Gottfried Thomasius and W. F. Gess, the emphasis at the time was not so much on squaring the doctrine of the incarnation with Leibniz's Law and concerns about incoherence. Rather, the goal was to incorporate the then-current research into the 'historical Jesus' into the life of faith, not in a way that would reduce the bold metaphysical claims of Chalcedon but instead as a means of using what was being newly learned about the life and times of Christ as a way to better understand his humanity. For God incarnate must be experientially rather than just metaphysically human if he is to truly join us in our condition.[8]

The fundamental biblical impetus for the kenotic perspective comes from an early hymn that Paul quotes in the second chapter in his letter to the Philippians. The relevant verses are these:

> *Let the same mind be in you that was in Christ Jesus*
> *Who, though he was in the form of God,*
> *Did not regard equality with God*
> *As something to be exploited*
> *But emptied himself,*
> *Taking the form of a slave, being born in human likeness*
> *And being found in human form,*
> *He humbled himself*
> *And became obedient to the point of death—*
> *Even on a cross.*[9]

The key to figuring out how to mine this passage of its christological import is in understanding what is meant by 'emptying'. It should be noted at the outset that the kenotic perspective can't be the entire solution to the incoherence objection that we've been discussing. For if we were to claim that in every instance of potential conflict, the divine property has been abandoned to allow for the taking on of a human nature, then the Son's divinity would be gutted and we would have abandoned one of our desiderata. So if kenoticism is to be helpful here it will have to be as a supporting role or perhaps as part of an ensemble. But as we've seen above, there are insights that a kenoticist can glean from the other views. In what follows, we will look at a major difficulty facing any account that is even partially kenotic and at how contemporary theorists have attempted to deal with it. In the end, I'll reject the favoured solution to the problem and offer in its place one of my own.

The kenotic perspective faces an obvious, potentially devastating objection before it even leaves the proverbial gate. Recall the second desideratum listed in this paper's first section, i.e., that any candidate account of the incarnation

---

[8] See Thompson (2006).
[9] Philippians 2: 5–8, New Revised Standard Version.

entail that God the Son had whatever properties are essential for divinity even during his earthly ministry. Inasmuch as the kenotic perspective attempts to deal with at least some varieties of the incoherence objection by claiming that God the Son lays aside some divine attributes in order to become human, it runs the risk of denying the divinity of Christ. For the doctrine of the incarnation is not simply the doctrine that God became human; were that all it asserted then perhaps we could be content with the idea that taking on humanity meant laying aside divinity. However, the doctrine requires that God incarnate be fully human and fully divine. So how is the kenotic perspective to even get started if what is fundamental to it is the Son's self-emptying of divine properties? Let's call this the 'Not Fully God' objection to kenoticism.

Let's look at a specific example, in particular the attribute of omniscience. The Christian philosophical tradition insists that omniscience is required for divinity. Put slightly differently, it is part of the job description, one might say, for being God that one be omniscient. On the other hand, being human plausibly entails finitude and that would seem to require being limited in knowledge. The kenotic perspective will advocate that we maintain that the Son empties himself of omniscience in order to take human form. The question, then, is why this doesn't entail that the Son surrenders his divinity. The answer that seems to have the most support among contemporary contributors to the analytic philosophical theological literature is essentially this:[10]

The incarnation teaches us some things about the nature of God. Whereas, in our recognition of God's limitlessness and infinite nature, we might have originally assumed that being omniscient was a requirement of divinity, we can infer from the fact that Jesus himself acknowledged that there are things he didn't know, together with the tradition's claim that Christ was divine, to the conclusion that omniscience is not necessary for divinity. However, this doesn't mean rejecting the idea that God is the Anselmian perfect being. If omniscience were essential for divinity, and if no omniscient person could be human (or could have a first-person understanding of what it is like to be human), then God could not become human while continuing to be God (or at least couldn't become a human who could empathize with other humans). Would a being who is incapable of such an incarnation be *greater* than a being who was able to be fully incarnated? It's hard to see that perfect being theology will require us to answer yes. Perfect being theology is guided by the conviction that we should attribute the greatest set of compossible great-making properties to God. Exactly which set is the greatest will be a matter of controversy even among those who hold to perfect being theology. Furthermore, even if the above reasoning shows that

---

[10] Morris was the first to suggest this possibility, although he rejects it in the end. Ronald Feenstra embraces it, as do Stephen Davis (2006a) and C. Stephen Evans (2006a).

omniscience *simpliciter* isn't an essential property of divinity, there is a reasonable facsimile at the ready. The kenoticist will agree that omniscience is generally a great-making quality which a perfect being would give up only if there was an overriding reason to do so. Armed with this insight, the kenoticist can claim that while omniscience *simpliciter* isn't an essential attribute of divinity, the related quality 'omniscient-unless-freely-and-temporarily-choosing-to-be-otherwise' is.[11] Our focus here has been on omniscience but there are other attributes for which a similar distinction can be drawn: omnipotence and omnipresence come to mind as possibilities.

No doubt it is obvious that this strategy can work for only certain ostensible properties of divinity: necessary existence and being creator of all that is other than God's self do not admit of kenotic renderings. But as we've seen, there are other, not implausible ways of dealing with these problems (it would seem to be consistent with taking on a human body and mind that one have these properties that Stephen Davis labels 'ungiveupable').

The question I want to address now, then, is not the extent to which kenotic understandings of the attributes can be generated, but their desirability. For the account of the divine essence that we will end up with if we give kenotic renderings of several of the traditional attributes will have an air of artificiality about it. Instead of the divine essence being composed (in part) of such unrestricted attributes as omnipotence, omniscience, and omnipresence, the kenotic perspective currently under consideration has it that each of these attributes is not, in fact, required for divinity, that divinity requires only the related property of having that attribute unless it has been freely given up. But there are two ways that such an account is problematic: first, it appears to be ad hoc, and second, the properties that are being claimed as kind essential for divinity are not sufficiently fundamental or basic. Let's look at these in turn.

The traditional Christian holds that Jesus Christ was fully God and fully human. Accounts of the incarnation that are purely additive are thus in principle acceptable because rather than removing anything from his divinity, God the Son simply adds on a complete human nature. However, the defender of the kenotic perspective as outlined above emphasizes the surrender of certain divine properties. The only way that she can do this and yet continue to claim that the Son was divine during his earthly ministry is to alter the standard account of the divine nature. As we've seen, she alters the account by adding a caveat clause that is specific to the problem she is thereby trying to solve. But this comes perilously close to being a paradigm of an ad hoc emendation. True, the advocate of the kenotic perspective who favours this response to the 'Not Fully God' objection will say that the incarnation has

---

[11] See Feenstra (1989).

taught us something about the nature of God. But that rejoinder, while effective against the complaint that altering the divine attributes is religiously objectionable, doesn't address the ad hoc nature of the changes. Learning something about divinity from the incarnation is fully appropriate, but one might have hoped that what we learn would be more general or maybe even deeper than the simple addition of a caveat clause on the traditional attribute. As we will see, I do think we can learn something about the divinity via the incarnation that takes us a good deal further.

This leads to my second objection: altering the divine properties in the way under consideration illustrates that the properties that are being claimed as constituting the divine essence are not suitably fundamental or basic to play that role. Consider the following case. Smith believes that an essential characteristic of tigerhood is 'being black-striped'. As long as every tiger Smith has seen had black stripes (and let's suppose that Smith has seen a lot of tigers), it might well be plausible for Smith that being black-striped is essential for being a tiger; that is, nothing could be a tiger that was not black-striped. But if his travels take him to India and he is confronted with a particular variety of white tiger, he'll have to change his perspective. (I take it that Smith's claiming they aren't tigers because they aren't black-striped would not be reasonable.) Suppose as a result of his encounter with the white tiger Smith alters his view of the nature of tigers. Instead of taking them to be essentially black-striped, he now believes 'being black-striped unless white' is essential for tigerhood. Surely, there is something too easy about making this particular change. Notice, though, his new belief might be true and rational. For if his experience with tigers is vast and if the only non-black-striped tigers are a certain type of white tiger, then it is not only true that every tiger is either black-striped or white, but it might well be true that nothing *could be* a tiger that fails to have this disjunctive property.

If the belief that 'being black-striped unless white' is essential for tigerhood stands a good chance of being true and is not irrational, then what is wrong with it as a response to seeing white tigers? I submit that the problem is that being confronted with the counterexample to the original belief should make Smith think that maybe being striped or non-striped doesn't bear a particularly significant relation to what it is in virtue of which a tiger is a tiger. Notice that for any kind, there are terrifically unenlightening properties that are essential to it. For instance, being coloured and opaque are both essential to tigerhood (nothing non-coloured and transparent could be a tiger), although I think no one would want to say that they tell us anything interesting about the essence of being a tiger. To be a tiger is to have the natural kind essence that tigers have. To use the current biological lingo, it is to have the tiger genome.

As far as I can tell, one who adopts a kenotic reading of the divine attributes is guilty of doing essentially what Smith does above. For if we are to learn something about the nature of divinity from the incarnation, and essentially what we learn is that the Son is able to divest himself of some of the standard divine attributes, then we should conclude that those attributes do not compose the deep essence of divinity, and we should suspect that perhaps the attributes in question were not of the right sort in the first place. As with Smith's tigerhood belief, the problem with the particular kenotic response to the 'Not Fully God' objection we are considering is not that it isn't *true* that nothing could be God that wasn't omniscient-unless-freely-and-temporarily-choosing-to-be-otherwise and it might well be *reasonable* for one to think this. The problem is that one now lacks a reason for thinking that this particular property is a suitably deep or fundamental property capable of serving as (a part of) the essence of divinity.

AN ALTERNATIVE KENOTIC PERSPECTIVE

I will now sketch a position that will take insights from all three perspectives we've been considering. I begin by briefly developing an alternative kenotic answer to the 'Not Fully God' objection and will finish by outlining an account according to which God the Son was embedded in the human mind and body during the incarnation, working through the mind and body of Jesus of Nazareth.[12]

I begin with a simple but important point. The 'Not Fully God' objection gets its purchase not because the kenotic perspective claims that divine properties are surrendered, but because it seems to entail that properties *essential to divinity* are given up. If there is a good way to argue that what is given up are divine properties that are not *essential* to divinity, then the kenoticist might have a philosophically and religiously adequate response. I will now attempt to forge such a way.

As we've seen, Thomas Morris's distinction between cluster concepts and natural kind concepts plays an important role in seeing how to begin to argue for the coherence of the doctrine of the incarnation. We should think of humanity along the lines of tigerhood rather than bachelordom. What it is to have the essence of humanity is to have the human genome. However, when it comes to how to think about divinity, Morris and others continue to think in

---

[12] Some of the ideas in the next several paragraphs were first discussed in Senor (1991).

terms of a cluster concept. To be divine is to be omnipotent, omniscient, omnibenevolent, necessarily existent, and all the rest; the essence of divinity is nothing over and above the collection of those properties. However, it seems to me that thinking of divinity as a cluster concept is no better than thinking of humanity as a cluster concept. Let's reflect for just a bit on the relationship between natural kinds, essential properties, and other attributes.

Let's take water for example: what is essential to water is that it be composed of two parts hydrogen and one part oxygen. These are its essential characteristics. In addition, water has what I'll call standard attributes. These are properties that an object commonly or typically has but which are not properties in virtue of which the thing is an exemplar of its kind. Among standard attributes, some are *ceteris paribus* and some are secondary-essential. A *ceteris paribus* property is a property that an object will typically have (or maybe will have in its natural or paradigmatic state), but which is not essential to the object's being a member of its kind. So, for example, water has the *ceteris paribus* property of boiling at 100 degrees Centigrade and being tasteless. But if you add salt to the water, both of those properties will no longer be exemplified yet you'll still have water. On the other hand, a secondary-essential property is a property that is essential for kind membership, but which is derivative in a way the fundamental essential properties are not. So consider again tigers and suppose that given the tiger genome, the only way a tiger can fail to have black stripes naturally is if it is white. Then Smith's belief that 'being black-striped unless white is kind essential for tigerhood' is true, but only because it is a secondary-essential property: it necessarily supervenes on those properties that are fundamentally essential.

Given this conceptual machinery, I propose the following: we should think of divinity as a supernatural kind. To be divine is to have whatever it is that is at the essence of the being who created the world and became incarnate in Jesus Christ. It is to have the God 'genome'. The standard divine attributes are not, then, fundamental essential properties but are standard properties of divinity: they are properties that a being with that essence will paradigmatically instantiate. Some of these properties will be secondary-essential but some will be *ceteris paribus*. Being the absolute ground of all being, source of all power, and necessarily existent are prime candidates for secondary-essential properties: any being who is of the divine substance will necessarily exemplify them.

On the other hand, a good case can be made for saying that omniscience is only a *ceteris paribus* property. On reflection, omniscience was never well suited to be a fundamental essential property. For being omniscient reduces to having and exercising maximal cognitive power (the ability to have direct knowledge of all propositions and entities). One might suppose that having maximal cognitive power would be secondary-essential but why should we think that its exercise would be as well? Of course, one might say that typically or paradigmatically, the power is utilized, but if one thinks a certain kind of freedom is important for a divine being, one might well think that there are possible circumstances in which that power is not fully used.

Omnipotence is a tougher case because to be omnipotent requires only having power and not, as with omniscience, fully exercising it. To give up omnipotence, then, it isn't enough that one quit exercising the full range of one's powers (for those powers are never fully realized in any event), but one must give up the *ability* to exercise them. In short, the powers of omnipotence must be unavailable if omnipotence is to genuinely be given up. I don't have anything definitive to say here but I do want to note that there is an interesting middle ground between having the powers of omnipotence readily available to one even if one isn't fully using them, and not having them and being unable to get them back at the time should one change one's mind. Suppose Katie gives up chocolate for Lent. She does this successfully (if minimally) as long as she does not eat chocolate in the forty days before Easter. If Katie's will is just barely strong enough to pull it off, there will be lots of counterfactual instances in which her will is weak and she gives in. Her managing to hold out until Easter is, to a certain degree, a matter of luck. This then is a clear case in which Katie doesn't in fact eat chocolate but (as we might say) *could have* and even *would have* in the right circumstances.

Suppose Katie wants so badly to keep to her Lenten vow that she sees a hypnotist who induces in her a deep repulsion to chocolate to the point that she is unable to eat or touch it. Even if she were to want to eat or touch it (perhaps she's offered a thousand dollars if she would and she really wants the thousand dollars), Katie just wouldn't be able to bring herself to do so. In these circumstances, Katie doesn't eat chocolate; but more than that, given the efficacy of her hypnosis, she *can't* eat it either.

Finally, suppose Katie is a person of remarkable will power and commitment to her word. If she vows to do something, she always follows through on it. Unlike Katie in the first case, there is no luck involved in her not eating chocolate; in the first case, although Katie didn't eat chocolate, she could have and would have. Unlike Katie in the second case, in the third case nothing other than her will prevents her from eating chocolate; in the second case she didn't eat chocolate and she couldn't have eaten it. In the third case, however, Katie didn't eat chocolate and could have eaten it, but she *wouldn't* eat it. That is, at nearby worlds where Katie gives up chocolate for Lent, she doesn't eat chocolate (even though she could). Furthermore, since she knows that once her will is set there is no going back, Katie thinks like someone who can't eat chocolate. She doesn't see eating it as an option. This makes her very different from case-one Katie who is willing to bail out if the going gets too hard, and who knows that she really can (and even might) give in. Psychologically, case-three Katie is more like case-two Katie. In fact, we can make them even more psychologically similar if we say that, in case three, Katie comes to believe that she can't eat chocolate. Maybe the hypnotist of case two produces in Katie a false belief that she is physically unable to consume the dark treats. Now Katie will not only think that the strength of her will power will see her through, but she'll believe that she is *unable* to go against her vow (even though she actually is able to).

The application of the Katie example to the case of omnipotence and the incarnation is straightforward. Suppose that due to metaphysical scruples (i.e, a conviction that an omnipotent being could not cease to be omnipotent even temporarily), the friend of the kenotic perspective can't see omnipotence as a *ceteris paribus* property and hence giveupable in the incarnation. She can nevertheless maintain that something an awful lot like giving it up can happen. In taking on a human nature, God the Son lays aside the powers of omnipotence not simply in the sense that (like case-one Katie) he doesn't, in fact, make use of them in his earthly ministry but in the much stronger sense that he *would not* use them during that time (like case-three Katie). Thus, there is a strong counterfactual component to the setting aside of the divine powers even if he doesn't technically cease to be omnipotent during that time. Furthermore, if we include in the incarnational scenario that the Son has laid aside omniscience and is operating with a human mind, then there is no reason to assume that he believes he's omnipotent even if he still is. So he not only *would not* make use of those powers but he doesn't believe that even *could be* an option.

For those of us who are less metaphysically scrupulous, however, there is no good reason to insist that the Son remained omnipotent when incarnated. For if he didn't, then omnipotence is but a *certeris paribus* property of the divinity and that doesn't imply that Christ was not fully God.

PUTTING THE PIECES TOGETHER

I conclude with a bare-bones sketch of an account of the incarnation that borrows features from all three views we've been discussing. It has more in common with Morris's general christology than it does with the compositional account, but it is also pretty clearly a variety of kenoticism as outlined in the previous section. A more complete kenotic theory would have something to say about the sense in which immutability can be maintained even while divine attributes are given up and the effect of kenosis on the metaphysics of the Trinity. Those topics will have to wait for another time.

1. *Humanity is a natural kind; divinity is a supernatural kind.* One doesn't learn the essence of either by armchair reflection. This position is both independently motivated and provides the philosophical theologian with some conceptual slack. Yet it comes with attendant worries. For example, one learns about the nature of human beings via the natural sciences (at least). But how does one learn anything about the divine essence construed as (somehow) akin to a genome? We can't very well do science on God. There's no time to get into these matters sufficiently but let me make two quick points. Yes, it seems to me that if the supernatural kinds thesis is right, then we are likely to never know the essence of divinity; it will be a mystery. But that is fine with me and accords well with my fifth desideratum. Second, though, there is still a place for philosophical theology as long as we think that something about at least God's secondary-essential properties can be gleaned from the scriptures, the creeds, etc. What my position does suggest is that whatever we learn about the nature of God will be crucially dependent on revelation.

2. *God the Son assumed a human body and mind.* Rather than seeing the incarnation as primarily the taking on of a set of human qualities, we should think in the concrete terms that the compositional account asks us to think in. In order to be true to the councils and creeds we must ascribe to God incarnate a human mind in addition to the divine mind of God the Son. What made Morris's two-minds view problematic was (i) the thought that two centres of consciousness was inconsistent with there being a single person in the incarnation; and, more importantly, (ii) Morris turned out to have no answer to the uniqueness problem—what made the relationship between the divine mind of God the Son and the human mind he assumed unique? I'm going to wait just a bit before addressing the first problem but I want to tackle the more significant problem now. Morris tried to answer this by claiming that they shared a set of causal and cognitive powers, but that was rejected for its monothelitism. But there is a better answer that can be gleaned from the compositionalist camp. Both Leftow and Stump consider the following objection to their position: standardly, a human mind and body composite compose a human person. But if the human mind and body assumed by the Son also compose a human person, then there are two persons in the incarnation (the human and God the Son), and that is to court Nestorianism. Leftow's and Stump's replies are complex and subtle but the bottom line is this: they claim that because the human mind and body never exist independently of the Son, but are assumed by him at the moment each begins to exist,

the normal process of the composition of a human person is blocked. Counterfactually, they would have composed a human person had they not been joined to the Son, but as things stand they do not. So the relationship between the human mind assumed by God the Son and every other human mind are distinct: other human minds belong to distinct persons but the human mind and body of God the Son fail to compose a person; rather, they are assumed by God the Son.

3. *God the Son was embedded in the human mind and body in the sense that it was only through them that the Son acted while on earth.* The view I favour identifies God the Son with Jesus Christ (thus satisfying the first desideratum); both terms refer to a single person. Thus my view is not a version of the compositional account of the incarnation, since I'm not claiming that Jesus Christ has God the Son as a proper part. Furthermore, in taking on the human mind and body, the Son has a single centre of consciousness and locus of action: the human mind and body. The Son is not conscious of or through the divine mind during his earthly ministry. What he consciously knows of the world he gets from two sources—typical human cognition and revelation.

4. *There is no single way of dealing with the incoherence objection.* For some inconsistent pairs of properties, the right thing to say is that God incarnate had the divine but not standard human properties (being uncreated and necessarily existent, say); for others we should say that he had the human but not standard divine properties (omniscience, omnipresence, and maybe omnipotence). In all of these cases, though, we'll be able to say why it is tempting to ascribe the inconsistent properties (because typical or paradigm cases of beings of the kind in question have the relevant properties—i.e., the properties are *ceteris paribus* properties of that kind). For the incarnate God will continue to be intrinsically just as he was prior to the incarnation; the changes involved in his human embedding do not alter anything intrinsic to him.

CONCLUSION

Admittedly, the position I'm advocating is something of a hodge-podge. But it might be that the best we can do in constructing models of the metaphysics of the incarnation is to shoot for accounts that meet our desiderata, are apparently logically consistent (or at least are not apparently logically inconsistent!), and explain the relevant data as well as or better than their competitors.

I have argued here that each of the three main contemporary models is problematic even while being insightful. I've attempted to pull together the insights of the competing views of others while leaving aside their woes. In the end, what I have is loosely a kenotic view that distinguishes between the giving up of divine properties and the giving up of essential divine properties, allowing for the former but not the latter, and which has resources for responding to the incoherence objection while incorporating mystery at its core.[13]

---

[13] This paper has benefitted from the comments of the participants at the 2009 Logos Conference held in May at Notre Dame and at the incarnation conference held at the University of Oxford in September of 2009. In particular, I've been helped by conversations with and comments by Oliver Crisp, Brian Leftow, Tom Flint, Dan Howard-Snyder, and Mike Rea. Thanks also to Mike Rea and Anna Marmodoro for inviting me to participate in the aforementioned events.

6

The metaphysics of kenosis

Stephen T. Davis

I

This essay reaches toward a way of understanding the metaphysics of the incarnation of Christ along kenotic lines.[1] Let us say that a *christological theory* is an attempt to understand how God became human, i.e., how the second person of the Trinity, the Logos, became a human being so that Christ could legitimately be described (as the creeds require) as 'truly divine and truly human'. That is, Christ has all the properties that are necessary and jointly sufficient for being divine and all the properties that are necessary and jointly sufficient for being human. And let us say that an *orthodox* christological theory is one that affirms or presupposes the affirmations of the classical christological creeds, especially those of Nicaea I (AD 325) and Chalcedon (AD 451).

Next, let us distinguish between two sorts of christological theories, which we will call classical ones and kenotic ones. Roughly, *classical theories* try to understand the incarnation in terms of the Logos simply adding to itself a human nature. Often this is said to entail an expansion or enhancement of Jesus' human nature. No reference is made to the Logos giving up or setting aside any properties normally characteristic of divinity. But *kenotic theories* do move in that direction; they try to understand the incarnation in terms of limiting the divine nature in certain ways.

Classical theories have been predominant throughout most of Christian history. Although kenotic themes can be found in scripture and in various theologians in Christian history, kenosis as a christological theory did not exist until the early nineteenth century. The first explicit kenotic theologians

---

[1] In a few places, the present article presupposes or briefly reviews some of the points made in Davis (2006a).

were the Germans, Gottfried Thomasius (1802–75) and W. F. Gess (1819–91).[2] Later the theory was defended by a series of British theologians, including P. T. Forsyth (1848–1921), Charles Gore (1853–1932), H. R. MacKintosh (1870–1936), and Frank Weston (1871–1924).[3] Interestingly, one of the points emphasized by the early kenoticists, viz. that Jesus' temptations and sufferings were genuine, is now widely accepted. Within the past thirty years, kenosis has enjoyed a renaissance among a small group of theologians and philosophers of religion, including Hans Urs von Balthasar,[4] Brian Hebblethwaite,[5] C. Stephen Evans, Thomas R. Thompson, Cornelius Plantinga, and Ronald Feenstra.[6]

Some of the early kenotic theories were clearly intended as substitutes for, rather than interpretations of, Chalcedon. But the version that I will defend (in common with the views of the six scholars just mentioned) presupposes the full humanity and divinity of the one person of Christ. Accordingly, I am suggesting a kenotic theory as a way of interpreting Chalcedon. The name and essence of the theory derive from the christological hymn of Philippians 2: 6–11, where Paul says of Christ (in the NRSV): 'who, though he was in the form of God, did not count equality with God a thing to be grasped, but emptied himself [the Greek term Paul uses here, *ekenosin*, is a derivative of the word *kenosis*], taking the form of a servant, being born in the likeness of men'.

II

We need to define some metaphysical terms. Let us begin by asking this question: what are the ultimate constituents of reality? Some people—we'll call them Process ontologists[7]—hold that the ultimate constituents or units of reality are *events*. An event, we'll say, is a real change in a thing or a relational change between things. Others—we'll call them Aristotelian ontologists—hold that the ultimate constituents or units of reality are *things* or *substances*. A substance, we'll say, is an enduring object that has properties, relations, causal powers, and an identity apart from other things.

The Aristotelian ontology seems preferable as a way of understanding the world for the following reason: it is possible to explain what a substance is without mentioning or presupposing events; but it is not possible to explain

---

[2] See Welch (1965). [3] See, for example, Weston (1907).
[4] In such works as Von Balthasar (1990), (1992), and (1994).
[5] See Hebblethwaite (1987: 27–44). [6] See their essays in Evans (2006b).
[7] They are represented in the recent and contemporary scene by Alfred North Whitehead and his followers. See Whitehead (1978).

what an event is without mentioning or presupposing substances. That is, we can identify and individuate substances by means of their properties or relations; but we can only identify and individuate events by means of the substances to or about which the events occur. Or, more simply, it is possible for substances to exist without events (there are possible worlds in which only immutable things exist); but it is not possible for events to exist without substances. Therefore, substances are more ontologically ultimate than events.[8]

But for Christians at least, the broad concept of substance is not what is truly ultimate. We need instead to look at a certain sort of substance. This is because Christians hold that at one time nothing existed beside God and that only at the moment of creation did other things or substances beside God come into existence.[9] And what sort of substance is God? Let us say that God is a *person*.[10]

But what then is a person? Boethius famously defined a person as 'an individual substance of a rational nature'.[11] This definition is definitely on the right track, but needs expansion. Let us say that a person: (1) is a substance (and accordingly is a property-bearer and has relations, causal powers, and an identity apart from other substances) that (2) has a rational nature (i.e., can think, feel, believe, know, decide, formulate intentions, act, etc.), (3) is morally responsible (in the sense of potentially being legitimately praiseworthy or blameworthy for good or bad deeds), and (4) can be in relationship with other persons. God is a person in something like that sense, so Christians hold, and so are human beings, although God and humans are radically different sorts of persons. Accordingly, a Christian metaphysic must begin with the notion that what is ultimately real, what is ontologically basic in our world, is persons.

---

[8] Of course, a process ontologist might opt for a different definition of the word 'event', perhaps as 'any instantiation of a property in a substance at a time'. And on that view you cannot have substances without events any more than you can have events without substances. But I would reply that the proposed definition of 'event' is flawed because it is too broad. Take the property of *being prime*. Notice that it would be quite true to say that it is instantiated in the number three on January 14, 2009. But primeness being instantiated in the number three on January 14, 2009 is hardly an event. This is because the number three is prime at all times. There are no everlasting events. Accordingly, there can still be substances without events but not vice versa.

[9] If time came into existence with the creation of the physical universe, then God was alone prior to the creation in a non-temporal or logical sense of 'prior to'.

[10] From a Christian perspective, it is more precise to say that God is personal and consists of three co-eternal and co-equal persons, the Father, the Son, and the Holy Spirit. Still, I think there is little harm in speaking of God as a person.

[11] *De duabus naturis* 3. Aquinas adopts this usage: see ST, 3a, q. 2, a.2 obj. 3.

A human person, we can say, possesses a rational nature in a human body and a human soul.[12] But what then is a *nature*? A nature, we can say, is the set of the essential properties[13] of a substance, where an essential property is a property that the substance has in every possible world in which it exists.[14] Aristotle famously distinguished between primary and secondary substances.[15] A secondary substance is close to what we today would call a natural kind or a kind nature (a universal), like being human or being a horse. This typically gives the general nature of the thing. But an individual substance is the thing's nature as *this* particular human or *that* particular horse. We would call it an individual nature (a particular).

That is, a substance that loses any of its essential properties no longer exists as the thing that it is. A bit more precisely, a property of a substance that is essential *de dicto* to that substance is a property that is necessary to its being the kind of substance that it is. For example, it is often said that God would not be God without the property of being perfectly good. And a property of a substance that is essential *de re* to that substance is a property that is necessary to its existence, quite apart from whether or not it belongs to the kind in question.

Finally, let's say that a *common property of a kind k* is an attribute that all members of k have (e.g., for the natural kind 'human being' *having been born on earth* is a common property). Common properties may be essential (e.g., three-sidedness for a triangle) or accidental (normally living underground, for earthworms).

III

Before we get to a more thorough explication of kenosis, a preliminary question must be asked: in the incarnation precisely what do the properties of *being truly divine* and *being truly human* belong to or attach to? Precisely what substance has these properties?[16] There appear to be three possible answers: (1) the man Jesus; (2) the Logos (the second person of the Trinity); and (3) the incarnate Logos (the God/man).

---

[12] Many Christian theologians would deny that humans are *essentially* embodied, especially given the notion of an interim period between death and the general resurrection, but I will ignore that point here.

[13] I will leave the term 'property' undefined except to say that I take properties to be universals.

[14] See Plantinga (1974: 60).   [15] See Ackrill (1963: 5–6) (2a 11–18).

[16] This question is discussed helpfully in Cross (2009).

The first possibility is obviously unacceptable because the incarnation definitely does not mean that a man (or a human nature) became God. The man Jesus was certainly truly human but could not be truly divine. The second possibility is perhaps the normal way for theology to go: the idea is that in the incarnation the Logos takes on a human nature (whether it also gives up certain divine properties is a separate question). Although this second possibility seems acceptable for Christian theology, I think the third option is also possible. Here the idea is that the properties are attached not to the Logos but to the incarnate Logos. But does this third view tend toward the Nestorianism heresy?

Nestorianism is the theory (condemned in 431 AD at the Council of Ephesus) which says or implies that there were two distinct persons in Christ, the divine person and the human person. They exist in juxtaposition in the incarnate Christ and are linked by a willed union of love. It is a kind of moral union, not genuinely a hypostatic union. Whether Nestorius himself held this theory is a matter of scholarly debate, but it is clear that the third option mentioned above need not go in the direction of heresy. The claim that the two natures are natures of the incarnate Logos, the one Christ, in no way requires that the natures be two separate persons. (I will return to the threat of Nestorianism in section VIII below.)

All orthodox christological theories hold that Jesus Christ had a human nature. So whatever human nature is—and minimally we can say, as above, that it consists in having a rational human soul and body—Jesus Christ had it. Again, a kenotic christological theory is one that explains the incarnation in terms of the Logos temporarily 'giving up' or 'laying aside' or 'divesting itself of' or 'emptying itself of' certain properties that normally belong to divinity. What must be emphasized is the voluntary and redemptive aspect of kenosis: it was out of love for us and for the sake of our redemption that the second person of the Trinity 'emptied himself'. Some kenotic theorists take the divestment to be temporal and temporary, as I do, with the period of divestment corresponding to the time-span of the earthly life of Jesus. After Jesus' earthly life, i.e., in the exaltation, the Logos reacquires the laid-aside properties.

Kenotic theories of the incarnation differ on whether the incarnation of the Logos is to be distinguished from the kenosis, and on (so to speak) how long they last. The view that I am defending is that the kenosis is indeed distinct from the incarnation, with the kenosis lasting only for the some thirty years of Jesus' lifetime, and the incarnation lasting from the moment of Jesus' conception to eternity. That is, the statement, 'The Logos is God incarnate' is true at any temporal point after (say) 4 BC, while the statement, 'The Logos is kenotically incarnate' was only true from about 4 BC until about 29 AD, and indeed is now (i.e., as I write this sentence in January 2009) no longer true. The incarnation accordingly begins in time, but unlike the kenosis does not ever cease.[17]

Kenosis as a christological theory has been subjected to various criticisms, some of them bizarre. The kenotic theory that I wish to defend has no necessary connection whatsoever with: (1) making Jesus Christ a kind of demigod by enlarging his humanity with a few divine properties;[18] (2) implying that the Logos, absent some of its divine attributes in the incarnation, is temporarily excluded from the Trinity;[19] (3) affirming that God and humans are different forms of the same species or are at least not very different;[20] or (4) claiming that we too, like Jesus, can be incarnations of God.

IV

Let me now lay out a possible kenotic theory of the incarnation.[21] The core idea is that Christ was indeed truly divine and truly human, possessing all properties essential to divinity and humanity, and that this was made possible by the Logos emptying itself, during the period of Jesus' earthly life, of those properties that normally characterize divinity but are inconsistent with humanity.

Here are some properties that, by consensus of Christians, characterize God and human beings, respectively:

God	*Human beings*
1. Being necessary	1' Being contingent
2. Living forever	2' Living only for a finite time
3. Being omnipotent	3' Being non-omnipotent
4. Being omniscient	4' Being non-omniscient
5. Being incorporeal	5' Being corporeal

And the logical problem for all orthodox views of the incarnation is this: if properties 1–5 are essential to God (constitute part of the divine nature); and if properties 1'–5' are essential to all human beings (constitute part of human

---

[17] See Evans (2002).   [18] As is charged by Dietrich Bonhoeffer (1966: 97).
[19] As is charged by Wolfhart Pannenberg (1977: 311).
[20] This idea seems to be held in Mormon thought.
[21] It is explained in more detail in Davis (1988), (1983: ch. 8), and (2006a).

nature); and if the orthodox doctrine of the incarnation, which includes the 'truly divine and truly human' clause, affirms that Jesus Christ must simultaneously possess all the members of both sets of properties; and if (as it surely seems) it is logically impossible for any being simultaneously to have all the members of both sets of properties; then the orthodox doctrine of the incarnation is incoherent.

But how do we go about deciding which properties of humans are essential to them? And how do we go about deciding which divine properties are essential to God? 1'–5' certainly seem to be properties of human beings (although 2' and 5' can be debated); and 1–5 certainly seem to be properties of God, at least as Christians conceive of God. But must we affirm that 1'–5' are *essential* properties of human beings, either *de re* or *de dicto*? And must we affirm that 1–5 are *essential* properties of God, either *de re* or *de dicto*?

So how can we know which properties of any substance are essential to it and which are accidental to it? With abstract or mathematical objects (e.g., numbers, circles, sets, etc.) the decision is sometimes fairly easy. But for concrete things such as human beings, it is rarely easy. Now Christians accept the orthodox doctrine of the incarnation; i.e., they hold that Jesus Christ is 'truly human and truly divine'. Accordingly, Christians will probably want to *deny* that the properties listed above are essential properties of God and human beings, respectively. Moreover, Christian theology has always held that Jesus Christ is both the pre-eminent revealer of God and the model human being. Considering the incarnation of Christ, then, is one fruitful way (doubtless the best way) of finding out about divinity and humanity, of discovering which properties of God and human beings are essential and which are accidental. If Jesus Christ is 'truly divine and truly human', then perhaps the properties listed above are either not essential properties or else are somehow consistent with all the others after all.

Thomas Morris, who is not a defender of kenosis, has nevertheless made a helpful suggestion that kenotic christologists can use: perhaps the 1'–5' properties are essential properties not of *being human* but of *being merely human*.[22] And certainly orthodox Christians do not want to affirm that Jesus Christ was 'merely human'. You and I are indeed merely human, but not Christ. Perhaps then the 1–5 properties are essential properties not of *being divine* but of *being divine simpliciter*, by which I mean being divine without also being human. And orthodox Christians do not affirm that God is 'divine simpliciter'. This is because Christians hold that there exists no being who is divine simpliciter. In fact, the one and only God who exists is a God who

---

[22] Morris (1983: 457).

becomes incarnate in a human being. Not even God the Father, who does not become incarnate as a human being, is God simpliciter; God the Father is certainly divine but is not 'a God'. Therefore, what Christians want to say about Jesus Christ is that he was *truly human* but not *merely human*, *truly divine* but not *divine simpliciter.*

Here is where kenosis can help. The core idea is that Jesus Christ was 'in the form of God' as the Logos, the second person of the Trinity, and that at a certain point in human history he voluntarily and obediently 'emptied himself' of the divine glory and of certain other divine properties; he then took on 'human form', i.e., became a human being. The notion is that in the incarnation, Jesus Christ 'emptied himself' by temporarily giving up those divine properties that are inconsistent with being truly human while retaining sufficient divine properties to remain truly divine.[23] And he gave up those common human properties that are inconsistent with being truly divine but retained sufficient human properties to remain truly human. Accordingly, in the incarnation, Jesus Christ was truly human but not *a mere human*; he was truly divine but not God simpliciter. Perhaps it is impossible simultaneously to be a mere human and truly divine; and perhaps it is impossible simultaneously to be God simpliciter and truly human. But Christians hold that it is possible (indeed in the case of Christ, actual) to be 'truly divine and truly human'.

The notion depends on there not being any essential divine properties that no human being can have and on there not being any essential human properties that no divine being can have. And following another suggestion from Morris,[24] a coherent kenotic theory will accordingly hold that what is essential to God is not, for example, omniscience, but rather the more complex property of being omniscient-unless-freely-and-temporarily-choosing-to-be-otherwise. The same point will then be made with other divine properties such as omnipotence, omnipresence, etc.

What does it mean for God to 'give up' a property? Well, as long as the property in question is accidental, there is no insuperable problem. We give up properties constantly, for example, the property of having long hair when we cut it short, or the property of being seated when we stand. 'God gives up property p' would roughly mean that at a given point God has property p but at a later point, of God's own free choice, God does not have property p. Suppose, for example, that God is in fact omniscient but that God could still exist and still be divine if God were slightly less than omniscient (if there were some few

---

[23] As Peter Forrest points out, perhaps it would be impossible for God *permanently* to give up such properties, but that is not what is envisioned here. See Forrest (2000: 129).
[24] Morris (1986: 75).

things that God does not know). That is, suppose that omniscience is a divine property, but an accidental one. Then 'God gives up the property of omniscience' means that at one point God is omniscient and that a later point God voluntarily becomes non-omniscient, while still existing and remaining God.

V

But there is a difficulty here. While some properties can certainly be given up (e.g., having long hair, being seated), others, whether essential or accidental, seem to be (so to speak) 'ungiveupable'. This category would include time-indexed properties or properties one has because of events that occurred in the past, for example, properties such as *not having been created, having existed in the sixteenth century,* and *being the creator of the heavens and the earth*. They may or may not be essential properties of any being who has them, but the point is that they cannot be given up. Any being who has them at one temporal point must have them at all temporal points. Thus kenosis faces a problem, because it seems to make no sense to say, for example, that the Logos gave up the property of *not having been created* in order to be truly human or that Jesus Christ gave up the property of *having been created* in order to be truly divine.

In response to this difficulty, defenders of kenosis can refer to a traditional way of making christological affirmations, viz., that Jesus Christ has some properties *as* God and some *as* a human being. But it should be noted that this notion is not an ad hoc invention of clever twentieth-century Christian philosophers. Indeed, the Chalcedonian Definition itself implies the point; it says, 'of one substance with the Father *as regards his Godhead,* and at the same time of one substance with us *as regards his manhood*' (italics added). This way of making christological affirmations was explored in a preliminary way by P. T. Geach,[25] who calls them (following medieval usage) reduplicative propositions. He distinguishes between what we ought to say that God *as God* can do from what we can say that God *as a human being* can do. In sentences such as 'A as P is Q', Geach says, we are not to think of Q as a predicate attached to the complex subject 'A as P'—rather, we ought to read the sentence as 'A is, as P, Q'. Thus we can sensibly say such things as 'Jesus Christ is, as God, unable to die' and 'Jesus Christ is, as a human being, able to die' without uttering nonsense.

---

[25] Geach (1977: 25–8).

There are certainly dangers here: if the notion is pushed too far, Christ might seem to be divided into two persons, one of which was and the other of which was not able to die. To divide Christ like that would amount to Nestorianism. And if the unity of Christ's person is to be emphasized, the following objection might arise: 'Well then, is the one person Jesus Christ able to die or not? Surely it must be one or the other: which is it? If he is able to die, he is not divine; if he is not able to die, he is not human.'

Accordingly, in one sense (a sense that will lead to paradox), we can say that the one person Jesus Christ both was and was not able to die. Better, however, to say: he was, as human, able to die; he was not, as divine, able to die. Again, the one person Jesus Christ both was and was not created. He was, as human, created; he was not, as divine, created. Jesus Christ does not possess those inconsistent properties in the same way. It is true that sentences such as, 'The second person of the Trinity is able to die' are puzzling and seem to be incoherent. Nevertheless, I hold that when the sentence is well-formed ('The second person of the Trinity is, as a man, able to die, and is not, as God, able to die'), it is true. (I will return to reduplication and the danger of Nestorianism in section IX.)

There is no denying that there is paradox involved in the notion of incarnation. Kenosis cannot remove all mystery from the doctrine. Nor can any other christological theory, in my opinion. But kenosis does help us toward an understanding of incarnation. It helps provide a sense in which we can legitimately (although admittedly somewhat paradoxically) say: 'Jesus Christ is truly divine.' It helps provide a sense in which we can legitimately (although admittedly somewhat paradoxically) say: 'Jesus Christ is truly human.'

It is important to note that the kenotic theory defended here has nothing whatever to do with a human being becoming God (or the reverse) or with human properties changing into divine ones (or the reverse). Nor does it end up with the kenotically incarnate Logos as a lessened or reduced God. If the theory could be shown to deny the *homoousios* principle of Chalcedon, in my view it would not be worth defending. But it does not do so. The kenotically incarnate Logos is indeed 'of one substance with the Father' because the Father's nature just is the set of his essential properties, which the theory insists Christ had. And since we do not accordingly have a minimized deity who died on the cross and rose from the dead, there are no untoward salvific implications in the theory either.

Is the use of mystery allowable in theology? I would argue that the subject matter of theology makes mystery virtually inevitable; mystery is just what we should expect when discussing a transcendent God. Any view of the Trinity or incarnation that has no room for mystery is probably mistaken. But, of course,

Christians are epistemically obligated to reduce theological mysteries as much as possible. If we were to embrace mystery fully, we would not have to write books or hold conferences on the incarnation; we could just say, 'Well, Christ both was and was not created', etc., full stop. I would argue that we embrace mystery where: (1) we can see that it's probably not an outright contradiction, i.e., we can see how there might well be an explanation that we have not at present fully got; (2) we can see that scripture and Christian tradition teach it and that theological incoherence would ensue if we simply rejected it; and (3) we cannot at present reduce the mystery any further.

VI

Let me make three further points. First, kenosis is based on the idea that human nature has a natural receptivity to the divine nature. In this way, it is quite unlike an amoeba nature or a coyote nature or even a gorilla nature. It is possible for a human nature and a divine nature to be united in one person because human beings, unlike amoebas, coyotes, and gorillas, were created 'in the image of God' (Genesis 1: 27).

Second, some kenotic theorists, including me, are disinclined to claim that incarnation can *only* be explained via kenosis. Accordingly, they are not to be seen as enemies of classical theories of the incarnation. This is certainly true of those kenoticists who hold that: (1) the incarnation of the Logos is everlasting after Jesus' conception (i.e., it is still—in the year 2009—true that 'The Logos is God incarnate'); and (2) the kenosis lasted only for the period of Jesus' earthly life. Thus such kenoticists face the question how incarnation without kenosis (i.e., after the resurrection and ascension) is possible. Accordingly, they will have to appeal to non-kenotic theories to understand how it is true in the year 2009 that 'The Logos is God incarnate.'

Third, although classical theorists deny this point, I claim that every orthodox believer in the incarnation is also an affirmer of kenosis, whether wittingly or unwittingly.[26] What is at issue between witting and unwitting kenoticists is the extent of kenosis and the helpfulness of using it as a way of understanding the Gospel narratives about Jesus and the incarnation. My claim is that every orthodox believer in the incarnation must believe that the Logos gave up at least *something* in becoming incarnate in a man—*the usual*

---

[26] As Peter Forrest points out, any theist who believes in human libertarian freedom is already committed to a divine limitation or kenosis of a certain sort. What God gave up or set aside in creating human beings is the power to determine all things. See Forrest (2000: 130).

manifestations of the divine glory, for example. Or we might say that in the incarnation the Logos gave up *the normal incorporeal life of God*. Or we might say, following Philippians 2: 7, that in the incarnation the Logos gave up *the form of a non-servant*. Even Thomas Morris, stern critic of kenosis that he is, is an unwitting kenoticist. Reading chapter 4 of *The Logic of God Incarnate*, we form the distinct impression that on Morris's view the Logos, in the incarnation, gave up the *ability to have full, direct, and continuous access to the contents of the divine mind*.[27]

VII

The central purpose of the present essay is not to establish a biblical basis for kenosis. Nevertheless, something brief should be said on that point. This is because for many kenotic theorists, the primary motivation for the theory is not logical or metaphysical but biblical. That is, the theory helps make sense of the picture of Jesus presented in the Gospels, a Jesus who grew in wisdom (Luke 2: 52), could not do many great works in Nazareth (Mark 6: 5), and who did not know who had touched his garment (Mark 5: 30) or the date of the parousia (Mark 13: 32; Matthew 24: 36).

So far as any christological theory is concerned, we should not expect to find it explicitly taught in scripture. Whether in his incarnation the Logos emptied himself of certain properties normally characteristic of divinity or else simply added a new human nature to his already existing divine nature is not a question that concerned the biblical writers. What we would be looking for, then, would be scriptural *permission* for the theory. And that is precisely what defenders of kenosis claim that we do have, both in Philippians 2 and elsewhere (see, for example, John 17: 4–5, 20–6; II Corinthians 8: 9; Hebrews 2: 9, 17).

Despite disagreement on each point, there exists, I believe, some degree of consensus among Pauline scholars that Philippians 2: 6–11 is a unified text and contains a 'high' christology. And although not much rides on this next point for present purposes, there is also significant opinion that this text is pre-Pauline, with the possible exception of a few words (e.g., 'death on a

---

[27] See Morris (1986: 103). Morris will doubtless reply that in the incarnation the Logos retained its divine mind but also took on an additional noetic structure, a human one, which was Jesus Christ's chosen operative noetic structure during all or most of his ministry. He chose not to have direct access to the contents of the divine mind, although he could have chosen to access it at any time. But I would ask whether such a person would be 'truly human'.

cross'). That is, Paul was citing words that he did not compose; accordingly, the passage reflects beliefs of the very young church. So the text has the authority both of Paul and the pre-Pauline Christian community. On the other hand, the text is also an exegetical and especially lexical minefield, and there has been controversy about it from the early church until today.[28]

Here is my own rough analysis of the christological teachings of the text. (1) Christ Jesus was at one time, i.e., before his appearance in the form of a servant, in the form of God (*en morphe theou*). (2) But he did not count the status of equality with God (*to einai isa theo*) something to be grasped or held on to or exploited (*harpagmos*—a 'thing to be seized'). (3) Rather, he obediently emptied himself (*heauton ekenosen*), taking the form of a servant, being born in human likeness, and being obedient to God even to the point of death by crucifixion. (4) Accordingly, God has highly exalted him (*auton huperuphosen*) and has given him the name that is above every name (*to onoma to huper pan onoma*); that at the name of Jesus every knee should bow and every tongue should confess that Jesus Christ is Lord (*kurios Iesous Christos*) to the Glory of God the Father.

A plausible exegetical case can be made that part of what Christ Jesus emptied himself of in the incarnation was the divine glory and majesty; this was at least part of what was involved in taking on human likeness. But the specific issue we are considering—whether in the incarnation the Logos 'emptied' himself of some of the properties God normally has—does not appear to be answered by exegetical considerations alone.

Some who resist kenotic theories of the incarnation insist that what Christ Jesus emptied himself of was not any of the divine *attributes* but rather certain divine *prerogatives*, like the divine glory. But that solution can only work, i.e., this is a possible reading of the text, if one can formulate a coherent distinction between the divine attributes and the divine prerogatives. But it seems to me that 'having the divine glory' is just as much an attribute or property as 'being omnipotent' or 'being omniscient'. So if, as I believe, that distinction cannot be coherently formulated (if I am right that all prerogatives just are or entail properties) and if the text implies that he at least emptied himself of the divine glory, we are already halfway there to a kenotic interpretation of the incarnation.

Others who resist kenoticism argue that the 'emptying' spoken of in Philippians had nothing to do with the incarnate Logos temporarily *no longer possessing* certain attributes (like, say, omnipotence or omniscience). It had to do instead with the incarnate Logos *voluntarily not exercising* those powers for

---

[28] See the essays in Martin and Dodd (1998), especially the essays by Larry J. Kreitzer and Richard Bauckham.

the duration of Jesus' earthly life. And here the crucial issue is not exegetical but philosophical: is a person who at any time has the ability to be omnipotent but voluntarily and temporarily decides not to call on that ability 'truly human' (as the creed insists)? Again, I am inclined to say no.

I conclude that exegetical considerations do not explicitly confirm the kenotic theory. But neither do they rule out the idea that the Logos temporarily gave up certain properties that God normally possesses. The theory seems to be allowed by scripture.

VIII

But perhaps kenosis is unacceptable for other reasons. The best way to test for that possibility is to consider criticisms of the theory. Let me now turn to that task. I will discuss four of them.[29]

1. *In the kenotic theory, the earthly Jesus is not really divine.* This is a common criticism of kenosis; it impugns the orthodoxy of the theory because orthodoxy requires that the earthly Jesus Christ be 'truly divine'. The objection involves an insistence on the part of the critic that such divine properties as omnipotence and omniscience are essential properties of God. Since on kenosis the kenotically incarnate Logos 'emptied himself' of such properties, it follows (so it is said) that Jesus Christ was not 'truly divine'.

But this is surely too quick. It is quite true that the one and only God is omnipotent and omniscient. The statement, 'All the Gods that exist are omnipotent and omniscient' is true. But it hardly follows from that point that these are essential properties, i.e., that a being who was, say, nearly but not quite omnipotent cannot go on existing or cannot be divine. More crucially, it does not follow that a being who is temporarily non-omniscient but still retains the property of being omniscient-unless-freely-and-temporarily-choosing-to-be-otherwise cannot go on existing or cannot be divine. If this property is essential to God, kenosis remains unaffected by the present criticism, because kenoticists can affirm this point.

To repeat a point made earlier, Christians believe that Jesus was 'truly divine and truly human'. So if the claim that omnipotence simpliciter is an

---

[29] I will not consider here a criticism of kenosis that I have discussed elsewhere, viz. John Hick's claim that kenosis is inconsistent with traditional notions of divine immutability. See Hick (1993: 75). For my reply, see Davis (1999: 261–5).

essential property of God is inconsistent with Jesus Christ being 'truly human', most Christians will be inclined to say: so much the worse for the doctrine that omnipotence simpliciter is an essential property of God.

2. *Peter van Inwagen's criticisms.* In his essay on 'Incarnation and christology' in the *Routledge Encyclopedia of Philosophy*, Peter van Inwagen raises two criticisms of kenosis.[30] I will concentrate only on the second, because his first point—that on kenosis, the three persons of the Trinity must be distinct substances or beings—is in my view essentially correct. Kenoticists do need to adopt some version of the 'social theory' of the Trinity. I have argued elsewhere[31] (and so have other social theorists) that this theory need not entail tritheism.

The second criticism from van Inwagen is that kenosis entails a considerable weakening of the concept of divinity. He says: 'The incarnate Christ can indeed say truly "I am a divine being," but only because, for the kenoticist, it is possible to be a divine being at a certain moment without then being omnipotent, omniscient or omnipresent.' And here too van Inwagen is right if we are talking about having those properties simpliciter. That is indeed an implication of the theory. But, as argued earlier, it is not clear to me how this weakens the notion of God.

But van Inwagen then points to phrases from Chalcedon and the Athanasian Creed that he thinks kenosis violates. From the latter, he cites the phrase, 'not by the transformation of his divinity into flesh'. But kenoticists hardly suggest anything like that. It is true that Christians do sometimes rather loosely say things like, 'In the incarnation God became a man.' But kenoticists are quite clear that divinity does not *become* human flesh; rather, as all orthodox christologists hold, they believe that divinity *became incarnate in* human flesh. From the former, van Inwagen cites the phrase, 'the properties [that is, defining properties or essential features] of each nature being preserved'. But kenotic christologists do indeed preserve what they take to be all the essential features of divinity. The dispute, as I suppose, is the one I have been discussing, viz., which attributes of God are essential properties?[32]

---

[30] Van Inwagen (1998). [31] See Davis (2006b: ch. 4).

[32] Van Inwagen also suggests that had kenosis existed in the fifth century, the creeds would have been so worded as to exclude it. And that may be correct; the creed-writers presupposed that God is timeless and absolutely immutable, and no kenoticist can hold that. They can hold to a kind of immutability but not absolute immutability. But the proper question is not what the fathers of the church *would have thought* about kenosis. Obviously, we do not know that. The question is whether kenosis preserves what they were trying to preserve, viz. the full divinity and humanity of Christ. I hold that it does (and would abandon the theory if I came to believe it does not).

3. *Is the theory coherent?* But perhaps the theory that I am suggesting is not coherent.[33] The problem is that I affirm two points. First, I hold that the incarnation is permanent (Christ is still today the incarnate Son of God) while the kenosis lasted only for the some thirty years of his earthly life; accordingly, I must admit that incarnation without kenosis is possible. But, second, I also hold that the earthly Jesus could not have been 'truly human' unless properties like *being omnipotent* and *being omniscient* were somewhat limited. That is, a straightforwardly omnipotent and omniscient person could not be human. How then is Christ today 'truly human'?

But although I certainly affirm that the glorified Christ is omnipotent and omniscient, I do not think he is omnipotent and omniscient in a straightforward sense. A straightforwardly omnipotent and omniscient being—like the person of God the Father—is omnipotent and omniscient at all times. How do we know that? Well, let's imagine a being who can do anything logically possible except that all day tomorrow (and just tomorrow) it will be unable to lift a ten-pound weight. Such a being, I say, is not now straightforwardly omnipotent because it does not have the logically possible ability *to lift a ten-pound weight tomorrow*. But Christ today, in his exaltation, is an omnipotent and omniscient being who for a time possessed neither of these properties. So he is not now, as we might say, omnipotent and omniscient simpliciter. And I think those properties—being omnipotent and omniscient but not omnipotent and omniscient simpliciter—are indeed logically compatible with full humanity.

4. *Reduplication and Nestorianism.* Let me now discuss a criticism of reduplication; it will lead to a reconsideration of the Nestorianism charge. The claim is this: the apparent contradiction that led people to kenosis and reduplication in the first instance is still very much in place. That is, despite all reduplicative manoeuvres (e.g., Jesus Christ is uncreated as divine and created as human), it is still the case that the one person, Jesus Christ, is both created and uncreated, both did and did not come into existence.[34] And in a certain sense, the claim being made here is true—he both did come into existence (as human) and did not come into existence (as divine). But this point seems to me less of a criticism of kenosis than an implication of the theory. I have admitted that there is mystery here; the question is whether anything that is logically unacceptable remains.

We are used to reduplicative strategies in ordinary life. To use an example from real life that I have discussed before, the mayor of the city may also be

---

[33] This criticism was raised by William Lane Craig in a session on my book *Christian Philosophical Theology* (Davis: 2006b) that was held at the American Academy of Religion in 2007.
[34] Morris spells out the point nicely. See Morris (1986: 48–9).

the Director of Athletics at the local college. As mayor, he has certain civic rights and abilities (rights and abilities that he does not have as Director of Athletics), and as Director of Athletics he has certain academic rights and abilities in the Athletics Department (rights and abilities that he does not have as mayor). But this is not a good analogy to the incarnation, because there is no apparent logical difficulty in the notion of one and the same person's being both mayor and Director of Athletics. But there is a logical difficulty in the notion of one and the same person's being both divine and human.

In an important article, Eleonore Stump explains Thomas Aquinas's rather complex theory of the incarnation. In so doing, she provides a robust defence of the reduplicative strategy against the above criticism.[35] What follows is a response by me to the objection that we are considering. It is much inspired by her argument.

Notice that of all my properties, some of them are had by me directly or (as we might say) basically. These are properties that I have not because any of my parts has them but because I, the whole person Stephen Davis, have them. One such property is *being human*. It is true that I have a human brain and human feet, but my brain and feet in themselves do not possess the property of being human. But *I* do possess it. I am human, as we might say, simpliciter. And notice that other properties are had by me indirectly or non-basically, e.g., *having ten toes*. It is true that I, Stephen Davis, have ten toes, but I have that property only because it is had directly by those parts of me that are feet. The criterion in play here is accordingly this: a property is basic if I have it and no part of me has it; a property is non-basic if I have it only because some part of me has it. As Stump puts it, I have the property because I 'borrowed' it from those parts of me that have it directly.

Now unlike me (and all other substances), Jesus Christ has two natures. We can without confusion call them two parts of the one person Jesus Christ, although they are certainly not physical parts. The divine nature directly or basically has properties like *being omniscient, being omnipotent,* and *not being able to die.* The human nature directly or basically has properties like *being ignorant of some things, being limited in power,* and *being able to die.* The one person Jesus Christ has all these properties, of course, but has them indirectly or non-basically, i.e., because the two different natures have them directly.

It is quite true that we can still say things like *Jesus Christ is both able to die and not able to die* and *Jesus Christ is both created and uncreated.* But what we

---

[35] Stump (2002).

have done (following Aquinas and Stump) is separate the incompatible attributes; there is no contradiction here because we do not predicate them of Jesus Christ in the same way. Unfortunately, I am not able to give any helpful and innocuous analogies from ordinary life. This is because of the fact just noted: of all the substances that exist, Jesus Christ is the only substance that has two natures. Still, having segregated the incompatible properties as reduplication does, the charge that the contradiction still stands has been answered.

Thomas Senor distinguishes among three different ways of understanding the 'as' clause in reduplicative sentences.[36] It is the second of his ways that I am interested in. It claims that 'Christ is, as human, non-omnipotent' means 'Christ-as-human is non-omnipotent'. This usage takes the 'as' clause to be imbedded in the grammatical subject of the sentence. Senor admits that this manoeuvre solves the logical problem: omnipotence and non-omnipotence *simpliciter* are attributed to different subjects, viz., Christ's divine nature and human nature, respectively. But the problem, he claims, is that it succumbs to Nestorianism.

> This interpretation avoids the logical problems of the incarnation by predicating the incompossible properties of different subjects. It is not the single person, the Redeemer, who bears these properties, but rather the divine nature bears the divine properties and the human nature bears the human properties. So the bearers of the divine and human properties are at best two respective natures; this is Nestorianism pure and simple.

But it is hardly clear that this is Nestorianism. First of all, let's notice that kenoticists only need make use of reduplication in cases of what I called the 'ungiveupable' properties. As far as the others are concerned, we can say (for example): the pre-incarnate Logos was incorporeal, but Christ was not incorporeal at all. No reduplicative manoeuvres are required here. But on the ungiveupable properties, I do want to say (for example) that 'Christ-as-divine was uncreated' and 'Christ-as-human was created'. And this does entail, as noted before, that the one person Christ is both created and uncreated, although he has those properties indirectly because parts of him—the two natures—have them directly (simpliciter). Contrary to Senor, the Redeemer does have these properties (albeit indirectly).

Second, why say *à la* Nestorius that this means there are two persons in Christ? I certainly affirm the hypostatic union, and not just the moral union that Nestorius seemed to want. And there are no untoward salvific implications

---

[36] Senor (2002: 229–31).

here because I hold that the whole person of Christ, with both natures, suffered on the cross for our sins, and not just the human nature, as Nestorius taught. The charge of Nestorianism seems very much unproved. It is not Nestorianism just to say that there are two subjects of predicates in Christ; as we have seen, the definition of Chalcedon implies as much.

How then do we distinguish between (1) the claim that there are two subjects of predication in Christ (the two natures), which I am suggesting, and (2) the claim that there are two persons in Christ, which is heretical? Two points are critical here.

First, on the second claim, some actions will inevitably be attributed to one of the persons and not of the other while on the first, all properties of the two subjects are attributable, either directly or indirectly, to the one person. The actions that Christ did, both normal actions like walking and talking and abnormal actions like healing the paralytic, were done by the one person Christ, not by one or other of the natures or even by both natures. The natures, in themselves, do not have causal powers, as a person (the one person of Christ) does. Second, I earlier (in section II) defined persons (in part) as having natures: a human person has a human nature and a divine person has a divine nature. But the two natures of Christ do not have natures—they *are* natures.

IX

Someone might ask at this point: given your use of reduplication in trying to understand orthodox christology, why do you need kenosis at all, for reduplicative strategies can surely be used by classical christologists as well? And that point is correct. So far as I can see, there are no logical or metaphysical reasons that prevent classical christologists from using reduplication, and of course many have done so. As I noted above, reduplication seems first to have appeared in the creed of Chalcedon.

It might even be claimed that given my use of reduplicative strategies, it is hard to see what the second person of the Trinity gave up in the incarnation, since he is still omnipotent and omniscient, etc. (*qua* divine). But my reply is that what he gave up in the incarnation is omnipotence and omniscience simpliciter.

Moreover, I should again state that kenosis is not adopted primarily (at least by me) as a means of overcoming the contradiction charge. Kenosis can indeed help us toward an understanding—admittedly still somewhat paradoxical—of the claim that Jesus Christ was 'truly divine and truly human'. But the basic motivation for kenosis is the attempt to understand the picture of Jesus that is presented in the Gospels. I do not claim to speak for all kenoticists here, but my own reasons for following the kenotic route are primarily biblical.[37]

---

[37] I would like to thank Professors Tom Senor and Dale Tuggy for their helpful comments on an earlier draft of this essay.

7

Hylomorphism and the incarnation[1]

Michael C. Rea

The Christian doctrine of the incarnation tells us that the Son of God, the second person of the Trinity, became incarnate as a first-century man, Jesus of Nazareth. According to the doctrine, the Son took on a human nature while at the same time retaining his divine nature. Thus, he became a two-natured individual. He also acquired distinctively human parts and characteristics—among them, a human body and soul. What the doctrine does not tell us, however, is what the relations are supposed to be between the various 'elements' involved in the incarnation: the divine nature, the human nature, the body of Jesus, the human soul of Jesus, the man Jesus, and the Son of God.

The history of metaphysical speculation on the doctrine provides us with a bewildering variety of options. Some identify the human nature with the mereological sum of the body and soul; others insist that natures are abstracta and that the proposed identification therefore makes no sense. Some identify the Son with Jesus of Nazareth and Jesus, in turn, with the sum of his two natures. Others say that the Son merely 'inhabited' the human nature (construed as a concrete object) as if it were a sort of outer garment. Some say that the Son functioned as the soul of Jesus' body and in so doing became a human

---

[1] This paper began life as a handout presented to my 'Metaphysics and Christian Theology' seminar in Spring 2007. I am grateful to the students in that seminar—especially Andrew Bailey, Jennifer Martin, Luke Potter, and Luke van Horn—for helpful discussion. I have also been helped by comments from audiences at Wheaton College and Western Washington University, the 'Incarnation: Perspectives from the Philosophy of Mind' conference in Oxford, the Joseph Butler Society in Oriel College, Oxford, and the Baylor Philosophy of Religion Conference. On these occasions, Maria Rosa Antognazza, Trent Dougherty, Daniel Howard-Snyder, Hud Hudson, Joseph Jedwab, Shieva Kleinschmidt, Brian Leftow, Anna Marmodoro, Alex Pruss, Christopher Shields, Christina van Dyke, and Ryan Wasserman were particularly helpful. Finally, I am especially grateful to Oliver Crisp for valuable conversation in the early stages of my work on this project, and to Jeff Brower and Alex Skiles, who provided detailed and very helpful comments on earlier drafts.

soul. Others say that Jesus had two souls—one human and one divine. We could carry on with this list for quite a while.[2]

Discussion of the relations among the elements involved in the incarnation usually arises in contexts where the main question in view is something like, 'How can we coherently suppose that a fully divine being has some of the very specific and distinctively human limitations that Jesus is represented as having—e.g., ignorance of the time of the Second Coming, or the "ability" to *grow* in wisdom?' Addressing this question usually requires at least a brief foray into controversies about the nature of natures and about what, exactly, would be involved in having multiple natures; but, in the contemporary literature at any rate, these issues tend not to take centre stage. It is also common for views about the metaphysics of the incarnation to be developed independently of views about the metaphysics of the Trinity—in some cases with the result that an author's views about the incarnation are in tension with his or her views about the Trinity.[3] Both tendencies in the literature seem methodologically problematic, the latter especially so.

My goal in this paper, then, is to provide a metaphysical account of the incarnation that starts from substantive assumptions about the nature of natures and about the metaphysics of the Trinity and that develops in light of these a story about the relations among the elements involved in the incarnation. Central to the view I will describe are two features of Aristotle's metaphysics, though I do not claim that my own development of these ideas is anything of which Aristotle himself would have approved: (i) a hylomorphic understanding of material objects; (ii) a doctrine of numerical sameness without identity; and (iii) the view that the *nature* of a thing can appropriately

---

[2] For a valuable critical survey of the major positions in the contemporary and historical literature, including references to the sorts of views just mentioned, see Cross (2009). See also Adams (2006: ch. 5), Crisp (2007: ch. 2), and part I of Cross (2002) for further explanation and critical discussion of some of these views.

[3] For example, advocating the view that human persons are material whereas divine persons are (normally) immaterial, Trenton Merricks (2007) argues that the incarnation is best understood as involving the Son of God *becoming a material object*—namely, Jesus of Nazareth. Yet, with regard to the Trinity, he argues that the relation between the divine persons is to be understood on analogy with the distinct spheres of consciousness of a split-brain patient (Merricks, 2006). It is, at the very least, difficult to see how the *incarnate* second person of the Trinity (a material object) could be related to the (immaterial) other persons of the Trinity in the way that the spheres of consciousness of a split-brain patient are related. Or, to take another example, Thomas Flint, in the conference version of his contribution to the present volume, pp. 67–87 (Flint, 2009), sets up the central problem in his paper by assuming that the Son of God, the second person of the Trinity, is *identical to* the divine nature of the incarnate Christ. But, of course, if the Son is identical to the divine nature then it is very hard to see how the Son could also *share* his divine nature with the Father and the Spirit.

be identified with its *form*. These ideas, along with other important aspects of the metaphysical framework with which I shall be working, are laid out in the first five sections below, followed in the sixth section by a brief sketch of the account of the Trinity that Jeffrey Brower and I have presented in detail elsewhere. In the final section, I present my account of the incarnation.

1 THE BASIC FRAMEWORK AND THE NEO-ARISTOTELIAN THEORY

Central to Aristotle's metaphysics is the idea that every material object is a structured entity with two constituents, matter and form. Explanations of these concepts commonly encourage the thought that *matter* is the stuff of which something is made whereas a *form* is a property, like humanity or felinity, instantiation of which accounts for an object's being the kind of thing that it is. It is furthermore common to characterize Aristotelian forms as abstract, immanent universals. I won't comment here on the extent to which these common characterizations are correct as interpretations of Aristotle's views.[4] I note them simply to acknowledge awareness of them, even as I depart from them in articulating my own story about matter and form.

Natures, for Aristotle, are internal principles of change and rest; and talk of *the nature* of a material substance will primarily involve reference to its form. Although Aristotle acknowledges that both matter and form each have some claim to being called 'the nature' of a material substance, he indicates that form has the greater, or primary claim.[5] What tips the scale in favour of form is, in a nutshell, the fact that forms, on his view, determine kind-membership for a substance and provide more fundamental explanations of its behaviour and development.[6] For material substances, then, *sharing* a nature will primarily involve sharing a common form.

Within Aristotle's metaphysics, matter is shareable as well. The best-known examples used to illustrate this involve material substances (e.g., Socrates) and substance-accident compounds (e.g., seated-Socrates, which exists when

---

[4] But see, e.g., Witt (1989), wherein it is argued that forms are not properties and not universals but rather, individuals. Cf. also Koslicki (2008: 252ff.).

[5] *Physics* II.1, esp. 193b8-19. See also *Metaphysics* IV.4 1014a35-b19 and *Metaphysics* VII.3 1029a5–7, and Loux (1991: 81–2 and ch. 5).

[6] Cf. Waterlow (1982: 58–66) and Witt (1989: 65–79). These passages in Waterlow and Witt focus primarily on the *Physics*. On the case for form in the *Metaphysics* see Loux (1991, esp. chs 3 and 5).

Hylomorphism and the incarnation 137

and only when Socrates is seated) that are made of the very same stuff.⁷ Things that share matter in this way are, on Aristotle's view, numerically the same, but not identical—of which more below.

All that I have said in this section thus far (minus what I have called the 'common characterizations' of matter and form) is what I shall have in mind when I talk below of the 'basic (Aristotelian) framework'.

Like many philosophers, both contemporary and historical, I think that the basic framework offers fruitful resources not only for solving central problems in metaphysics, but also for explicating and solving problems with central doctrines of Christianity. My own use of it, however, depends on thinking of matter and form in such a way that even *immaterial* things might be said to have a matter-form structure. As shall become clear below, I also find it useful to allow that one and the same thing can be the form of one object and the matter of another. Thus, as I have already indicated, I find it difficult to endorse, without a lot of qualifying assumptions, the idea that matter is stuff and forms are kind-properties. I also find it difficult, for other reasons, to endorse various other familiar claims about matter, forms, and natures—for example, that matter is 'potentiality', or that forms (and therefore natures) are final causes or 'principles of life'.⁸ One reason why I am not inclined to endorse these claims is that the central terms, like 'potentiality' and 'final cause', either are, or are explained in terms of, primitive concepts that I think many contemporary metaphysicians will find unintelligible. Though I am somewhat sceptical of claims to the effect that 'my primitives are more intelligible than yours', I would prefer to develop a metaphysic that retains some of the central aspects of the basic Aristotelian framework (in particular, a place for some of the central *roles* associated with the concepts of matter, form, and nature, as well as the relation of numerical sameness without identity) but whose explanations invoke primitives whose intelligibility is more widely acknowledged by contemporary metaphysicians.

For the purposes of this paper, then, I want to work with what is probably best thought of as a *neo*-Aristotelian theory of natures and substances. This theory can be roughly divided into two parts: the *Aristotelian* part and the *neo* part. The 'neo' part of the theory attempts to forge connections between contemporary ideas about *powers* and *fundamental properties* on the one hand and, on the other hand, certain Aristotelian ideas about natures and forms— namely, that whatever plays the role of form is also suited to play the role of

---

⁷ See, e.g., *Topics* I.7 103a23–31 and *Metaphysics* IV.6 1015b16–27. Perhaps all of Aristotle's examples are like these, but I cannot claim to have examined the entire corpus.
⁸ Cf. Witt (1989: 68, 126ff.).

nature, that natures are intimately connected with the distinctive powers and capacities of their corresponding natural kinds, and that natures are principles of unity.

Let us start, then, with the Aristotelian part of the theory.

(T1) Every substance that is not a nature is a compound of matter and form.
(T2) Forms are *constituents* of objects, not transcendent universals.

I have discussed these two claims to some extent already at the beginning of this section; but let me add here just two further comments. First, note that T1 allows that natures are substances. I believe that this is Aristotle's view as well, but there are controversies in the neighbourhood that I have neither the space nor the expertise to discuss in appropriate detail.[9] I do not here mean to take a position on those controversies. Second, hylomorphic compounding is not the same as composition, or mereological summation.[10] In my terminology, matter and form are constituents of material objects, but not parts. I don't suppose that there is any pre-theoretical distinction to be drawn between parts and constituents. But I do think that there is a substantive, and probably pre-theoretical, distinction to be drawn between composition (or summation) construed as an operation on concrete particulars and the sort of compounding that might take place between stuff and a form or between a concrete particular and a form. Even a child can grasp the idea of imposing a form upon a piece of clay; but it would be a substantially further step—and one that I am not inclined to take—to regard the form of a statue as one of its *parts*.[11] The terminological distinctions between parts and constituents and between summation and compounding are meant to help us keep track of that difference.

The *neo* part of the theory involves three further claims about the nature and function of *natures*:

---

[9] But see, for starters, Loux (1991).
[10] Whether composition and mereological summation are the same depends in part on whether one wants to reserve the term 'mereology' for, for example, classical extensional mereology while at the same time denying that composition obeys the axioms of that system. My point here is just that compounding should not be assimilated to either. Alternatively, one might endorse *compositional pluralism*, the view that there are multiple fundamental composition relations; and one might then say, for example, that mereological summation and compounding are two such relations. (Cf. McDaniel (2009), as well as the remarks about Fine in note 11.) I am not, in principle, opposed to this way of talking; but it does represent a different terminological choice from what I have opted for here.
[11] My hylomorphism differs in at least this respect, then, from that of Johnston (2006) and Koslicki (2008). Fine (2008) suggests that forms are parts, but not the sorts of parts that are joined by *fusion*. (Cf. also Fine 1999.) Perhaps, then, our difference on this score is merely terminological. There are, of course, other differences, however.

(T3) Natures are fundamental powers.[12]
(T4) The natures of composite objects *unite* other powers (in particular, the powers that are the natures of their parts).
(T5) Natures can enter into compounds with *individuators*, and with *distinguishing properties*. In compounds with *individuators*, natures play the role of form; in compounds with *distinguishing properties*, they play the role of matter.

Each of T3–T5 requires comment and, in the case of T4 and T5, explication of central terms. I'll take each in turn.

2 NATURES AS FUNDAMENTAL POWERS

In saying that natures are fundamental powers, I mean three things. First, they are perfectly natural properties—not in the sense that contrasts with 'supernatural', but rather in the sense of marking objective similarities and joints in nature (cf. Lewis, 1983.) Second, they are not reducible to other powers. The power to tell a lie, for example, is reducible (if it is a genuine power at all). It is nothing over and above the more basic powers involved in its exercise: the power to form beliefs, the power to speak, the power to entertain false propositions and to intend to report them as true, and so on. Negative charge, on the other hand, is plausibly non-reducible, and so fundamental. Third, they ground non-natural powers or, if there are no such things, they explain the truth of (putative) non-natural power attributions. For example: fundamental particles have the power to repel other fundamental particles. If there really is such a thing as *the power to repel other fundamental particles*, presumably it is a non-natural power that is grounded in one of two plausibly fundamental powers—negative or positive charge. (For the purposes here, I'll follow George Molnar in my understanding of grounding: 'The ground of a power, P, is the set of properties (all of which are conceptually distinct from P) by virtue of which a thing has P' (2003: 147).) On the other hand, if there is no such thing as the power to repel other fundamental particles, still, the claim that fundamental particles have that power will be made true by facts about fundamental powers; and so the fundamental powers will explain the truth of that power attribution. I take it that the difference between reducible powers and non-

---

[12] I have located 'T3' in the 'neo' section not because I think that Aristotle would disagree with it (I don't). Rather, I have located it here simply to avoid having to defend the claim that it belongs in the 'clearly Aristotelian' part.

reducible non-natural powers roughly corresponds to the difference between conjunctive properties and irreducibly disjunctive properties.[13]

I should also say what I don't mean by the claim that natures are fundamental powers. Most importantly, I don't mean to say that natures are 'basic' in the sense of being entities upon which all other things depend for their existence. For example, it might turn out that the natures of composite objects depend in some sense upon the natures of their parts. Also, I don't mean to take any position on the question of whether there are fundamental empirical properties beyond those investigated by physics. If there are, then perhaps there are biological and chemical natures as well as physical natures; or perhaps there are mental natures. If there aren't, then the only natures exemplified by material things are natures of physical objects. Of course, the doctrine of the incarnation is committed to the existence of human nature and the nature of God. But I don't think anyone would say that the divine nature is a fundamental *empirical* property; and it is an open question both philosophically and from the point of view of traditional Christian doctrine whether humanity is.

In saying that natures are powers *and* that natures can play the role of form, it might seem that, from the point of view of traditional hylomorphism, I have got my metaphysics upside down. For *powers*, one might argue, are dispositions, or potencies, not 'acts' or 'manifestations'; but the role of 'potency' is commonly associated with *matter*, whereas the role of 'act' is commonly associated with form. Addressing this concern in detail would take us too far afield; but let me offer just two brief remarks. First, Aristotle himself distinguishes between *active* (causal) power and mere potentiality, and it is the latter, not the former, that is associated with the matter role.[14] This makes intuitive sense, too. *Being feline*, for example, might just be a certain complex power or capacity to develop and behave in certain ways, even if, at the same time, *felinity* is the actualization of the potentiality on the part of some matter for being a cat. Second, the metaphysic of properties with which I am working in this paper is a version of *dispositional monism*, according to which *all* properties (and hence all *manifestations of dispositions*) are powers, and therefore dispositions. There are, of course, well-known difficulties for dispositional monism, not least of which are the threat of infinite regress and the (related) problem of ungrounded dispositions. I cannot possibly hope to articulate and defend my own responses to these problems here; but I can at least refer interested readers to promising responses already available in the literature.[15]

---

[13] This is not to say, of course, that there is no overlap between the two; i.e., if there are indeed both conjunctive powers and irreducibly disjunctive powers, then surely too there are irreducibly disjunctive conjunctions as well.

[14] Witt (2003: esp. ch. 2).   [15] See Molnar (2003) and Bird (2007).

3 NATURES AS UNITING OTHER POWERS

Thesis T4 is meant to express and do justice to that part of traditional hylomorphism that says that natures are principles of unity. The relation of *uniting* is to be understood roughly as follows: one power—a nature—unites some other powers just in the case that the nature is so connected to the other powers that its manifestation depends upon the cooperative manifestation of the united powers and, furthermore, the latter do not confer any powers on the object that has the nature that are both intrinsic to the object and independent of the nature. A bit more precisely:

A power p_0 of an object x unites distinct powers $p_1 - p_n$ $=_{df}$ (i) p_0 is intrinsic to x,[16] (ii) each of $p_1 - p_n$ is a nature of at least one of x's parts, (iii) p_0 is grounded in or identical to a certain sort of cooperative manifestation (CM) of p_1-p_n,[17] (iv) every power intrinsic to x that is at least partly grounded in CM is identical with, reducible to, or at least partly grounded in p_0, and (v) there is no power intrinsic to x that is distinct from both p_0 and CM and that grounds p_0.

Consider a human organism, for example, and suppose that *humanity* is indeed a biological nature. The manifestation of humanity in a region depends causally upon the cooperative manifestation of the natures of the simple parts of the human organism. Not just any sort of cooperative manifestation will do, however. Take all of the simple parts of a human and force-fit them into a one-quart cylindrical container and you will not have a human organism, even if, at that time, the natures of the erstwhile parts of the human being are engaged in some sort of cooperative manifestation. Thus, the presence of humanity in a region depends upon a particular *sort* of cooperative manifestation of the natures of the relevant parts. (Perhaps it just *is* that sort of cooperative activity. I don't commit to this; but neither do I intend to rule it out.) Finally, every power intrinsic to a human being whose manifestation depends upon the relevant sort of cooperative activity—e.g., the capacity for rational thought, the power to grow and develop as a human

---

[16] This might be a problem if, as some think, dispositions—and therefore powers—turn out to be extrinsic. Jennifer McKitrick (2003), for example, argues for the thesis that dispositions are extrinsic. Molnar (2003), on the other hand, argues that they are intrinsic, and Bird (2007) provides replies to McKitrick's arguments. Obviously I'm taking sides with Molnar and Bird.

[17] In other words: let CM be a property such that, necessarily, CM is had by an object x iff p_1-p_n manifest in a particular sort of way. Then x's having p_0 is grounded in or identical to x's having CM.

organism, the power to run and dance—is plausibly dependent upon the power that is humanity; and humanity is not itself so dependent upon some further uniting power.[18] Thus, humanity unites the natures of the parts of a human being in the sense described above. This is the sense in which I think that humanity is a 'principle of unity', and it is part of what is involved in its being a nature.

At this juncture, it may be helpful briefly to contrast my own understanding of principles of unity with another one available in the literature. Mark Johnston, in developing his own version of hylomorphism, also regards forms as principles of unity; and he regards principles of unity as relations. Thus, for example, he writes:

> Consider HCl, a kind of molecule. The principle of unity for individual hydrogen chloride (HCl) molecules is the relation of *bipolar bonding*.... The principle of unity holds of the ions, and its holding is the essential condition for existence of the molecule. It is simply an essentialist elaboration of a proposition of chemistry that what it is for a given hydrogen chloride molecule to be is for there to be a hydrogen ion and a chlorine ion together in a bipolar bond. (2006: 653)

On the assumption that relations can be identified with polyadic properties and properties with causal powers (both controversial, of course), Johnston's version of hylomorphism comes out in one respect very similar to my own: principles of unity, and so the forms of material objects, turn out to be powers. But it should also be clear that, on my view, relations like *bipolar bonding* will not at all be the right sorts of powers to function as *natures*. To see why, one need only attend to the fact that HCl and NaCl both have their parts united (in Johnston's sense) by the bipolar bonding relation, and yet they don't share a nature. As I see it, a nature should be something that *unites the powers* of the parts of the object in the sense described above. But it is hard to see *bipolar bonding* as playing that role. HCl and NaCl have very different causal powers, after all; thus, even if *bipolar bonding* satisfied conditions (i–iv) of the definition of power-uniting, it is hard to imagine that it would satisfy condition (v). Presumably condition (v) is satisfied in each case by a more 'all-encompassing' power—i.e., a power that we would normally name by reference to a kind, like *being hydrogen chloride*, or *being sodium chloride*.

---

[18] I don't, of course, mean to suggest that these powers are *unique* to human beings; only that they are intrinsic.

4 NATURES, 'INDIVIDUATORS', AND 'DISTINGUISHING PROPERTIES'

According to the version of hylomorphism that I am developing, the natures of material objects play the role of form, and they enter into compounds with things or stuffs that play the role of matter. On one common way of understanding the roles of form and matter, forms are constituents that are shared among objects of the same kind, whereas matter is what individuates objects of a kind. I can unqualifiedly endorse the claim about forms, but not the claim about matter. In accord with the spirit of that claim, I want to say that (for material objects, anyway) what natures enter into compounds with are *individuators*. But for those of us who endorse the view that *distinct objects* might nevertheless share the *same matter* in common, and for those of us who believe that immaterial things might have a hylomorphic structure, the claim that 'matter is what individuates objects of a kind' cannot be affirmed without qualification. Individuators can't be seen as accounting for distinctness, since distinct items can have the same individuator as a constituent. Furthermore, *matter* can't always be what individuates, since immaterial things have no matter, strictly speaking. (Another way of putting this is that it is not always matter, literally speaking, that plays the matter role.) Let me therefore say a few words about how I'm thinking about individuators, about matter-sharing, and about the hylomorphic structure of immaterial things.

Let us begin by considering simple material objects. A simple material thing—a point-sized particle, for example—will have a nature which it shares with other particles of the same kind. But what accounts for the fact that there are *many* particles with the same nature rather than just *one* scattered, mereologically complex particle located wherever we find the nature in question? The answer, I take it, is just this: the nature itself doesn't divide across disconnected regions of spacetime; it is a power that must be, in some sense, wholly or fully concentrated at, or attached to, point-sized regions (or, better, line-sized ones for the typical case of a *moving*, spatially point-sized particle), rather than to scattered regions. In light of this, it is natural to suppose that, in the case of each particle of the relevant kind, the nature has compounded with some further constituent that accounts for its concentration at or attachment to the region in question. From here, the story might be fleshed out in a variety of different ways. My own inclination is to think that, for simple objects, the individuators are regions—presumably point-sized, but perhaps not—of spacetime. I think of the powers of simple material objects as physically locatable properties—qualities that exist at multiple regions of spacetime. Thus, it is natural to regard the objects themselves as compounds whose matter is a spacetime region and whose form is the quality located at that region.

What about complex material things? Here, it seems, we have fundamentally the same situation, but on a larger scale. What is it that accounts for the fact that there are many distinct human beings, rather than just one spatiotemporally scattered human being? Presumably it is that human nature doesn't divide widely across spacetime; it is the sort of power that is fully and completely located in what we think of as human-shaped regions.[19] More precisely: it is a power that *unites* only the natures of certain kinds of objects standing in certain kinds of relations, and it is this fact that explains why human nature concentrates at human-shaped regions rather than scattered regions. Unlike the case of simple particles, however, it is *not* so natural to suppose that the individuating constituent of a human being is its region of spacetime. The reason is just that there is an intuitively better candidate available—namely, the collection of objects whose powers are united by the nature. (By using the terms 'a better candidate' and 'the collection of objects', I don't mean to commit to the claim that 'the collection' is an individual thing distinct from the human being it constitutes.) Thus, in general, the individuators for mereologically complex things will just be collections of objects whose powers are united by the natures of those things.

But what if we believe that distinct things share all of the same matter in common? Suppose, for example, you think that a clay statue is distinct from the lump of clay that constitutes it. (Perhaps you think that the lump can survive things—squashing and reshaping, for instance—that the statue cannot, and that by virtue of this difference, the lump cannot be identical to the statue.) In that case, it will be at least somewhat misleading to say that matter individuates. Matter would *not* be what accounts for the distinctness of the two objects. Nevertheless, if you also believe—as I do—in a relation of *numerical sameness without identity*, you might think that there is still a perfectly good sense in which matter *does* individuate. Proponents of numerical sameness without identity say that, in the statue/lump case, though the statue and the lump are distinct, they nevertheless count as *one material object*. They are *two* hylomorphic compounds, two things, two entities, etc.; but they are, nevertheless, one material object. Thus, on this view, *material*

---

[19] But, one might wonder, *how* is it located at those regions? For some such region R, does the nature *entend*, *pertend*, or *span* the region? (Roughly, this question boils down to the following: 'Is the nature wholly present at every subregion of the region in question, or does it have parts at every subregion, or neither?' For definitions of *entension, pretension,* and *spanning*, and related notions see Hudson (2005: 99–101). See also Parsons (2007).

objects are individuated by their matter. That is, whether x and y count as the *same material object* just depends on whether they share the same matter. I have defended this view elsewhere and do not have the space to rehearse that defence here. But what I want to note is just this: if one has this sort of view, the right thing to say about individuators is *not* that they account for *distinctness simpliciter*, but rather that they account for *absence of numerical sameness*. In the case of material objects, matter plays that role. (What, then, accounts for distinctness simpliciter? Perhaps divergence of properties.)

We have considered simple material things and complex material things. But there is one further sort of case we must consider, given our present interest in the Trinity and the incarnation. What should we say about simple *immaterial* things?

The nature of a simple immaterial thing will not be located anywhere in spacetime, so there is no literal sense in which matter could individuate such things. One option then is simply to deny that immaterial things have a hylomorphic structure. If we say this, then we can go on to say one of the following three things: that they have matter but no nature, that they have neither matter nor nature, or that they are identical to their natures. Affirming the first option would be extremely bizarre if what motivates us to deny that immaterial things have a hylomorphic structure is the fact that they have no literal matter. Taking the second option commits us to the view that some substances have natures, but not all of them do. It is hard to see what the motivation for such a view might be. Thus, it seems that the last alternative would be the clear choice.

But suppose we believe in immaterial things that *share* a nature? We cannot appeal to matter or spatiotemporal separation or anything of the sort to individuate them—i.e., to account for an absence of numerical sameness among them. Thus, a natural thing to say, given that we already accept a relation of numerical sameness without identity, is to say that immaterial things that share a nature are, on that account, one in number, and they are distinguished from one another by their possession of some further property—let us call it, uncreatively, a *distinguishing property*.

Note, however, that on this view there is a clear sense in which the nature of an immaterial thing does, or can, *play the role of matter*. Just as matter-sharing explains numerical sameness among distinct material objects, so too nature-sharing explains numerical sameness among distinct immaterial objects. Likewise, the property (perhaps complex or conjunctive, or perhaps a mere thisness) that accounts for the distinctness of these objects plays at least part of the role of form. Differences in form account for major differences in character among material objects; and, in the case of two distinct things that count as the same material object, it will be differences in form that fundamentally account for the distinctness of those things. And so too in the case of the distinguishing properties of immaterial things that share a nature in common. Thus, it turns out that immaterial objects have a hylomorphic structure after all.

5 FURTHER TERMINOLOGY

Having now finished commenting on theses T1–T5, I want to close my discussion of hylomorphism as such by explaining (in light of the foregoing) my use of terms like *constituent, matter-form compound, matter,* and *form*:

x is a constituent of $y =_{df} x$ plays in y the role of matter or the role of form.

x is a matter-form compound $=_{df} x$ has constituents that play the roles of matter and form.

m plays the role of matter in $x =_{df}$ (i) m is an individuator that exactly overlaps x or, if there is no such individuator, m is a nature of x and (ii) it is not possible for a distinct thing to share m with x without being numerically the same as x.

f plays the role of *form* in x iff f is a nature of x (or a sum of natures of x, in the case of multi-natured beings), or a distinguishing property instantiated by x, and f does not play the role of matter in x.[20]

As noted earlier, I allow that mere pluralities—collections—can function as individuators, and hence can play the role of matter. But, in light of the above definitions, this poses a small terminological problem. Consider the collection of particles, C, that plays the role of matter in some particular cat. Suppose the xs are the members of the collection. Given that C is a mere collection, 'C' is just a device for referring collectively to the xs. Thus, the xs play the role of matter. But now do we say that the xs *are constituents* of the cat? If we do, the definitions imply (falsely) that *each* of the xs plays the role of matter in the cat. If we don't—if we say, instead, that the xs are *a constituent* of y—then we violate grammar. There is no substantive issue here. We just need to recognize that, just as 'the collection' is only apparently a singular referring expression, so too 'being a constituent of the cat' only apparently picks out a role that can

---

[20] In the case of multi-natured beings, I say that the two natures (or more) comprise *one* form because, as indicated above, different forms account for the distinctness of objects that share the same matter in common. Thus, if Christ's two natures were two forms that inform the same matter, then there would be no way to account for the fact that Christ is a *two-natured person* who is distinct both from the compound of his matter plus the human nature and the compound of his matter plus the divine nature.

be played just by an individual. (Analogously: we can't grammatically say that the members of the Notre Dame football team are *the winner* of Saturday's game. We have to say either that the team itself was the winner or that the members of the team won. The problem in the case of constituency is just that there is no corresponding verb analogous to 'won'. We could invent one; but once the point here has been appreciated, there is no need to.)

There is one additional notion that ought to be introduced here as well: the notion of *consubstantiality*. It is important to talk about consubstantiality because, according to the tradition, Jesus is supposed to be *consubstantial with the Father* with regard to his divinity and *consubstantial with us* as regards his humanity. It is generally taken for granted that the *substance* or *essence* of a thing is its nature, and that what it is for objects (material or immaterial) to be consubstantial is for them to share a nature. I affirm all of this. Given what I have said above, distinct but consubstantial immaterial things will stand in the relation of numerical sameness without identity—they will be counted as *one* F, where F specifies the nature they share in common.[21] But consubstantial *material* things will not stand in that relation: matter-sharing (in general), not nature-sharing (in general) is what puts things into the relation of numerical sameness without identity.

Since God is an immaterial thing, it will follow from all of this that x is the same God as y if and only if x and y share a divine nature (and there will be exactly one God if and only if there is exactly one divine nature, as traditional Christian doctrine maintains). Obviously, we are now in a position to say something about the metaphysics of the Trinity.

6 THE TRINITY

So let me provide a brief sketch of the 'constitution model' of the Trinity that I favour. In several other papers (Rea, 2003, 2006, and 2009; Brower, 2004a, 2004b; Brower and Rea, 2005) Jeff Brower and I have tried to motivate this model by highlighting its intrinsic virtues, defending it against objections, subjecting its main rivals to criticism, and arguing that the view is at least

---

[21] This, of course, implies that if (say) angels are immaterial and share a common nature, then all angels are the same angel, even if they are distinguishable under some other sortal. One way to avoid this consequence is to suppose that 'angel' isn't a natural kind, and that each of the beings we characterize as angels in fact has its own distinct nature. Another possibility is to deny that angels are immaterial. But if these options are somehow untenable, I am content to accept the consequence.

consistent with and in salient respects similar to views defended by some of the most important patristic and medieval figures writing on the Trinity. For present purposes, however, I'll leave all of that aside and simply present the main lines of the model.

According to the model I favour—'Constitution Trinitarianism'—each divine person is an immaterial substance whose constituents are the divine nature (or substance) and a 'person-making' property (let's refer to the relevant properties as *Fatherhood, Sonship,* and *Procession*). The divine nature plays the role of matter, and the person-making properties each play the role of form in the senses just described. Since each divine person is *a* substance, the persons cannot be regarded as mere aspects of a common substance, and so the heresy of modalism is avoided. Moreover, though the persons are distinct from one another, they nevertheless count as *one God* and as numerically the same divine substance, and so the heresy of tri-theism is avoided. This, again, is because immaterial things are individuated by their nature, and Father, Son, and Holy Spirit share the same divine nature. The relation between the persons of the Trinity is, therefore, *analogous* to the relation of material constitution—the relation between objects that share all of the same matter at the same time. Thus, on this view, there is just one divine substance, and so the view allows us to affirm, along with the creed, that there is '. . . one God, the Father almighty . . . and . . . one Lord Jesus Christ . . . begotten, not made, being of one substance with the Father . . .'.

Elsewhere I have said this about the model:

> What is it that plays the role of matter in the Trinity? And is it a substance itself? Here I want to offer only a *partial* view that might be developed in a variety of different ways. What plays the role of matter in the Trinity is *the divine nature*; and the divine nature *is* a substance. It is not a fourth substance, for reasons already discussed; nor is it a fourth person (since it is not a compound of 'matter' plus a person-defining property). But it is a substance, since (again, taking cues from Aristotle) *natures* are substances. What I don't want to take a position on here is the question of what, exactly, a nature is. Is it concrete or abstract? Is it particular or universal? Is it a property or something else? These questions I will not answer. I think that they must be answered in a way that allows the divine persons to be concrete particular non-properties; but I think that there are various ways of answering these questions that are compatible with that view. (Rea, 2007: 420)

In the present paper, obviously enough, I am not leaving all of these questions open. I have come down in favour of the view that natures are powers. I have not said whether natures are universals or particulars—I have said that they are sharable and multiply locatable, but nothing beyond that. This might suggest that natures are universals; but I don't want to commit to this, partly because I am unsure whether I buy into the universal/particular distinction.[22]

7 THE INCARNATION

I turn now, at last, to the metaphysics of the incarnation. Recall our central question: 'How are the elements involved in the incarnation—the divine nature, the human nature, the body and human soul of Jesus, the man Jesus, and the Son of God—related to one another?' I'll begin with some abbreviations that I think will make the presentation of the model go more smoothly; then I'll lay out the model.

Here are the abbreviations:

'X++Y' abbreviates 'the matter-form compound whose matter is X and whose form is Y'
M = Jesus' physical matter
DN = the divine nature
S = The Son
Sonship = the person-making property in the compound that is the Son
HN = humanity—Christ's (and our) human nature.

Now for the model.

As should already be clear, I do not identify the human nature of Jesus (as some do) with either his body, or his soul, or the mereological sum of his body and soul. The human nature of Jesus is a power, and it is something that he is supposed to *share* with us. On the present view, then, humanity—HN—is one of two *formal* constituents of Jesus (the other being DN), and Jesus himself is a compound of those formal constituents and a material constituent—M. One might wish to identify M with Jesus' body; or one might wish to identify Jesus' body with the compound, M++HN. Which alternative one chooses depends in part upon what one says about Jesus' soul.

What should one say about Jesus' human soul? At the very least, I want to say that, for all x, x has a human soul iff x is identical to a matter-form compound whose form is a human nature. But it is not clear to me what more to say. I am reluctant to take on commitments because I suspect that with minor modifications here and there, my model is indifferent between a variety of options (including an option according to which 'having a soul' doesn't

---

[22] On this issue, see Ramsey (1925) and MacBride (2005).

imply the existence of anything that would ordinarily count as a soul). That said, though, here is an option that I mostly like: a human soul is something with two modes of existence—material and immaterial. In the immaterial mode, the soul is a compound whose matter is the human nature and whose form is some distinguishing property—perhaps a thisness. In the material mode, the human nature plays the role of form in a compound whose constituents are humanity and some matter, and the (same) distinguishing property becomes simply a property of the whole compound.

One likely consequence of this view is that Jesus' human soul is identical to the compound that was the Son prior to the incarnation. The reason this is a likely consequence is that there is no candidate other than Sonship in the incarnate Jesus for being the relevant 'distinguishing property'. Thus, on this view about human souls, what happens in the incarnation is that the compound that *was* the Son becomes the human soul of Jesus. Since this view is consistent with—indeed, entails—that the incarnate Christ has a human soul, there is nothing obviously heretical about it. And I find it intuitively rather satisfying as an account of what the incarnation fundamentally involves.

A consequence of this view that I strongly *dislike*, however, is that all human souls that exist in the immaterial mode count as *the same human being*.[23] On the other hand, views in the neighbourhood of this pervade the patristic and medieval literature on original sin; so perhaps it deserves to be taken seriously. At any rate, the consequence is mitigated by the fact that God can easily see to it that no human being ever exists in that immaterial state by seeing to it that the relevant distinguishing property is only ever exemplified by a genuine matter-form compound. (This might be part of why resurrection is so important.)

Leaving aside concerns about the nature of the soul, what should we say about the relations between Jesus, the Son, and the two natures of Jesus? On the present model, Jesus is identical to the Son; and prior to the incarnation, the Son is identical to the matter-form compound whose constituents are the divine nature and the person-making property, Sonship. After the incarnation, the Son is identical to a matter-form compound with the following features: (i) his matter is M; (ii) his form comprises *two natures*, DN and HN; and (iii) he has the individuating property, Sonship.

One might worry that this view implies the following claim, which appears at first glance to be incoherent:

(C1) S = DN++Sonship = M++(DN&HN).

---

[23] Or, at any rate, the same *something*, if being human requires having a body.

One might also worry that Sonship seems simply to disappear in the incarnation. To the latter worry, I reply that Sonship doesn't disappear; it simply ceases to be a constituent. Prior to the incarnation, Sonship is the formal constituent of S; after the incarnation, it is merely a property of S. To the former worry, I reply that the claim is implied, but it is not incoherent. If '++' represented mereological summation (understood according to standard axioms of mereology), then the claim *would* be incoherent, since standard mereology includes an extensionality axiom. But there is no reason to think that hylomorphic compounding obeys the same rules as mereological summation. Compounds are not defined by their constituents—or, at any rate, to say that they are is to *add* a substantive and controversial thesis to one's hylomorphic theory.

One might also worry that C1 violates Leibniz's Law. After all, DN++Sonship has the property *having DN as matter*, whereas M++(DN&HN) lacks that property. I reply that the 'problem' here is to be solved in whatever way we solve ordinary problems with material change. Let M_F be the eight-pound lump of matter that is Fred's matter when he is newborn. Now, *Newborn Fred* has the property *having M_F as matter*; *Adult Fred* lacks that property. But, as is well known, we can solve the problem by indexing either the property or the having of it.[24]

One might furthermore worry that, post-incarnation, the Son is no longer the *same God* as the Father, since Father and Son no longer share the same matter: the Son has M for matter, whereas the Father has DN. I reply that, because the compound DN++Sonship is present in Jesus—because Jesus still has as a constituent the very thing that plays the role of matter in the Father—that is sufficient for Jesus still to stand in the immaterial analogue of the matter-sharing relation with the Father. (And likewise for the Spirit.) Thus, the doctrine of the Trinity is preserved. Moreover, because HN is present in Jesus, he shares a nature with us and so counts as human; and because Jesus exemplifies Sonship, he counts as the Son incarnate.

Finally, one might object that the official story about the incarnate Christ is not consistent with what I am inclined to say about ordinary cases of material constitution. Consider, for example, a block of marble ('B') that constitutes both a statue ('X') and a pillar ('Y'). Since the pillar could survive erosion that would destroy the statue, X and Y are distinct. Thus, it looks like we have two

---

[24] For discussion, see, for example, Rea (1998b). There are other ways of solving the problem in Fred's case, too: invoke temporal parts, appeal to presentism, or (following a recent suggestion of Jeffrey Brower's [forthcoming]) account for the change by positing different compounds (i.e., *Newborn Fred* and *Adult Fred*), which have different properties but have Fred himself as a common constituent. Each of these strategies, however, seem problematic as applied to the incarnation.

matter-form compounds that share the same matter. So far so good. But now let F1 be the 'statue form' and let F2 be the 'pillar form'. Given what I say about the incarnation, it seems that I ought to be willing to say that, in the region occupied by the statue, there is a two-natured object—a statue-pillar, perhaps—whose matter is B and whose two natures are F1 and F2. In other words, I ought to say that there is a thing S* such that S* = B++(F1&F2). But it looks as if I do not say this—I say, instead, simply that X and Y stand in the relation of numerical sameness without identity. So, one might think, I am not giving uniform treatment to similar cases.

There are two ways to reply. One is to take two-natured beings to be metaphysically rare and special, and to insist that (unlike in the case of the incarnation) in the case of X and Y, there is simply no reason to believe that there is a third thing, S*, that has two natures and stands in the relation of numerical sameness without identity with them. The view, then, would be that sometimes when two natures inform the same matter, a two-natured being results, but most of the time that doesn't happen. One would then appeal to divine revelation (i.e., the Christian scriptures and the arguments that move from them to the doctrine of the incarnation) as our reason for thinking that the incarnation is one of the special cases where a two-natured being results.

Alternatively, one might say that two-natured beings aren't all that special after all—that, for example, when a statue and a pillar coincide, what we have is a statue, a pillar, and a statue-pillar, all of which are the *same material object*, and likewise for other cases of material constitution. One might then also concede that, in the incarnation too, there are three compounds—M++DN, M++HN, and M++(DN&HN)—all of which coincide, all of which count as the *same material object* (and perhaps the same F for a variety of other Fs), but only one of which counts as a person.[25] Overall, this second reply strikes me as more natural and more easily motivated for a believer in numerical sameness without identity, so I am inclined to favour it. But those who dislike the almost indiscriminate proliferation of multi-natured beings might prefer the first reply instead.

---

[25] Note that, on this view, DN and HN do not together compose a third, hybrid nature; rather, M++(DN&HN) is to be understood as a genuinely two-natured being. Note too that belief in multiple hylomorphic compounds—or even belief in many multi-natured beings—in the incarnate Christ poses no problem for orthodoxy. What matters for orthodoxy is that there is *one person* in the incarnate Christ, and that *that person* has exactly two natures.

8

The coherence of the Chalcedonian Definition of the incarnation[1]

Richard Swinburne

By the middle of the fifth century AD it had become a largely universal Christian belief that the second person of the Trinity (the Son), while remaining divine, became human as Jesus Christ. Christians had two main reasons for holding this belief. The first was that they thought that many New Testament passages confirmed by a tradition of church teaching entailed it. The second was that they thought that—as church teaching and the New Testament claimed—God had provided reparation for human sins, and that he could only have done so by God the Son becoming human and living a perfect human life. The Council of Chalcedon in AD 451 expressed this largely universal view by asserting that Jesus Christ was one 'hypostasis' (ὑπόστασις) who had two natures (φύσεις), a divine nature and a human nature, joined together, so that 'at no point was the difference between the natures taken away though the union, but rather the property of both natures is preserved and comes together into a single person and a single subsistent being'.[2] Christ had 'a rational soul and a body', and—Chalcedon seems to be saying—his humanity consisted in his having these.

The Chalcedonian 'Definition' caused two Christian groups to break away from mainstream Christianity, initiating schisms which have remained until today. A minority group insisted that there were in Christ two hypostases, and they evolved into a small Middle-Eastern church now called 'the Church of the East'. The other minority group insisted that there was in Christ only one nature, and they evolved into a number of larger monophysite 'churches' in

---

[1] This essay incorporates much material from Swinburne (1994), especially chapter 9, revised in a simpler form in Swinburne (2008: ch. 3).
[2] Tanner (1990: I 86).

the Middle East, such as the Egyptian Copts, the Ethiopians, and the Armenians. But there have been recent theological discussions between high-level official representatives of the Roman Catholic Church and the Church of the East, and of the Orthodox Church and the 'monophysite churches' which have revealed surprising agreements to the effect that really these groups now claim to hold the same doctrine, although using different words to express it; the 'schisms' resulted from different understandings of φύσις and ὑπόστασις. The Church of the East claimed that its insistence on two 'hypostases' was in effect an insistence on Christ being both fully human and fully divine. The 'monophysites' claimed that their insistence on 'one nature' was an insistence on the unity of the person of Christ. It is plausible to suppose that all these groups have always been deeply conscious of what they were affirming on this issue, which to a considerable extent constituted their separate identity, and so plausible to suppose that the schisms arose primarily because members of the council of Chalcedon had different understandings from each other of their technical terms and perhaps not only of ὑπόστασις and φύσις. So (given that none of the groups have changed their views since Chalcedon) it turns out that the core claim of Chalcedon was common to virtually all Christianity for the thousand years between Chalcedon and the Reformation and for the vast majority of Christians since then. But it also follows that there is no point for those of us who wish to be faithful to church tradition by accepting the Chalcedonian Definition, to try to do so by seeking to discover what the council members meant by their technical terms, for they had no common understanding of them. Rather, we must ask which of the possible ways of understanding the technical terms lead to a coherent doctrine in the spirit of Chalcedon.

What all groups agreed (or at any rate now agree) is that Jesus Christ is a 'person', and that person is the second person of the Trinity. The 'Common christological declaration' of 1994 signed jointly by Pope John Paul II and the Catholicos-Patriarch of the Church of the East affirmed that 'the divinity and humanity are united in the person of the same and unique Son of God and Lord Jesus Christ'.[3] He is eternally Son of God, retaining his divinity during his early ministry; but he acquired his humanity at his human birth. If the divinity and humanity are united in a particular person, they are united in a particular individual of a certain kind (a rational kind). This is how those council members who supported the Chalcedonian Definition seem to have understood 'hypostasis'; others expressed that unity in a different way. (I will understand 'hypostasis' in the way understood by the supporters of the

---

[3] See the website of the Church of the East: <http://www.cired.org/>.

definition in future). But what were the divinity and the humanity which were thus united? The Chalcedonian Definition described them as 'natures'. The joint statement signed by official representatives of the 'monophysite' churches and of the Orthodox Church affirmed that the Son of God united his 'divine nature' to a created 'human nature'; and accepted in all other respects the Chalcedonian formula, subject to the qualification that the natures were 'distinguished in thought alone'—presumably meaning that they are now inseparable. (This was a formula clearly designed to satisfy the 'monophysites', but one with which the Orthodox representatives were happy.)[4] So the 'two natures' command general assent.

And what is a 'nature'? Minimally it includes a set of properties which make the individual who has them an individual of a certain kind. So the Son's divine nature, all would have agreed, included his having a set of properties which constitute being divine, such as omnipotence, omniscience, perfect freedom, perfect goodness, eternity, and necessity (although what in detail each of these properties amount to would have been, as it still is, a matter of much dispute). This divine nature was, all agreed, part of the essence of the Son (and, indeed, of any other being who was divine); the Son was necessarily divine. But the Son needed something further to individuate him, and thus distinguish him from the two other divine persons. It was, I think, a common view among those who considered this issue in patristic or medieval times, that the Son was the Son in virtue of a relation to something else, that is the relation of being 'begotten' from the Father, defined as that divine person who is the source of the divinity of the other persons. That distinguished him from the Spirit who 'proceeded' from the Father (and maybe also from or through the Son. While 'and the Son' (*filioque*) was favoured only by western fathers, 'through the Son' was favoured by some eastern fathers.). And what is the difference between being 'begotten' and 'proceeding'? There were two answers given. One answer, given by Gregory of Nyssa,[5] was that there is no difference. The Son's being begotten from the Father is simply his being caused to exist by and only by the Father; whereas the Spirit's proceeding from the Father is the

---

[4] For the official statements resulting from the Orthodox 'monophysite' meetings, see Chaillet and Belopopsky (1998). The citation is from p. 63.6.

[5] 'That is the only way by which we distinguish one Person from the other, by believing, that is, that one is the cause and the other depends on the cause. Again, we recognize another distinction with regard to that which depends on the cause. There is that which depends on the first cause and that which is derived from what immediately depends on the first cause. Thus the attribute of being only-begotten without doubt remains with the Son, and we do not question that the Spirit is derived from the Father. For the mediation of the Son, while it guards his prerogative of being only-begotten, does not exclude the relation which the Spirit has by nature to the Father'. Gregory of Nyssa, 'An answer to Ablabius: that we should not think of saying—There are three Gods', trans. C. C. Richardson in Hardy (1954: 266).

Spirit's being caused to exist by the Father either 'and the Son' or 'through the Son'. The other answer, given by Augustine,[6] was that it was a mystery known to God alone. (Those Orthodox who deny that the Son is involved in the 'procession' of the Spirit had to give the 'mystery' answer to this question.) This individuating property, however understood, was essential to the Son; the Son could not exist without being the Son. So analysed, the divine nature of the Son is minimally simply a set of essential properties, both kind properties and an individuating one. I will return shortly to the issue of whether it is anything more than a set of properties.

Far more problematic is: what is human nature? This too certainly included a set of kind properties. These days we think of being human as having (actually or potentially) certain fairly limited powers of bodily control and knowledge acquisition through senses (not too much greater than those of actual humans), being to some extent rational, and belonging to the same species as the other earth inhabitants we call 'human' as a result of a common origin or at least subsequent interbreeding. But that would be far too narrow an understanding of humanity for the members of the Council of Chalcedon. Christ's nature, they held, was an unfallen nature. Unfallen humans, such as Christ, could have, they would have considered, far greater powers than ours. Less than two centuries later Maximus the Confessor, a theologian given enormous reverence in the Orthodox tradition, claimed that we humans while remaining human could become divine, which he understood as 'becoming all that God is, except for an identity in essence';[7] and so presumably having the divine properties but not essentially. That might have been an extreme view of human potentiality, but even the later western tradition claimed that Christ in his human nature could do and know a vast amount more than we do. Thus Aquinas claimed that the 'soul' of Christ, which is part of his human nature, could know all the past, present, and future; but that it could not know all the possible actions which God could do but does not do.[8] And so he denied that the soul of Christ was omnipotent since, 'being omnipotent is exclusive to God'.[9] And certainly most Christians of AD 451, influenced by Plato rather than Aristotle, would have affirmed that there could be humans without bodies, since there were saints in Heaven whose dead bodies were still in their graves. I do not think that they would have

---

[6] Thus Augustine, while acknowledging that the members of the Trinity differed in respect of which one was the source of the divinity of two others, which of one other, and which of none, considered that there was a further distinction between 'being begotten' and 'proceeding'. But he wrote that he was unable to say what that distinction was. See *Contra Maximinum* 2.14. (PL 42: 770).

[7] Maximus, *Book of Antiquities*, 41. (PG 91: 1308.)

[8] Aquinas, *Summa Theologiae* 3a.10.2.   [9] Ibid., 3a.13.1.

accepted Aquinas's apparent claim in his dictum 'my soul is not me',[10] that these saints were not humans. Gregory of Nyssa claimed that it was not essential to having the same nature to have the same origin or kind of origin. He claimed that just as Son and Spirit originating in different ways from the Father does not mean that they do not have the same nature, so Adam's origin from Earth and Abel's origin by sexual generation being different from each other, and Christ's origin from Mary and the Spirit being different from the origin of other humans, did not mean that they did not have the same nature.[11] All told, perhaps the most that the fathers might agree with respect to what human nature consisted of was that it was a rational nature limited in its powers of control and knowledge acquisition, and apt for exercising them through a human body (and perhaps necessarily doing so when first instantiated).

I pass over the question of whether for ordinary humans, their human nature is essential to them. My own answer is that it is not; a human being is essentially an animate being (a being capable of being conscious), and so exists only as long as he is capable of being conscious, but is not essentially a human being—any human could become a crocodile, for example. But whatever the kind to which humans essentially belong, there must be some further feature which individuates, which makes a human the particular human he is. My own view is that it is not a relation or any intrinsic property (in the sense of a universal or a conjunction or disjunction of universals) which makes a human who he is, but a 'thisness'.[12] That is, it seems to me evident that there could have existed instead of me a different human connected to the body which is currently mine and who had exactly the same mental and physical life as I have had. Hence the difference between us cannot consist in the properties which have characterized our lives—for these would have been exactly the same. So what makes me me is a 'thisness'; my being me is not analysable further.

However, no individuating human properties and no human-type thisness could have made the incarnate Son who he is. For all the fathers thought that he existed before his incarnation, and was already who he was in virtue of his particular divine nature. He can only have acquired the human kind properties, and not the human individuating properties or (more widely so as to include 'thisness') features. But he could still have acquired a particular human nature, even if not one which individuated him. This nature—Chalcedon seems to be saying—consisted of 'a rational soul and body'. And clearly the Son acquired a particular body. But what did his acquiring a

---

[10] Aquinas, *In I Cor*, 15: 1–2.   [11] See the citations in Daley (2002).
[12] See Swinburne (1997: new appendix D); and more adequately, Swinburne 1986, rev (2007).

rational soul amount to? One possibility is that it consisted simply in having whatever is involved in having a human nature beyond having a body, which I've suggested amounted to limited powers of control and knowledge acquisition apt for exercising through a human body, that is a human way of acting and thinking. This would be an Aristotelian account of having a soul. Alternatively, it might be a particular thing, a 'substance' in a wide sense underlying and causing those mental properties.

Ancient philosophers had some ideas on the nature of the soul wildly different from each other;[13] and it would be a bad mistake to suppose that the fathers of Chalcedon had a common view about the nature of 'the soul', any more than they had about 'nature' and 'hypostasis'. But when talking about ordinary human souls in a non-christological context, the fathers for the most part clearly didn't think that the human soul was merely a set of properties of the kind mentioned. For almost all of them held that the soul could be separated from the body and that, if it were so separated, the human went where his soul went, although it might need the original body or some similar body in order to live again.[14] Origen stated as 'the church's teaching' that 'the soul, having a substance and life of its own, will be rewarded according to its deserts after its departure from this world'.[15] So there seems to be a widespread view that the soul constituted the principle of individuation for an ordinary individual human. A set of properties such as those mentioned are shared by all humans and are quite insufficient to distinguish one human from another one. But, to repeat my point with respect to the 'rational' soul which I made with respect to the 'human nature' which included it, they couldn't have thought that Christ's human soul, however construed, constituted the principle of individuation for Christ whom they all thought to have existed before his incarnation. The only conclusion one can reach is that the fathers of Chalcedon had not thought things through very thoroughly, although—as far as anything I have discussed so far is concerned—their 'difficulties' are compatible with an understanding of 'soul' which makes their definition coherent—the Aristotelian one, according to which the acquisition of a 'rational soul' consists in the acquisition of a set of properties, the possession of which was essential for ordinary humans but only contingent for Christ. This understanding does, however, mean that they

---

[13] See Sorabji (2006: chs 1–6).

[14] See Kelly (1977: ch. 17). All Christians believed in the general resurrection of the dead at the 'last day', but there were different views about what happened to dead people before they were reunited with their bodies. However, the vast majority of Christians held that their 'souls' continued to exist and to have a conscious life during that period.

[15] Origen, *On First Principles*, book I. Preface, Latin text, in Butterworth (1966: 4).

have to understand other humans having souls in a different sense from Christ having a soul.

The medievals needed a more consistent account. Hence Aquinas's account, that ordinary humans are who they are in virtue of their individual substantial form (their soul) and the matter which it normally configures (which forms the human's body). However, in his incarnation, the divine nature of Christ configures a human soul and its matter. This human soul of Christ does not form the principle of individuation of the person, but is a thing which would have become the principle of individuation if it had not already been configured by the divine nature of the second person of the Trinity.[16] This removes any overt contradiction, and allows 'soul' to play a similar role (although not the same role) in the constitution of Christ to the one it plays in the constitution of ordinary humans. We can make some sense of the resulting picture as follows. It's not unreasonable to suppose that a foetus which is not yet conscious is not a particular human; only when it becomes conscious will there be a truth about whether that human is one who will suffer or enjoy life later. But maybe there is truth before that first moment of consciousness about which future human that foetus will become (barring divine intervention). And maybe that is determined by some immaterial feature possessed by the early foetus. If all that makes sense, then it makes sense to suppose that at Christ's conception the second person of the Trinity acquired both the foetal matter and the immaterial feature already individuated as that of the ordinary human whom it was destined (together with the matter) to become (barring divine intervention). But the act of the Son in assuming the foetal matter prevented that ordinary human person from ever existing; although this nature, thus prevented, remained a composite part of Jesus Christ. This immaterial feature is the cause of the resulting person having the human mental properties interacting with a body which it has, both in ordinary humans and in Christ, but in ordinary humans is also the principle of individuation.[17]

---

[16] See Stump (2002) and Adams (2006: 133–47). The theories of Duns Scotus and Ockham are similar to Aquinas's theory—see Adams (2006: 135).

[17] A. F. Freddoso (1986) points out that none of Aquinas, Scotus, or Ockham affirms that Christ is a 'human person' which they understood as a suppositum, that is an 'independently existing ultimate subject of characteristics'. From that it seems to follow that any human nature is only contingently the nature of a human person. Freddoso argues that Aquinas, though not Scotus and Ockham, might be inclined to deny this, and claim that any human nature is either necessarily a human person (and so presumably a particular human person) or necessarily sustained by a divine person. But that raises the question of what individuates the individual human nature which a divine person assumes. The view which I am commending that human nature is just a set of universal properties avoids all these difficulties.

But although we may be able to make sense of this medieval way[18] of resolving Chalcedon's problem, I see no reason at all for believing it to be true. And there is a much simpler way of resolving Chalcedon's problem, which is to interpret Christ's human soul merely as a set of properties, a human way of thinking and acting instantiated in the second person of the Trinity and conjoined in a human body.[19] In contrast, on the medieval account this human soul is the cause of Christ having the mental properties of human nature, the human way of thinking and acting which it has in addition to its divine properties. And so on both accounts, the issue arises as to whether the divine and human properties are compatible with each other.

I have argued in various places that all the traditional divine properties (including perfect goodness) follow from the properties of essential omnipotence, omniscience, and perfect freedom.[20] There is no contradiction in an omnipotent God choosing to have a set of human powers which he executes through a unique body in order to produce effects which he could also produce in a more direct way if he so chose; or an omniscient God choosing

---

[18] Brian Leftow (2002) advocates this kind of medieval view. But, no doubt expressing here too the view of most medievals, he combines it with the view that the second person of the Trinity is timeless, yet, in acquiring a human soul, becomes also a temporal being who had a temporal life and presumably therefore also a temporal consciousness. He experienced things at particular moments of time. Starting from a view that God, although timeless, 'can have causal relations with temporal things, for example in creating and sustaining them', Leftow writes: 'I now simply pose a question: given that causal relations unite parts into substances and a timeless God can have causal relations to a temporal being, is there any good reason a priori to think that a timeless God's causal relations to some temporal being(s) could not be such as to form with them a single substance? I cannot think of one' (p. 288). But, even if 'a timeless God's causal relations to some temporal being', e.g., a body, could be 'such as to form with them a single substance', more is surely needed than causal relations to form a single person. If at a given time a person with one consciousness also has a second consciousness, he must be able to co-experience the experiences which occur in both consciousnesses at that time. He may, of course, choose to keep the consciousnesses separate or be prevented by some psychological obstacle from co-experiencing, but it must be a possibility that he can co-experience both sets of experiences. If it isn't, I'm lost as to what it means to say that both consciousnesses belong to one person. Further, if a person does co-experience experiences of two consciousnesses, those experiences must happen at the same time. Now consider some temporal experience of Christ at a moment of time t during his human life. Is the second person of the Trinity even able to co-experience that experience together with some experience of his divine consciousness? An answer 'Yes' is not possible, since t is not a moment simultaneous with any moment in the timeless divine consciousness. But an answer 'No' entails that, although in his divine consciousness he may be timelessly aware of everything which happens at t (including his own experiences in his human consciousness at t) he cannot himself have an experience at t. But the second person only exists as long as he has a divine timeless consciousness; so he cannot have that experience at t at all.

[19] I appreciate Marilyn Adams's discussion of the two ways of interpreting Christ's human nature and her acknowledgement that either my way or her preferred medieval way is sufficient to rebut the 'charge that the notion of a God-man is unintelligible' (2006: 108).

[20] See for example, Swinburne (1994: 150–8).

to acquire knowledge through human sense-organs and reasoning as well as in virtue of his divine nature. God's perfect freedom is the freedom to choose between alternatives uninfluenced by irrational desires, that is, causes which incline him to do actions with a force out of proportion to their worth, for example, incline him to do what he believes to be a bad action or one less good than a best action. Almost all the fathers, following New Testament texts, held that Christ was subject to normal human desires arising from our embodiment, for example, hunger (the desire to eat), tiredness (the desire to rest), and so on. Although they could also have held that there can be a human nature not so subject (and Adam was depicted as much less subject to such desires before the Fall than all humans were after the Fall), they seem to have held that in this respect Christ was subject to the consequences of the Fall. They also held that (as the New Testament claims) he was subject to temptations (at least at the beginning and end of his ministry), that is, desires to do actions which were not the best. There would still be no contradiction in supposing that Christ was perfectly free and also subject to tempting desires if one supposed that although he felt the desires they could not influence his choice. To use an imperfect analogy—like Odysseus, he could hear the Sirens' voices but was unable to respond to them. And it was an essential Christian belief that Christ never did yield to temptation to do wrong,[21] for if he had done so he would not have lived the perfect life which would secure our salvation. It would seem to follow that if he had even opened himself to the possibility of doing wrong, he would have risked failure in his mission; and so it is natural to suppose that not merely did he not yield to temptation, but he could not have done so.

This seems to be the way that in these three respects many Christians picture the incarnation; but for two reasons this does not seem a very satisfactory way. It does not picture God as fully sharing the limitations involved in our actual fallen condition (even if in some sense sharing our human nature); and it does not fit well with what is said about Christ in the New Testament. We humans have very limited powers and knowledge (including false beliefs on many matters), and bad desires exercise on us an influence to which—given that we have free will (as is the majority Christian view)—we frequently yield.

St Mark reports that in a visit to his own country Christ 'could do then no mighty work',[22] and that Christ claimed that he, 'the Son', does not know

---

[21] The Letter to the Hebrews (4: 15) claimed that Christ was 'one who in every respect has been tempted as we are, yet without doing wrong' ($\chi\omega\rho\iota\varsigma\ \dot{\alpha}\mu\alpha\rho\tau\iota\alpha\varsigma$). The latter phrase is usually translated 'without sin', but as 'sin' may be construed as 'wronging God' and as (in my view) no one can wrong himself, I prefer my translation which carries no implication about the relation of Christ to God.

[22] Mark 6: 5.

something which the Father does know—'the hour' at which 'heaven and earth shall pass away'.[23] Luke reports that as he grew older, Jesus 'increased in wisdom',[24] implying that he was not totally omniscient in his earliest human years. And temptations to which one cannot yield are not such full-blooded temptations as those to which one can yield. Many of the fathers gave these passages a meaning other than the natural meaning, but others of them saw them as telling us that Christ in one nature could do or know things which he could not do or didn't know in his other nature.[25] But if Christ was not to be deceiving us in his claim of ignorance, and the inability was in any sense a real inability, we are led to a 'two minds' view; and to understand the separation of the two natures as implying that not merely did he do different actions but he acquired different and sometimes contradictory beliefs when acting with his divine powers than when acting with his human powers.

It was Freud, the modern founder of psychoanalysis, who helped us to see how a person can have two systems of belief to some extent independent of each other. Freud described people who sometimes, when performing some actions, act only on one system of beliefs and are not guided by beliefs of the other system; and conversely. The Freudian account of the divided mind was derived from analysis of cases of human self-deception, where a person does not consciously acknowledge either the beliefs of one belief system or the belief that he has kept its beliefs separated from his other system, and where the self-deception is a pathetic state from which that person needs to be rescued. But the Freudian account of such cases helps us to see the possibility of a person intentionally keeping a lesser belief system separate from her main belief system, and simultaneously doing different actions guided by different sets of beliefs, of both of which she is consciously aware—all for some very good reason. Indeed, even people who do not suffer from a Freudian divided mind seem to be able sometimes to perform simultaneously two quite separate tasks (for example, having a conversation with someone and writing a letter to someone else) in directing which quite distinct beliefs are involved, which we can recognize as 'on the way to' a divided mind in which they have two different sets of beliefs.

Now the second person of the Trinity, in assuming a human nature, could acquire the capacity to acquire beliefs by normal human routes; and some of the resulting beliefs would then be different from and contradictory to his divine beliefs. (Since it's odd to talk of one person believing both one proposition and its negation at the same time, strictly speaking the human

---

[23] Mark 13: 31–2.   [24] Luke 2: 52.
[25] For some differing patristic views on Christ's ignorance, see Tixeront (1923: 117–19); and Hovorun (2008: 32–6).

beliefs are best described as 'inclinations to belief'; but having made that point, I will ignore it henceforward for the sake of simplicity of exposition.) The second person of the Trinity would then do his divine actions by his divine powers guided by his divine beliefs. He would do his human actions by his human powers guided by his human beliefs. The beliefs belonging to the human perspective would guide the public statements of the incarnate Christ, which would be honest in virtue of reflecting those beliefs of which he was conscious in his human acting. The separation of the belief systems would be a voluntary act, knowledge of which was part of God incarnate's divine belief system but not of his human belief system. And the separation of belief systems could go with separation of 'minds' also in other respects—sensations, desires, intentions, and occurrent thoughts, as later Christian tradition affirmed that it did in Christ.[26] We thus get a picture of a divine consciousness and a human consciousness of God incarnate, the divine consciousness being fully aware of the human consciousness, but the human consciousness not being fully aware of the whole divine consciousness. (The human consciousness would at times need to be aware of some of the divine consciousness, in order that Christ might reveal to us truths otherwise known to God alone.)

So far, so good. But what about Christ's temptations? All the fathers who considered the matter claimed that not merely did Christ do no wrong, but he could not have done wrong, and so could not have yielded to a temptation to do wrong; and the synodical letter of the Council of Nicaea affirmed that the Council had anathematized those who claimed that Christ 'by his own power is capable of evil ($\kappa\alpha\kappa\iota\alpha$) and goodness'.[27] The fathers would have been horrified at the suggestion that there was a risk that the incarnation might not have had its intended effect, through a failure on God's part. But the difficulty is that it seems that if Christ couldn't do wrong, then living a perfect life would have been so much easier for him than for us that it would hardly have been as perfect as the perfect life we ought to have led.

---

[26] That Christ 'suffered' (and so had human sensations) was an item of the Nicene creed. But since it was normally claimed that the Father did not suffer the same sufferings as Christ did, and since it was also normally held that the members of the Trinity in their divine nature shared a divine life, it would seem to follow that Christ did not suffer in his divine nature. The Third Council of Constantinople affirmed that there were in Christ 'two natural volitions or wills' and 'two natural principles of action' (often translated 'energies')—see Tanner (1990: I 128). Two 'principles of action' merely implies, in addition to the divine way, a human way of thinking and acting (as discussed above) and so, as well as two sets of beliefs, two kinds of occurrent thought. Two 'wills' involves Christ in his human nature being subject to temptation (see below), which in turn requires that Christ in his human nature is subject to human desires (e.g. thirst), none of which, of course, characterized the divine nature.

[27] Tanner (1990: I 17).

I believe that there is a way out of this dilemma if we distinguish between two kinds of good actions—those that are obligatory (or duties), and those that go beyond obligation and which we call 'supererogatory'. I am obliged (it is my duty) to pay my debts, but not to give my life to save that of a comrade—supremely, 'supererogatorily' good though it is that I should do so. To fail to fulfil an obligation is to do something objectively wrong; to fail to fulfil what the agent believes to be an obligation is to do something subjectively wrong (and that is blameworthy). Often, of course, actions are both objectively and subjectively wrong. A person is not, however, meritorious merely for fulfilling her obligations. But she is objectively meritorious for doing what is supererogatory; and she is subjectively meritorious for doing what she believes is objectively meritorious (and that is praiseworthy). Positive obligations normally arise because of benefits received (I owe my parents much because they have done much for me); or because of commitments, explicit or implicit (I must keep my promises and pay my debts because I have explicitly committed myself to doing so; I must feed my children because by bringing them into existence I have implicitly committed myself to doing so). Negative obligations—obligations not to do things—normally concern not damaging other people. It is wrong to steal or kill (possibly subject to some qualifications). Obligations are a limited set of good actions, and most of us can fulfil all our obligations. Although God cannot always do the best action, because sometimes there is no best action,[28] he can always fulfil all his obligations. As the source of the existence of all other beings, he does not owe anyone anything as a result of benefits received or for any other reason; and since there is good reason to ensure this, he will ensure that he never enters into commitments which he could not fulfil.

Now it would, I suggest, have been wrong of a perfectly good divine person to allow himself to become incarnate in such a way as to open the possibility of his doing objective or subjective wrong. For it is wrong of anyone to put themselves in a position where they are liable to do wrong to someone—intentionally allow themselves to forget their duties, or to take drugs which would lead to their being strongly tempted to do some wrong, or simply be unable to stop themselves from doing wrong. That is why it is wrong to drive a car when you have drunk too much alcohol; you put yourself in a position where you are likely to kill or injure others. It follows from God's perfect goodness that he would not put himself in a position where he could have

---

[28] This may be either because two incompatible actions open to God might be equally good actions, and better than any other incompatible actions; or because there are an infinite number of such actions open to God, each less good than some other action. For fuller discussion of this point see Swinburne (1994: 65–71, 134–6).

chosen to do wrong. So in becoming incarnate, God must have ensured that in his human actions he had access to such true moral beliefs as would allow him to be aware of his duties, and he must have ensured that he would never be subject to too strong a desire to do any action which was wrong.

While it is wrong to put oneself in a position where one is liable to do wrong, there is nothing wrong in putting oneself in a position where one is liable not to do some supererogatory action. Indeed, an action which had the foreseen consequence of putting oneself in that position might itself occasionally be the (objectively and subjectively) best thing to do. A generous person might well, as a supererogatory good act, give away so much money that she would be so short of money in future that she would be much tempted not to do any more supererogatory good acts. And, the normal view is, Christ did not win our salvation merely by fulfilling his obligations. His life, culminating in allowing himself to be crucified, was one of supererogatory (subjective and objective) goodness. So in becoming incarnate, God could have allowed himself to be tempted not to do such an action, and could have yielded to that temptation. And if he could have yielded to a temptation not to do a supererogatory action but didn't, his life would have been the truly perfect life which we could have led but didn't—as the fathers claimed that it was. I illustrate the point by the three temptations to which, according to the Gospels of Matthew and Luke,[29] Christ was subject in the wilderness. Christ could not have yielded to the temptation to worship the Devil—for that would have been wrong, but he could—on this account—have yielded to the temptation to command a stone to be made bread, or to throw himself down from the pinnacle of the temple—for there would have been nothing wrong in his doing these things. But if he did these things, he would not have shown us how to live in difficult circumstances and so provided for us the heroic example which would constitute a perfect life of the kind that ordinary humans could have lived but have failed to live: life would have been too easy for him to provide much of an example for us. Yet it follows that if Christ had yielded to these temptations to do less than the best and still sought to save us by living a perfect life, he would have needed to try again.

None of the fathers of the early centuries seem to be sensitive to the distinction between a temptation to do wrong and a temptation not to do a best act. But their description of the acts which Christ could not have done (ἁμαρτία, κακία) are clearly of acts which were wrong. I do not think that they ever considered the possibility that he might have been tempted not to do a supererogatory act. I do not think that many of them would have welcomed

---

[29] Matthew 4: 1–11 and Luke 4: 1–13.

this suggestion, but they never ruled it out. A major reason why they would have found it unacceptable is that they would have thought that it was incompatible with the perfect goodness of God the Son to put himself in a situation where he might do less than a best action, where there was a best (or equal best) action available to him. Hence if there were supererogatory best acts available to him and such acts as allowing himself to be crucified were such acts (as I and they assume), he would inevitably do them. But what I am suggesting is that it could be a best supererogatory act for God to allow himself to be tempted not to do the best and so not to do some supererogatory best act (in such a way that he might yield to that temptation).[30] If my suggestion is accepted that a perfectly good God could have put himself in such a position, then God incarnate in Jesus Christ could have been in such a position, and could by resisting temptations not to do some supererogatory acts to which he could have yielded have led a perfect human life of the kind we could have led but didn't. That life would indeed have been a perfect offering to the Father sufficiently costly to secure our salvation. But if God incarnate because of his perfect goodness could not have made it possible that he would live a less than perfect human life, then we must say that he led the nearest life he could to the perfect life which we could have led; that is, did the actions required, endured the suffering, and felt the temptations which we do not to be perfect—although he could not have yielded to them.

The point of God the Son becoming incarnate and living a perfect life was—however it is spelled out—to provide reparation for our sins, a perfect life instead of the imperfect lives we have led. Many of the fathers and subsequent theologians agreed that God the Father could have forgiven us without demanding a reparation of the kind actually made by the life and

---

[30] Allowing this possibility requires a slight alteration in the definition of God's 'perfect freedom'. As I defined it earlier, God's perfect freedom is the freedom to choose between alternatives uninfluenced by irrational desires, that is causes which incline him to do actions with a force out of proportion to their worth, e.g., incline to do what he believes to be a bad action or one less good than a best action. Hence, given his knowledge of the objective worth of actions (following from his omniscience) he will always do a good action and the best action or an equal best action where there is one, and never do a bad action. But to allow the above possibility, we need to understand a perfectly free person as one subject to no irrational desires except insofar as, uninfluenced by such desires, he chooses to allow himself to act while being influenced by irrational desires to do (what he believes to be) good actions which are less than the best (though not compelled to yield to them). This preserves the point of the original definition that such a person is at the highest level uninfluenced by any considerations except those of reason in determining how he will act, but allows that he may rationally choose to allow himself to do certain acts while open to the influence of irrational desires. But on this definition of perfect freedom it follows that God could be less than perfectly good, though could not do wrong.

death of Christ.[31] It is surely up to a wronged person to determine how much (if any) and of what kind reparation is needed before he will forgive the wrongdoer. It follows that it was up to God to determine what sort of good life would constitute adequate reparation for sins. And, if in virtue of his perfect goodness, Christ led the most perfect human life that he could lead, God the Father would surely be satisfied with Christ doing the best that he could do (even if, given his free decision to become incarnate, he could not have yielded to any temptation to do less than the best). I conclude that, even if my suggestion that Christ could have yielded to a temptation not to do some supererogatory acts is not accepted, that does not damage the coherence of the Chalcedonian account of the incarnation.

---

[31] Thus Augustine claimed that 'the mode by which God deigns to free us through the mediator of God and man, the man Jesus Christ, is good and suitable to the dignity of God' but denied that he needed to show that 'no other mode was possible to God to whose power all things are equally subject' but merely affirmed that there was no 'other mode more appropriate' (Augustine, *On the Trinity*, trans. A.W. Hadden (1873), book 13, ch. 10).

9

The incarnation and unity of consciousness

Joseph Jedwab

'In the beginning was the Word, and the Word was with God, and the Word was God... And the Word became flesh and dwelt among us...' (Jn 1: 1, 14). So the Word, though with God, somehow also was God, and became flesh; and the Word, who became flesh, is the Lord Jesus Christ. This doctrine of the incarnation is central to Christian belief. It has developed through many twists and turns in church history. One key statement of it is the Council of Chalcedon's Definition of Faith (AD 451), which says:

> ... we all with one voice teach the confession of one and the same Son, our Lord Jesus Christ: the same perfect in divinity and perfect in humanity, the same truly God and truly man, of a rational soul and a body; consubstantial with the Father as regards his divinity, and the same consubstantial with us as regards his humanity; like us in all respects except for sin; ... one and the same Christ, Son, Lord, only-begotten, acknowledged in two natures which undergo no confusion, no change, no division, no separation; at no point was the difference between the natures taken away through the union, but rather the property of both natures is preserved and comes together into a single person and a single subsistent being; he is not parted or divided into two persons, but is one and the same only-begotten Son, God, Word, Lord Jesus Christ...[1]

So, in the incarnation, one person (i.e. the Son) has two natures (i.e. deity and humanity). The Son has a complete divine nature and takes on or assumes, in addition, a complete human nature, which involves both a human rational soul and body. And so there are two main errors to avoid in any properly orthodox account of the incarnation. First, one must avoid Nestorianism: the claim that the human nature that the Son assumes is or involves a distinct person in its own right. Secondly, one must avoid Monophysitism: the claim

---

[1] Tanner (1990: 186).

that the Son has only one nature and so lacks either deity or humanity or both.

What do we mean by 'person' and 'nature' here? First, in the ordinary sense, a person is anything to which a personal pronoun applies: that is to say, a person is a someone. It is clear that the Son and Jesus are persons: for they are someones, objects one can personally address. And it is also clear that the Son is the same person as Jesus. If the Son were a different person from Jesus, the Son couldn't truly say of himself 'I am Jesus', which is false. Secondly, the word 'nature' is ambiguous: it means a kind and it also means a substance. Every kind (for example, deity and humanity) is a property, which is an abstract being: a being that lacks causal powers. So deity is the property of being divine and humanity is the property of being human. And every substance (for example, God or a human) is a concrete being: a being that has causal powers. So God is a substance who has the property of being divine and every human is a substance who has the property of being human. So, in its abstract sense, a human nature is an abstract being: the property of being human by having which something is a human. And, in its concrete sense, a human nature is a concrete being: a substance by being or assuming which something is a human. Such a concrete nature either is a human, or is intrinsically just like a human, or would have been a human if unassumed. On the view known as Abstractism, the Son comes to have an abstract human nature by becoming a concrete human nature, but not by assuming a distinct concrete human nature. On the view known as Concretism, by contrast, the Son comes to have an abstract human nature by assuming a distinct concrete human nature.

PROBLEMS

This doctrine gives rise to philosophical problems: e.g., the number problem and the modal problem. The number problem is this. The Son is a person who has a divine intellect and will. But it might well seem that the human nature that the Son assumes involves a distinct created human rational soul and body that has a human intellect and will, and so that such a nature is or involves a distinct person in its own right. But then how can there be *one* person and *two* natures? And the modal problem is this. It might well seem that anyone divine is necessary, simple, eternal, omnipresent, immutable, impassible, omniscient, omnipotent, and perfectly good. That's what classical theists think. And it definitely seems that anyone human is not at least some of these. But then how can someone *possibly* be both divine and human?

These are important problems and much work has been done on them. But we won't pursue these here. Instead, we focus on a different problem.

The Son is divine and human and so has a divine intellect and will and a human intellect and will. Most importantly for our purposes, the Son must have a divine conscious life and a human conscious life. But what's the relation of these conscious lives to each other? This is a compulsory question for all who want to offer some detailed proposal of the incarnation. There are two possible views here: what I call the Two-Spheres View and the One-Sphere View. And there are three versions of the One-Sphere View: what I call the Divine-Sphere View, the Human-Sphere View, and the Divine-Human-Sphere View. I argue for the comparative advantage of the last.

CONSCIOUSNESS: PHENOMENAL, ACCESS, AND INTROSPECTIVE

But first I need to say what I mean by 'consciousness', 'unity of consciousness', and 'a sphere of consciousness'. There's no one thing consciousness is. Rather there are different kinds of consciousness. Or better: there are different senses of the word 'conscious'. In one sense, it applies only to mental subjects or thinkers. Only subjects are conscious; for example, you are conscious and so am I. In another sense, the word 'conscious' applies only to mental states or events. Only states are conscious; for example, your auditory experience is conscious and so is my visual experience.

Among those senses that apply to states, there is a now standard distinction that Ned Block draws between phenomenal and access consciousness. A mental state is phenomenal-conscious just if there's something it's like to have it; for example, there's something it's like to have a visual experience of a sunset. And there are two kinds of phenomenal-conscious states: experiences and acts of will; for example, seeing an apple involves an experience, which is something that happens to me; reaching for the apple involves an act of will, which is something that I do. So a mental state is phenomenal-conscious just if it's either an experience or an act of will. Henceforth, unless qualified, by the word 'conscious', I mean phenomenal-conscious, which most agree is the fundamental sense that applies to states.

Access (or A-) consciousness is supposed to be the cognitive counterpart of phenomenal (or P-) consciousness. Block originally defines it thus: 'A state is access-conscious if, in virtue of one's having the state, a representation of its content is (1) inferentially promiscuous, that is, poised for use as a premise in reasoning, (2) poised for rational control of action, and (3) poised for rational control of speech.'² So, as Block has it, a mental state is access-conscious just if, by having it, its content is poised for rational use. David Chalmers modifies this original definition thus: 'A good start is the modified notion of direct availability for global control. That is, a content is A-conscious in the modified sense when it is directly available for use in directing a wide range of behaviors, especially deliberate behaviors.'³ So, as Chalmers has it, a mental state is access-conscious just if, by having it, its content is directly available for global control. That the content is *available* implies that it is accessible, that one has the cognitive power to access it. And that the availability is *direct* rules out the content's being accessible only with effort. So, for example, if I believe that there is an apple before me and I desire to grasp it, and I so act on the basis of my belief and desire, then my belief, desire, and act of will are all access-conscious.

In addition to phenomenal and access consciousness, there is introspective consciousness. A mental state is introspective-conscious just if one introspects it. Introspection is a kind of attentive awareness of one's own mental states. Such an attentive act is itself phenomenal-conscious: there's something it's like to notice, focus on, or attend to one's mental states. And on the basis of such an act, one can form or sustain beliefs about those mental states; for example, if I see an apple, I can attend to my visual experience and on this basis form the belief that I am having that experience. Moreover, there are degrees of introspective consciousness. We can attend to more or fewer of our mental states. We can attend to more or fewer aspects of our mental states. And we can also attend more or less intently to the mental states or their aspects to which we do attend. Finally, conscious states that one introspects form what we can call the phenomenal foreground. And conscious states that one doesn't introspect form what we can call the phenomenal background.[4]

UNITY OF CONSCIOUSNESS

With the concepts of consciousness in place, I can introduce the concepts of co-consciousness, unity of consciousness, and a sphere of consciousness. We are aware in ourselves that not only do we have conscious states but some make up larger conscious states and that all the conscious states that we have at some time make up a largest conscious state then; for example, my perceptions, sensations, thoughts, and feelings involve experiences that make up a largest

---

[2] Block (2002: 216 n. 7).
[3] Chalmers (1997: 421).
[4] See Dainton (2000: 29).

experience that includes all of these. The largest experience we have at some time provides the total conscious perspective or point of view on the world that we have then. Here are the definitions:

Co-consciousness: conscious states are co-conscious with each other if and only if they are parts of the same conscious state.[5]

Unity of consciousness: a subject has unity of consciousness at some time if and only if all the conscious states she has then are co-conscious with each other.

A sphere of consciousness: a conscious state is a sphere of consciousness if and only if it isn't part of any other conscious state.

Co-consciousness is, by definition, reflexive and symmetric: every conscious state is co-conscious with itself, and if one state is co-conscious with a second state, the second is co-conscious with the first. Co-consciousness, however, isn't, by definition, transitive: it doesn't follow, just by definition, that if one state is co-conscious with a second and the second is co-conscious with a third, that the first is co-conscious with the third. Nevertheless, that co-consciousness is transitive is a further claim that some are strongly inclined to accept.[6]

As there is access and introspective consciousness, so there is also access and introspective co-consciouness and unity. Here are the definitions:

Access co-consciousness: access-conscious states are access co-conscious with each other if and only if they are parts of the same access-conscious state.

Access unity: a subject has access unity at some time if and only if all the access-conscious states she has then are access co-conscious with each other.

Introspective co-consciousness: introspective-conscious states are introspective co-conscious with each other if and only if some subject, by the same introspective act, introspects them.

Introspective unity: a subject has introspective unity at some time if and only if all the introspective-conscious states she has then are introspective co-conscious with each other.

There are many connections between these concepts. Here are two, relevant to later discussion, that concern the relation of unity of consciousness and introspective unity. First, all (phenomenal-) conscious states that are introspective co-conscious with each other are also (phenomenal) co-conscious with each other. So, for example, if I have a visual experience and a tactile experience, and, by the same introspective act, I introspect both experiences together,

---

[5] See Lockwood (1989: 88), Foster (1991: 245–6), Hill (1991: 236); cf. Bayne and Chalmers (2001).

[6] See Dainton (2000: ch. 4) and Bayne and Chalmers (2001).

then both experiences are parts of the same visual-tactile experience. Secondly, I suggest that, intuitively, all introspective-conscious states that are (phenomenal) co-conscious with each other are also introspective co-conscious with each other. So, for example, again, if I have a visual experience and a tactile experience, and I introspect each experience, and both experiences are parts of the same visual-tactile experience, then, by the same introspective act, I introspect both experiences together. Perhaps I could have two spheres of consciousness, and by one introspective act, introspect part of one sphere, and by a different introspective act, introspect part of the other sphere, but, by no introspective act, introspect both parts together. It's hard to see, though, how I could have only one sphere, and by one introspective act, introspect one part of that sphere, and by another introspective act, introspect another part of that sphere, but, by no introspective act, introspect both parts of that sphere at once. So that's consciousness and unity of consciousness.

THE DIVINE MENTAL LIFE

Now I need to say briefly what divine and human subjects are and what their mental lives are like. A mental subject is divine just if it's a perfect mental subject: it couldn't be that something is a better subject than it is. I shall assume that, being perfect, every divine subject is eternal, omniscient, omnipotent, and a sustainer of the world. There are two senses of the word 'eternal'. In one sense, to be eternal is to be omnitemporal, and neither begin nor cease, and not persist through only a finite temporal interval. In the other sense, to be eternal is to be atemporal. I assume, for ease of exposition, that every divine subject is eternal in the first sense. I could, so I believe, recast my discussion in a way consistent with the claim that every divine subject is atemporal. But it would take longer to put things that way and so I won't. As to the other divine attributes, here's a rough characterization of each. A subject is omniscient just if it knows, in the circumstances, every truth. A subject is omnipotent just if it has the power, in the circumstances, to do any intentional act.[7] And a subject sustains the world just if it causes the world to continue to exist as long as it does. Moreover, according to venerable tradition, some divine persons proceed from others. The Father generates

---

[7] Perhaps it's better to replace these with the definitions for maximal knowledge and power. A subject has maximal knowledge just if it couldn't be that, in the circumstances, some subject knows more truths. And a subject has maximal power just if it couldn't be that, in the circumstances, some subject has more power to do intentional acts.

the Son and the Father through the Son spirates the Spirit. And so the Son has a role in spirating the Spirit.

The Son is a divine subject and so has a divine mental life. Let's say the divine mental life has a default setting. The default is what the divine mental life is like unless the divine subject has reason to cause or permit itself to be otherwise. What's the default divine mental life? Every divine subject, being omniscient, has beliefs, and being a sustainer of the world, does intentional acts, and so has beliefs and desires, and does acts of will. And the Son, having a role in spirating the Spirit, again does intentional acts. Finally, perhaps every divine subject attends to all things, including its own mental states, and so has attentive acts. I know of no good reason to think that any divine subject, apart from incarnation, has any other mental states. So I shall focus on these.

First, every divine subject has conscious states: for acts of will are conscious states—there's something it's like to do them.[8] And every divine subject also has non-conscious states: for beliefs and desires are non-conscious states—there's nothing it's like to have them. Indeed, we can have beliefs and desires in the absence of any conscious states at all; for example, in dreamless sleep. Of course, if I act on the basis of a belief and desire, my belief and desire are access-conscious. And if I introspect my belief and desire, they are introspective-conscious. But, in neither case does it follow that they are themselves conscious states.[9]

In addition, perhaps by default, every divine subject attends to all and so has attentive acts, which are also conscious states. So one might think that, as a mark of the perfect mental life, every divine subject attends to the highest degree to all things and so also introspects to the highest degree all its mental states. Note, though, that if so, then if attentive acts are also mental states and if attentive acts are distinct from what they are about, which seems right, then such a divine mental life lacks introspective unity: for then there is no introspective act by which the divine subject introspects all its mental states together. That's worrisome in itself. But here's a further worry. For suppose some divine subject introspects all its conscious states. And suppose all its conscious states are co-conscious with each other. Then all its conscious states are introspective-conscious and (phenomenal) co-conscious with each other. But, since its conscious life lacks introspective unity, not all its conscious states are introspective co-conscious with each other. As noted before, however, intuitively, all introspective-conscious states that are (phenomenal) co-conscious with each other are also introspective co-conscious with each other. Now clearly, we shouldn't give up the claim that every divine subject, by

---

[8] But for an account of divine acts of will on which they are not conscious states, see O'Connor (1999).
[9] See Crane (2001: § 32).

default, has unity of consciousness. So, rather, I suggest that we should give up the claim that every divine subject introspects all its conscious states. And we can easily do so by saying that every divine subject, by default, attends to, not all, but all apart from the attentive act by which it attends to all else.

But then again, perhaps by default, every divine subject doesn't attend to anything. So, instead, one might think it a mark of the perfect mental life that no divine subject attends to anything. We attend in order to acquire abilities and knowledge. That is the function of such attention in humans. And it's hard to see what else it could be for. But no divine subject has any such need so to attend. Every divine subject has the abilities and knowledge that it does directly without acquiring these on the basis of any attentive act. And if no divine subject needs to attend, then, as a matter of theoretical simplicity, it is perhaps best to posit no such attentive acts. Of course, being omniscient, every divine subject knows all and so is, in this sense, aware of all. But it doesn't follow from this that any divine subject is attentively aware of all. So, as to the default divine mental life, it seems that either every divine subject attends to all things apart from the attentive act by which it does so, or else every divine subject attends to nothing.

Secondly, every divine subject has access-conscious states. Beliefs, desires, and acts of will in God are all access-conscious. And if any divine subject has attentive acts, these are also access-conscious. By having them, their contents are poised for rational use and directly available for global control; for example, in report. Thirdly, as it's unclear whether any divine subject attends, so it's also unclear whether any divine subject has introspective-conscious states.

Finally, it's clear that, by default, as a mark of the perfect mental life, every divine subject has unity of consciousness at any time it exists: all conscious states that it has at some time are co-conscious with each other then. Also, by default, the divine mental life has access unity: all access-conscious states that the divine subject has at some time are access co-conscious with each other then. And if every divine subject does attend to all else, then the divine mental life has introspective unity: all introspective-conscious states that the divine subject has at some time are introspective co-conscious with each other then. So that's a divine subject and its mental life.

THE HUMAN MENTAL LIFE

Now I need to say what a human subject is and what its mental life is like. A mental subject is human just if it's humanly embodied. We are, I take it, either organisms, or embodied souls, or constituted by organisms, or constituted by embodied souls, or we are composites of an organism and a soul, or composites of matter and form. (I think that just about covers it.) The Son, in becoming human, either becomes or assumes one of these.

The Son is a human subject and so has a human mental life. But what's a human mental life like? When God renews all things, he will renew heaven and earth, and humans too (see Rom. 8). Our bodies will be imperishable (see 1 Cor. 15). And there will be no more sin, suffering, or death (see Rev. 21). But for all that, we will still be human. So our condition now in the present age is not the same as our condition will be in the age to come. What's a human mental life in our present condition like? We are all intimately aware of this in our own case. By various means, including but not restricted to introspection, we know how it is with our conscious life. We have conscious states; for example, the experiences that we have and the acts of will that we do. At times, though, we have no conscious states at all. We also have access-conscious states; for example, the beliefs and desires that guide intentional acts or those that are ready so to guide intentional acts that we are ready to do. Many of our beliefs and desires, though, are not access-conscious and require some, if not great, effort to access. And sometimes we have introspective-conscious states; for example, our own experiences to which we attend. Many of our experiences, though, indeed the vast majority of them, are part of our phenomenal background: that unintrospected part of our conscious life.

Finally, normally, we have unity of consciousness at any time we have conscious states: all conscious states that we have at some time are co-conscious with each other then. And, normally, our mental lives have introspective unity at any time we have introspective-conscious states.[10] But do we have access unity at any time we have access-conscious states? Not obviously. Arguably, there are so-called access bottlenecks. So, for example, in George Sperling's experiment, a subject sees a matrix of three rows of four letters each for a quarter of a second, after which a tone sounds to indicate which row's letters the subject is to report. On average, when the subject reports the letters of one row, she correctly reports 3.3 of 4, but when the subject reports the letters of the whole matrix, she correctly reports only 4.5 of 12. So it seems that, for each row the subject has a mental state that represents the letters in that row, and each such state is access-conscious, but no mental state that represents all the letters together is access-conscious.[11] So that's a human subject and its mental life.

---

[10] Arguably, there's conscious disunity and introspective-conscious disunity in cases of commissurotomy, hypnosis, or dissociative identity disorder. In each case, though, there's a plausible alternative account: i.e. the switch model. See Bayne (2007) and (2008a).

[11] See Bayne and Chalmers (2001: 15).

THE SON INCARNATE'S MENTAL LIFE

Now I apply all this to the Son incarnate's mental life. The way I see it, all should accept at least this much. The Son's mental life is divided. He has two systems of powers, beliefs, and desires: a divine one and a human one. Each divine intentional act he does (for example, sustaining the world), he does on the basis of the divine system, not the human one. And, at least for the most part, each human intentional act he does (for example, praying to the Father), he does on the basis of the human system, not the divine one. Perhaps though, some human intentional acts he does, he does partly on the basis of the divine system and partly on the basis of the human system. So perhaps when the Son does miracles (for example, when he feeds the five thousand, Mt. 14: 13–21; Mk 6: 30–44), he does so partly on the basis of his divine power. And perhaps when the Son prophesies (for example, when he predicts Peter's denial, Mt. 26: 34; Mk 14: 30), he does so partly on the basis of his divine beliefs. But perhaps instead when the Son does miracles or prophesies, he does so in the same way that merely human prophets (for example, Elijah and Elisha) do. Such prophets don't do so on the basis of some divine system they have, for they don't have any such divine system.

Moreover, the powers and beliefs of the human system are limited. And so, with respect to his human system, the Son is limited in power and knowledge. The New Testament supports this. At times, Jesus was limited in human power. Luke's Gospel says that the boy Jesus became strong (Lk. 2: 40). And the same says that, on the Mount of Olives, when Jesus prayed for the Father to remove the cup of God's wrath from him, an angel appeared and strengthened him (Lk. 22: 43–4). Also, at times, Jesus was limited in human knowledge. Luke's Gospel says that the boy Jesus increased in wisdom (Lk. 2: 52). And, in Matthew's Gospel, Jesus, unlike the Father, didn't know the day and hour of the Son of Man's coming (Mt. 24: 36). Moreover, the desires of the human system are not only limited, but some are, so it seems, disordered. And so, with respect to his human system, the Son is able to be tempted. Again, the New Testament confirms this. According to the Synoptic Gospels, Jesus, after his baptism, was led by the Spirit into the wilderness, where he was tempted by Satan (Mt. 4: 1; Mk 1: 13; Lk. 4: 2). And Hebrews says that because Jesus was tempted, he is able to help those who are tempted (Hb. 2: 18). And the same says that, in Jesus, we have a high priest, who is able to sympathize with our weaknesses and in every way was tempted as we are, yet without sin (Hb. 4: 15). It seems that, when tempted, what the Son desired was contrary to what he believed must be done, which implies that his desire was, in some respects, disordered. For example, in the garden of Gethsemane, Jesus prayed to the Father that the cup pass from him, but Jesus says 'not as I will but as you will' (Mt. 26: 39; Mk 14: 36), which implies that he desired not to drink the cup, but believed that to do so was, in the circumstances, what must be done. Finally, at least for the most part, the Son's human system includes the cognitive power to access only the contents of human mental states, not divine ones, and also includes the cognitive power to introspect only human mental states, not divine ones. And so, at least for the most part, with respect to his human system, the Son's divine mental states are neither access-conscious nor introspectible. Again, perhaps when the Son prophesies, he has, as part of the human system, the cognitive power to access and introspect the contents of divine beliefs. But again perhaps instead when the Son prophesies he does so as merely human prophets do, which does not involve any cognitive power to access or introspect any divine belief they have.

How does the Son's conscious life differ from the default divine setting? Suppose that, by default, the Son's only conscious states are acts of will or such acts together with attentive acts. Then, when incarnate, the default differs because, instead, the Son has additional kinds of conscious state: human thoughts, human perceptual, bodily, and emotional experiences, and human acts of will. And suppose that, by default, the Son attends (to the highest degree) to all apart from the attentive act by which he so attends.

Then, when incarnate, the default differs because, instead, the Son doesn't attend to some mental states that he has and doesn't attend to the highest degree to some mental states to which he does attend; for example, he has human experiences that he doesn't introspect. And, finally, suppose that, by default, the Son attends to nothing and so no mental state that he has. Then, when incarnate, the default differs again because, instead, the Son does attend to some mental states that he has; for example, he has human experiences that he does introspect.

All this concerns the Son incarnate's mental life. But what, in particular, is the structure of his conscious life? There are two main views here: the Two-Spheres View and the One-Sphere View, which we now look at in turn.

The Two-Spheres View

On the Two-Spheres View, the Son has two spheres of consciousness: one divine and the other human. The divine sphere is typical of a default divine conscious life and the human sphere is typical of a human conscious life in our present condition. The spheres are either discrete from each other or overlap. One sphere, though, can't be part of the other sphere. For, by definition, a sphere or a total conscious state is a conscious state that isn't part of another conscious state.[12]

On this view, the Son's conscious life differs from the divine default in two further ways. First, of course, instead of having one sphere and so one conscious perspective on the world, the Son has two. Secondly, suppose that, by default, the Son, by one introspective act, introspects every conscious state that he has except the introspective act by which he so introspects. Then, when incarnate, though the Son, by one introspective act, introspects every such divine conscious state, by another introspective act, he introspects every human conscious state that he does so introspect, and by no introspective act does he introspect every conscious state he has. So there is not only conscious disunity here, but also introspective-conscious disunity. As noted before, if two conscious states are introspective co-conscious with each other, they are also (phenomenal) co-conscious with each other. So if two conscious states are not (phenomenal) co-conscious with each other, they are not introspective co-conscious with each other either. And so if the Son has two conscious states (one divine and the other human) that are not (phenomenal) co-conscious with each other, they are not introspective co-conscious with each other either.

But the Two-Spheres View faces a worry. If such a view holds, then it is appropriate to say that Nestorianism holds, which we should avoid if we can. Suppose the Son has not only two systems of powers, beliefs, and desires, but also, and associated with such systems, two conscious spheres and so two conscious perspectives on the world. Then the Son, though strictly speaking one person, is otherwise just like two persons. Consider Derek Parfit's famous example of someone who has a divided conscious life. In the example, Parfit has a device by means of which he can divide and then reunite his conscious life. Suppose he uses the device.

Then in one conscious sphere, correlated with his left cerebral hemisphere, he controls the right side of his body, including his right hand. And in the other conscious sphere, correlated with his right cerebral hemisphere, he controls the left side of his body, including his left hand. In the story, Parfit is taking a physics exam and has only fifteen minutes left to answer the last question. There are two ways to tackle the question. So he divides his conscious life to try out each way. Parfit continues:

---

[12] This rules out what Tim Bayne calls the Standard Inclusionist model of the incarnation, which he also rejects. See Bayne (2001).

Consider my experiences in my 'right-handed' stream. I remember deciding that I would use my right hand to do the longer calculation. This I now begin. In working at this calculation I can see, from the movements of my left hand, that I am also working at the other. But I am not aware of working at the other. I might, in my right-handed stream wonder how, in my left-handed stream, I am getting on. I could look and see. This would be just like looking to see how well my neighbour is doing, at the next desk. In my right-handed stream I would be equally unaware both of what my neighbour is now thinking and of what I am now thinking in my left-handed stream. Similar remarks apply to my experiences in my left-handed stream.[13]

This seems to me exactly right. From the right-handed point of view, looking to see how I'm getting on in the other stream is just like looking to see how another person is getting on. And so, though I am one person, having two spheres at once is otherwise just like being two persons at once. And so again if the Son has two spheres at once, though he is one person, he is otherwise just like two persons at once. Strictly speaking, there's only one person here and so, strictly speaking, Nestorianism doesn't hold. But, since the Son is just like two persons, it is appropriate to say that the Son is two persons and so it is appropriate to say that Nestorianism holds. And this is a worry for the Two-Spheres View.

Moreover, on my own view of the Trinity, there is only one divine subject that has three divine lives, which includes three divine conscious lives.[14] On this view, the divine subject has three conscious spheres and so three conscious perspectives, in virtue of which it is right and proper to say that there are three divine persons: the Father is the divine subject from the first sphere's perspective, the Son is the divine subject from the second sphere's perspective, and the Spirit is the divine subject from the third sphere's perspective. But, on this view, if there's a fourth sphere, which is human, it's hard to see how to avoid the result that if it was before appropriate to speak of a trinity of persons, it is now appropriate to speak of a quaternity of persons, which is, again, something to avoid if we can. Insofar then as there is good reason to accept such a view of the Trinity, which I think there is, there is good reason to reject the Two-Spheres View of the incarnation.

The One-Sphere View

The other views we shall consider are different versions of the One-Sphere View, according to which the Son has only one conscious sphere. There's a

---

[13] Parfit (1984: 247).
[14] For similar accounts, models, or pictures of the Trinity, see Craig (2003), Leftow (2004), and Merricks (2006).

spectrum of versions of the One-Sphere View. On one end, there is the Divine-Sphere View, on which the Son has one sphere typical of a default divine conscious life. It clearly won't do here to say that the Son has only a divine conscious life and is in no way associated with anything that has a human conscious life. But there are two views I can think of on which, though the Son does indeed have only a divine conscious life, there is a human conscious life in the neighbourhood. First, Peter van Inwagen has a Relative-Identity account of the incarnation, on which he proposes that, though nothing is divine and human, something divine (i.e. the Son) is the same person as something human (i.e. Jesus).[15] Van Inwagen could say, though he doesn't go into this explicitly, that the Son has a divine conscious life and Jesus a human conscious life, but nothing has both. On this view, however, the Son is not human. Perhaps we can say that, though the Son is not in the strict sense human, he is in a loose sense human, because he is the same person as something human. But if the Son is not strictly human, then, at least so it seems to me, the Son is not strictly incarnate and so the doctrine of the incarnation is not strictly true. Secondly, Thomas Flint has a concretist account of the incarnation, on which he proposes that the human nature that the Son assumes is a human being that has a conscious life in its own right, and, in some sense, the Son has the conscious life that the human nature does because the Son assumes this nature.[16] One way that Flint could develop his view, though he doesn't explicitly address the matter, is to say that the Son has a divine conscious life, his human nature has a human conscious life, and, though the Son doesn't strictly speaking have a human conscious life, it is appropriate to say that the Son has such a conscious life because of the peculiarly intimate association between the Son and the human nature that he assumes. Compare the dualist who thinks that we are embodied souls. For such a dualist, I have mental properties, my body has physical properties, and, though I lack physical properties, it is right and proper to say that I have physical properties because of the intimate relation between me and my body. But if Flint were to take this line, then, again so it seems to me, since the Son strictly lacks a human conscious life, he doesn't strictly take on our humanity in the right way.

On the other end of the spectrum, there is the Human-Sphere View, on which the Son has only one sphere typical of a human conscious life in our present condition. But, likewise, the problem here is that the Son lacks those conscious states that are necessary to be divine.[17] Now one might think that,

---

[15] Van Inwagen (1995: 275–6).
[16] See Flint (2001).
[17] If this is right, this rules out what Bayne calls the Restricted Inclusionist model of the incarnation. See Bayne (2001).

in actual fact, no conscious states are necessary for a subject to be divine. I have, though, already assumed that this is false. Every divine subject, being divine, sustains the world, which involves a conscious state. Moreover, the Son, being the divine person he is, has a role in spirating the Spirit, which again involves a conscious state. Now one might think that a divine subject needn't sustain the world so long as another carries on the work. But, so it seems to me, it is part of being perfect that a subject sustains the world. And so the Son, being perfect, can't leave this to another. If two agents are qualitatively the same, except that one sustains the world and the other doesn't, and all else such difference implies, then, in that respect, the first is better than the second. So if the Son doesn't sustain the world, it seems we can imagine a better agent, one who is just like the Son except that it also sustains the world and whatever such difference implies. But, of course, if the Son is perfect, we can't imagine a better agent. Moreover, the Son can't leave the work of his role in spirating to another. The same venerable tradition that tells us that the Son has a role in spirating also tells us that the Spirit is the divine person he is partly in virtue of this role that the Son has. So if the Son didn't perform his role in spirating the Spirit, the Spirit wouldn't exist, which is false.

Another version of the One-Sphere View combines the Divine-Sphere and Human-Sphere Views: the Switch Model. According to this model, the Son first has a divine sphere, then switches to a human sphere, then switches back again to a divine sphere, and so on. This model, however, as far as I can see, simply inherits the problems of the Divine-Sphere and the Human-Sphere Views. On this model, the Son is only ever divine or human but never both. But, first, every divine subject is permanently and essentially divine and so the Son can never cease to have a divine conscious life. And, secondly, the doctrine of the incarnation implies that the Son is both divine and human at once.

The Divine-Human-Sphere View

Between these two extremes lies the Divine-Human-Sphere View, according to which the Son has one sphere of consciousness, one part of which is, in itself, typical of a human conscious life in our present condition, and the other part of which is, in itself, as typical of a default divine conscious life as being a human in our present condition allows. What such a version looks like in detail, however, depends on what the default divine conscious life is like. Let's look at divine attentive acts and divine conscious states in turn.

So, first, what of divine attentive acts? Suppose that, by default, every divine subject attends (to the highest degree) to all apart from that attentive act. There are two kinds of attentive act. There are attentive acts directed on one's own mental states and there are attentive acts directed on what is not one's own mental states. Let's focus on the claim as it concerns attention to one's own mental states, i.e., introspection. So suppose that, by default, every divine subject attends (to the highest degree) to all its mental states apart from that attentive act. Then, on this version, when incarnate, the Son attends to all his divine mental states apart from that divine attentive act. This, of course, creates a problem. For if the Son does so attend, then his sphere will not look, from the inside, much like a human sphere in our present condition. In this case, we must say that the Son, albeit for good reasons, further alters the divine default setting. In this case, we must say that the Son either attends to no divine mental states or else attends to them to such a low degree that it hardly registers in his conscious life. The Son, if you like, turns the attentive light aimed at his divine mental states off or down so low that his total conscious state looks, from the inside, as much like that of a human sphere in our present condition as possible. And what goes for attentive acts directed on one's own mental states, goes for attentive acts directed on what is not one's own mental states. So suppose that, by default, every divine subject attends (to the highest degree) to all that is not its own mental states. This raises the same problem as before. Of course, the Son, when incarnate, attends to what is not his own mental states in much the same way that any human typically does. But apart from this, again the attentive light is either turned out or turned down as low as possible.

But suppose that, instead, by default, every divine subject attends to nothing. Then, on this version, when incarnate, the Son attends to no divine mental states, but he does attend to some human mental states. In this case, we don't face the same problem as before. The Son doesn't have to turn the attentive light off or down, as the light is already out. Rather, he turns the light directed on some of his human states on.

One alternative to this is that, though the Son has conscious unity, he has introspective-conscious disunity. Though the Son has one conscious sphere, by one introspective act, he introspects (to the highest degree) every divine conscious state that is not itself that introspective act, and by another introspective act, he introspects every human conscious state that he does introspect. The Son, if you like, divides the one introspective light into two and shines one beam onto the divine part of his sphere and shines the other beam onto the human part of his sphere. But, as I suggested before, it's hard to see how this could be. Intuitively, if two introspective-conscious states are (phenomenal) co-conscious with each other, they are introspective co-conscious with each other too. So if the Son has a divine (phenomenal) conscious state and a human (phenomenal) conscious state that are (phenomenal) co-conscious with each other, and he introspects each state, then, by one and the same introspective act, he introspects both conscious states together.

Secondly, what of divine conscious states? Suppose that every divine conscious state is unintrospected. Then such divine conscious states, together with any human conscious states that the Son doesn't introspect, form a phenomenal background: a region of unintrospected conscious states. In this case, the one sphere looks, from the inside, like a human one. And suppose that, instead, every divine conscious state is introspected, but to the lowest degree. Then such conscious states never form part of the Son's phenomenal background. But, though they are introspected, they hardly register in the Son's conscious life. And so again, in this case, the one sphere looks, as near as makes no matter, from the inside, like a human sphere in our condition. The one sphere has a divine part and a human part, and so differs from a typical human sphere, which has no divine part. But, since every divine conscious state is unintrospected or nearly so, and since the only conscious states that are introspected are human ones, such a sphere looks, to the subject, human.

The Divine-Human-Sphere View does raise at least one worry. Can a subject do an intentional act but not attend (to any degree) to what it does? Some versions of this view do imply that the Son performs divine acts but doesn't introspect doing so. But one might think that, though perceptual, bodily, and emotional experience can be part of the phenomenal background, intentional agency can't. But this seems wrong. Consider a long-distance driver. She drives a long way without taking a break. Her thoughts wander here and there. After some time, she realizes that she has been driving for a while without attending to what she has been doing. Clearly, she was intentionally acting. For she kept the car on the road, used the gas pedal and brake, and perhaps even changed lanes and signalled to do so. But all the while, she was unaware of her doing any of this.[18] Moreover, consider two disorders of agency: the so-called anarchic hand syndrome and utilization syndrome. In each case, there's an inability to prevent an intentional act. With the first syndrome, the patient, for example, will take food from the plates of others or undo the buttons of his own shirt that were just done up. And with the second syndrome, the patient, for example, will put sunglasses on top of sunglasses already being worn. Such acts either don't satisfy the patient's conscious intentions or frustrate them. These two syndromes, however, lead to very different reports. Those with the first disown their acts, but those with the second don't. So it seems that with the two syndromes, the patient's experience of the acts differ. In the first, the patient doesn't experience herself as the

[18] Cf. Armstrong (1999: ch. 10.3).

agent of the act (or perhaps experiences herself as not being the agent of the act). But, in the second syndrome, the patient does experience herself as being the agent of the act (or perhaps doesn't experience herself as not being the agent of the act).[19] One way or another, though, we have cases here where a subject does an intentional act but doesn't introspect doing so. And I see no reason why the Son can't sustain the world or play his part in spirating the Spirit, and so do intentional acts, but not introspect doing so.

So when it comes to the structure of the Son incarnate's conscious life, it seems the One-Sphere View comes out better than the Two-Spheres View, and among versions of the One-Sphere View, it seems the Divine-Human-Sphere View comes out better than the other versions.[20]

---

[19] See Bayne (2008b: 186).
[20] I'm grateful to Brian Leftow, Robin Le Poidevin, John Lizza, and Richard Swinburne for helpful comments.

10

Vehicle externalism and the metaphysics of the incarnation: a medieval contribution

Richard Cross

In what follows I will use some insights from the medieval philosophers to develop an account of the incarnation that makes central the notion that Christ's human nature should be thought of as an *instrument* of the second person of the Trinity. Some medieval thinkers, especially those influenced by Aquinas, made this notion central to their doctrine of the hypostatic union. But the relevant accounts of instrumentality are developed with sufficient detail only by Duns Scotus. So I combine the insights of the (Franciscan) Scotus on the nature of instrumentality with the accounts of the incarnation proposed by some of his (Dominican and Thomist) opponents. Indeed, as I shall show, Scotus himself explicitly rejected the notion that Christ's human nature could be an instrument of the divine person, and had some powerful reasons for so doing. So I shall try to propose, on behalf of Scotus's opponents, replies that they could offer to Scotus's objections, in some cases using further insights derived from Scotus's inventive and creative philosophical theology.

THE METAPHYSICS OF THE INCARNATION

The thinkers I shall be interested in here all suppose that the incarnation is a relation between two individual substances: the second person of the Trinity, and a concrete human nature. They claim too that the relevant relation is one of *dependence*. But they differ on the relevant kind of dependence—specifically, whether the dependence should be thought of in specifically *causal* terms. Scotus, for example, thinks not:

The relation [between the human nature and the Word] is one of order or dependence of a different kind from every sort of dependence in the order of caused to cause...And although it is difficult to see that there is some such dependence, nevertheless it seems to appear somehow in subject and accident. For an accident has two sorts of relation to its subject: namely, of what informs to what is informed (and this necessarily includes imperfection in the informed subject, since [the subject has] potentiality in relation to a qualified (i.e. accidental) act); and [the accident has] another [relation] as of what is naturally posterior to what is naturally prior, on which it depends as on a subject, not as on some cause...If therefore these two relations of an accident to a subject are distinguished from each other, one is necessarily to the subject under the description of some sort of imperfection in the subject—viz. of potentiality—whereas the other does not necessarily posit any imperfection in it, but only natural priority and substantification in relation to the accident. The relation which is the dependence of the human nature on the divine person is most similar to this.[1]

The opposing view—that the relevant kind of relation is a causal one—is spelled out very clearly by Hervaeus Natalis, a slightly younger contemporary of Duns Scotus:

We should see the kind of mode in which the human nature is understood to be united to the Word and dependent on the divine *suppositum* (*innixa supposito divino*). It is impossible for a human being to explain this sufficiently. But among those modes, the union of soul to body is closest to this union: not as the body relates to the soul as a proper subject relates to its form, but as it relates to [the soul] as an instrument naturally joined [to the soul], through which the other [viz. the soul] in some way operates, even though the one relation is not without the other in an animate body. So it is necessary to imagine some such dependence of the humanity on the divine *suppositum* without its being the case that one is properly speaking a part in relation to the other, or that there is any kind of composition properly so-called. In order to express this relation, the relation of an instrument to that which operates through it is most appropriate—especially when the instrument is naturally united.[2]

The idea is that there are two ways in which soul and body are related. The soul is the form—the *structure*—of the body; and it uses the body in bringing about its consciously chosen activities: it is an efficient cause, and the body is its instrument. (The example Hervaeus goes on to give just after the passage just quoted is that of a human being and his hand—an example deriving from Aquinas).[3] Scholastic accounts usually appeal to relations of the former

---

[1] Scotus, *Ordinatio* [= *Ord.*] 3.1.1.1, nn. 15–16, in Scotus, *Opera omnia*, ed. C. Balić et al. (Vatican City: Vatican Press, 1950–), IX, 6–7.

[2] Hervaeus, *In quatuor libros sententiarum commentaria* [= *In sent.*] 3.1.1.4 (Paris, 1647), 283b.

[3] See Aquinas, *Summa theologiae* [= *ST*] III/1, 111b-112a. For this kind of instrumentality account of the incarnation, see too Giles of Rome, *Lectura* 3.1 (in C. Luna, 'La Reportatio della

kind—formal, not efficient causation—to explain the unity of an item: hence Scotus's preference for seeing the human nature as something like an (accidental) *form* of the second person of the Trinity, rather than something that depends 'in the order of caused to cause'. The second person of the Trinity and the human substance, for example, are supposed to be just *one* subsistent thing, and seeing the human nature as something like an accident provides some sort of account of how this might be: just as Socrates and his whiteness, for example, are one subsistent thing—namely, Socrates himself. So while it is easy to see how Hervaeus's account might give an account of Christ's intentional human activity, it is hard to see how it might give an account of unity—given that unity is customarily explained in terms of forms and their subjects.

In the next section, I consider an alternative account of unity, proposed by Duns Scotus—one that would have served Hervaeus very well. I develop, too, a fuller account of the efficiently causal relation between soul and body that would allow a more complete account of the hypostatic union—again, based on insights from Scotus. But first, I want to consider an objection to any account that sees the incarnation as a relation between two concrete substances. On the face of it, human persons are concrete human substances, and if Christ's human nature—a concrete human substance—is a person, it looks as though Nestorianism will be true. Medieval theologians from Scotus onwards generally denied Nestorianism by arguing that a necessary condition for a substance's being a person—what the medievals referred to in technical language as a *suppositum* (= hypostasis)—is *failing* to depend on some other substance. Hervaeus sets the position out as follows:

'*Suppositum*'...means in reality that which has existence independently (*non innixum*) of any other *suppositum*: it is dependent on another neither by inherence (like an accident on a substance), nor as a part on a whole is (e.g. an arm on a body), nor somehow as something like a part on a whole is (e.g. the human nature dependent on a *suppositum* in Christ).[4]

Nestorianism is thus ruled out by *fiat*; but not in a wholly unprincipled way. Hervaeus, for example, claims that the human substance is an *instrument* of

---

lettura di Egidio Romano sul Libro III delle Sentenze (Clm. 8005) e il problema dell'autenticita dell' *Ordinatio*', in *Documenti e studi sulla tradizione filosofica medievale*, 1 (1990), 181): 'A human nature separated from the divinity is an efficient cause, and constitutes [a *suppositum*]; but the human nature joined to the divinity does not constitute a *suppositum*, but is as it were an instrument of the divinity, grounded in its hypostasis, through the mediation of which [viz. the human nature] the God-man does everything.' For the development of the model in the later Thomist tradition, see Nieden (1997: 160–75).

[4] Hervaeus, *Quodlibeta* 3.6 (Paris, 1513), fo. 76rb. The *locus classicus* is Scotus, *Ord*. 3.1.1.1, nn. 46–7 (Vatican, IX, 20–1).

the divine person, and there may be good reasons to suppose that a substance that satisfies *all* the requirements for being an instrument of the relevant kind lacks some feature that we might label 'personhood'. (By 'all the requirements', I mean to include more than just the kind of instrumental relation highlighted by Hervaeus. I return to this issue later, when I have made clear what causal relations I think are necessary in this case.)

INSTRUMENTALITY, SUBSTANTIAL UNITY, AND THE INCARNATION

Clearly, Hervaeus wants to use this causal relation to account for the hypostatic union. Thus, he needs some way to secure the fact that an instrument somehow becomes part of the person that uses it. Sadly, Hervaeus nowhere develops an account of instrumentality sufficient to guarantee this. But Scotus—who, as we shall see, explicitly rejects an instrumentality view of the incarnation—provides just the sort of account that would have proved useful to Hervaeus. Scotus claims that, in certain cases, a soul (or a whole body) can use a conjoined instrument in just the same way as it uses a part of the body. The context of the discussion is a particular problem in Scotus's theory of cognition. According to Scotus, when we call stored mental content to mind, the relevant occurrent cognitive act is caused jointly by the intellect and the stored content itself. Scotus labels such stored content an 'intelligible species'. So his view is that the occurrent cognition is caused by the intellect and an intelligible species. But the occurrent cognition inheres in the intellect, so it seems that a partial cause of something inherent in the intellect—the occurrent cognition—is something else inhering in the intellect—the intelligible species. And this seems to raise problems about self-motion. Scotus's reply is that the inherence of the cause makes no difference to the causal story, and he illustrates his claim with a very striking example:

That [the species] perfects this intellect is accidental to the species, in so far as it is a partial cause with respect to the act of cognizing, concurring with the intellect as the other partial cause. For even if it perfects [the intellect], it does not give the intellect any activity pertaining to the intellect's causality. Example: the motive power in a hand can use a knife to cut up a body, in so far as [the knife] is sharp. If this sharpness were in the hand as its substance, then the hand could use it for the same operation, and nevertheless it would be accidental to the hand (in so far as the motive power is in it) that sharpness is in it, and vice versa, because the sharpness gives the hand no perfection pertaining to [motive] power. This is apparent, because the motive power is equally perfect without such sharpness, and it uses [the sharpness] in the same way when it is in some other thing joined to the hand—such as a knife—as it would use it if it were in the hand.

So it is in the case at hand. If the species could exist in the intellect without inhering in it in the manner of form, and if by that mode of existence in [the intellect] it were or could be sufficiently conjoined to the intellect, these two partial causes, conjoined to each other, could [tend] to the same operation to which they now can when the species informs the intellect. This is also apparent if we posit some intelligible [object] present without a species. That object is a partial cause that does not inform the intellect (which is the other partial cause); but these two partial causes, close to each other without the informing of the one by the other, cause one common effect by their required proximity alone.

If this latter is posited, perhaps there is a reason for it to be impossible that an accident, which is an immanent and not a transient (*transiens*) principle, be sufficiently joined to the substrate unless it is in it subjectively—which is why it is called an accident. But surely the divine essence in the intellect of a blessed—which is neither immanent in the essence [of the blessed] nor in something of which it is a form—is a principle of intuitive cognition.[5]

The idea is that the knife and the body form something with a unity as tight as would obtain in the case that the blade was straightforwardly a *part* of the body (in the manner, say, of Johnny Depp's Edward Scissorhands character). The knife and the body become one subsisting thing. Presumably, the only significant difference is that the knife is easier to detach than (say) scissorhands would be. But if this is correct, it has a striking consequence for an account of substantial unity. For there is no unity in form between the knife and the body (even if there is in the case of Edward Scissorhands). So whether or not relations of formal causality sufficiently explain unity, they cannot be necessary conditions for unity. Unity can be explained equally by relations of *efficient* causality.

The application to the incarnation is obvious. By being an instrument of the Word, the human nature and the Word become one subsisting thing. Furthermore, the human nature and the Word become the subsisting thing that is the Word—just as the knife becomes (in effect) a part of the body. The body *extends itself* to include the knife; the Word *extends himself* to include the human substance.[6] Hervaeus's position on the incarnation, then, marks a considerable advance in explanatory power over the one proposed by Scotus.

---

[5] Scotus, *Ord.* 1.3.3.2, nn. 500–1 (Vatican, III, 296–7).

[6] On the relevant notion of extension, see e.g. Clark and Chalmers (1998: 7–19). Clark and Chalmers talk of the *self* extending itself to include, for example, external memory devices. Scotus's suggestion here uses the notion of an extended self in contexts other than merely cognitive use, and I need this suggestion for my argument here. I owe to Anna Marmodoro, with gratitude, the idea that it would be possible to use the Extended Mind theory to model the metaphysics of the incarnation.

Scotus can claim that the union is *like* that of substance and accident; Hervaeus could claim (if he adopted Scotus's account of instrumentality) that the union simply consists in an instrumentality relationship. The nature's being an instrument of the divine person explains the union.

This view of the incarnation requires occasionalism to be false, since in effect it posits something like occasionalism in the case of the incarnation, and if occasionalism obtained generally, it would entail on Hervaeus's account that God is incarnate in the whole universe. Now, the medieval theologians all have strong accounts of God's primary causality, and of his causal concurrence with every creaturely act. Scotus, for example, claims that, barring special divine intervention, God and creatures are what William A. Frank has labelled 'autonomous co-causes' of creaturely effects.[7] God is the primary cause of such effects, and creatures secondary causes: a creature acts 'through a form that is proper and intrinsic to the agent, even though in acting through that [form the agent] is subordinated to a higher agent cause'.[8]

What Scotus has in mind is that the divine activity and the creaturely activity are necessary and jointly sufficient for the effect. Both God and the creature act by means of their intrinsic causal powers ('through a form proper and intrinsic to the agent'). The picture is most easily grasped in the case that God *fails* to co-operate with the created cause—for example, the story of Shadrach, Meshach, and Abednego:[9]

There is an example in the case of the fire in the furnace, which did not act to bring about the destruction of the three boys—not because of some impassibility intrinsic to the boys, or because of some lack of passive potency [in the boys], or because of some intrinsic contrary impediment, but because God, through his will, did not cooperate in the action.[10]

The excluded options are *intrinsic impassibility* (the boys were simply such that they cannot be affected by anything external); *lack of passive potency* (the boys are such that they cannot be destroyed by fire); and *an intrinsic contrary impediment* (there is some kind of internal block on destruction).

The subordination claim, made in the last quotation but one, is not to be understood in any particularly strong sense. For example, it is not the case that God *causes* the creature to act. An example that Scotus often gives is that of the causal roles of father and mother in procreation:

---

[7] See Frank (1992).   [8] Scotus, *Ord.* 4.1.1.un., n. 119 (Vatican, XI, 43).
[9] Daniel 3: 24.
[10] Scotus, *Ord.* 4.49.13, n. 9, in Scotus, *Opera omnia*, ed. L. Wadding, 12 vols (Lyon, 1649), X, 587.

If it is posited that a mother has active causal power in the generation of a child, that power and the active power of the father cooperate (*concurrunt*) as two partial causes—but ordered, because one is more perfect than the other. But the less perfect does not receive its causality from the more perfect cause; neither does the total causality belong more eminently to the more perfect cause. Rather, the less perfect cause adds something, to the extent that the effect can be [produced] more perfectly from the more and less perfect causes [together] than [it would be if it were] from the more perfect cause alone.[11]

The idea in the last sentence is that the proper causal structure of the world requires the cooperation of both causes; if just one of the two were the cause of the effect (for example, in the case of occasionalism), the causal structures would be violated.

So God and creature are two distinct and independent causes of any given effect; God contributes more (as the more perfect cause), but the secondary cause is an independent contributor: it is not moved by the primary cause. Scotus explicitly contrasts this with the case of instrumental causation. In this kind of causal cooperation, the lower cause is moved by the higher cause—it has a causal role in the production of the effect only because it is made to do so by the activity of the higher cause:

That which lacks an active form in its order, even when it depends on a higher [agent] in its activity, can be called an instrument. Rather, it acts only through the actual motion of some other mover, as is clear in the case of artificial instruments, such as an axe or a saw, and such-like, because if an instrument is posited to be active properly speaking (*proprie*) to some end result, it is necessary for it to have some intrinsic active form, either in *esse quieto* prior to any motion of another agent, or in *fieri*, when it is wholly moved by a higher agent. For if it has an active form in neither sense, then it would not in any way act properly speaking.[12]

A form active in *esse quieto* is a causal power in virtue of which something can act independently unless impeded by some external agent or circumstance (assuming God's primary causality, as just outlined, of course). In the case of a voluntary agent, the relevant power is such that the agent can contingently place itself in a situation where it causes unless prevented by something external.

Talk of *esse quietum* is a way of picking out the fact that the relevant cause is not *moved* by anything else; so too is talk of 'an active form in its order'—we do not need to worry too much about these rather ugly bits of jargon. A non-instrumental cause has such a power. Instruments lack such a power. But they

---

[11] Scotus, *Ord.* 1.3.3.2, n. 496 (Vatican, III, 294).
[12] Scotus, *Ord.* 4.1.1.un., n. 120 (Vatican, XI, 44).

do have causal powers or internal structures such that, when moved, they can have a genuinely causal role in the production of an effect. Scotus's technical term for such a power or structure is 'a form active *in fieri*': a form that has a causal role when moved. His reason for this is that, if the instrument had no such power, then the internal structure of the instrument would make no difference to the kind of effect that is produced, and (absurdly) any instrument would do for any effect:

> For when a first act is the principle of some second act that has no *per se* active first act in that order, then it cannot bring about any second act in that order: otherwise anything could be said to be an instrument with respect to anything – and it could be said that God might create an angel through a fly as his instrument, which is nothing: for if it is repugnant to some nature that it is the active principle of certain actions, then it is not possible that, through any power whatsoever, it is the principle of them. For even if God can absolutely create a cold thing, he cannot [do this] by means of heat, such that heat is an active cause, in some order, in relation to coldness; or in some other example, where there is such repugnance to acting. From this it is clear that an instrument, if it is posited to act properly speaking to some effect, or [if it] has an active form in *esse quieto* prior to motion (as a secondary cause), or at least receives, in an actual motion, an active form by which it acts in its order of acting...then in this way this proposition is always true: 'Every instrument, which is active properly speaking...attains the principal result through some intrinsic form, whether that intrinsic form precedes the motion or merely is in [the instrument] while it is actually moved.'[13]

('First act' here refers to a causal power, and 'second act' to an effect of such a power, and the point of the awkward first two lines here is that a cause cannot use an instrument in causing an effect unless the instrument itself has some relevant causal power.) So not even God can use just any instrument in the production of any effect: there must be some structural feature of the instrument that enables it to be used in the production of such and such an effect. In the case of the incarnation, the intrinsic powers of the human substance are such that the divine person can do things that human beings can do—for example, touch things—that he cannot do unless incarnate.

What the knife example adds to all this is a stipulation that the instrument and the principal cause become one substance for the duration of their conjunction. Viewed in terms of Hervaeus's twofold account of the relation of body and soul—as subject and form, on the one hand, and instrument and agent, on the other—Scotus's view would be that the fact that the soul can use the body as an instrument is sufficient to guarantee their union as one person,

---

[13] Scotus, *Ord.* 4.1.1.un., nn. 121–2 (Vatican, XI, 44–5); see too Scotus, *Ord.* 4.1.1.un., n. 44 (Vatican, XI, 19); *Ord.* 4.6.3.1, nn. 118, 122–3 (Vatican, XI, 331, 332).

irrespective of the fact that the soul *informs* the body, or is the form of the body. So here instrumentality explains unity, irrespective of questions of inherence.

It would be an easy matter to give an account of the incarnation if we could show that every human activity fits this paradigm: that every human activity is such that, in the case of an incarnate divine person, it is caused directly by that person. I do not know what Hervaeus would say. Scotus would have a hard time accepting it, for as he sees it a necessary condition for being human is not merely being able to do the kinds of thing that humans can intentionally do, but also being causally dependent on certain internal causal structures and devices necessary for continued human functioning. Hervaeus's account of the incarnation does not posit any such dependence in the case of the second person of the Trinity. For example, according to Scotus a human substance is dependent on the continued functioning of its organs:

> A part [is] an instrument, and properly active with respect to the whole. And being the principle of an operation pertains primarily to the part, and to the whole only through the part. And in this way the Philosopher calls the organs those parts according to which an operation pertains to the whole...[The organ's] active form belongs to it and to the whole: but it belongs to [the organ] primarily, and to the whole essentially (*per se*) but not primarily...The same power is participated in different ways in the whole and in the part, and...it can be conceded that such a part does not properly have...another action than the whole, acting through the part, [does]; but it has the same [action] in a different way...An example...: the organ of the nutritive power and the whole animal with respect to nutrition.[14]

The idea is that there are certain kinds of part—here the organs of bodily functions over which we do not habitually exercise conscious control—whose activities belong to the part and by piggybacking belong to the whole. But because the relevant organs are parts of the whole, they count as *instruments* of the whole. For example, the efficient causality of a heart is a partial cause of an animal's persistence. But because the heart is a part of the animal, there is clearly a sense in which the relevant efficient causality belongs to the whole animal as a (partly) self-sustaining thing: the animal, including all its relevant parts, has a necessary but non-sufficient causal role in its own persistence. That the whole stands in a certain causal relation to these various parts is necessary for the continued existence of the whole animal. Scotus seems right to think that there will be a difference in causal story between this case and that of (for example) using a knife: the instrumentality of my heart (in keeping me alive) is different from that of my arm holding a knife, or of my Scissorhands-style

---

[14] Scotus, *Ord.* 4.6.3.1, nn. 120–1, 123 (Vatican, XI, 331–2).

modified arm. And the difference seems to be exactly the one he highlights: my heart is some kind of efficient cause of which my persistence is the effect; whereas in the knife case I am the efficient cause such that some external object is the effect.

Be that as it may, Scotus does not spell out the relevant conditions for the sort of parthood he has in mind here. He does, however, make it clear that the different organs have different forms ('[The organ's] active form belongs to it...primarily'), and elsewhere he makes it clear that the organs count as part of one whole on the grounds that there is a form of the body, potential to the organic forms: just as the bodily form inheres in matter, so the organic forms inhere in the composite of matter and bodily form.[15] But it seems to me that this inherence account is not the only possible account that would allow for the kind of organic instrumentality that Scotus defends here. For it is easy to imagine external vehicles having just the same causal role as bodily organs, but without such vehicles satisfying the inherence requirement. There are, for example, artificial devices that could perform the roles of the various organs: some are implanted (for example, artificial hearts such as the Jarvik-7), but some (such as incubators or dialysis machines) are fully external. And the causal story in both such cases will be much the same as obtains in the case of natural bodily organs: the organs/vehicles are in some way *efficient causes* of the persistence of the whole. If we adopt Scotus's (efficiently) causal account of substantial unity, we could say that such artificial devices become part of the substance that uses them. And these devices—unlike the knife—are necessary for the continued *human* existence of the person that uses them.

The discussion provides a way of fleshing out (as it were) Hervaeus's account of the incarnation. On the knife-style instrumentality that seems relevant to Hervaeus's account, we could provide what would be an account of the conscious activity of the second person of the Trinity: the person's using the human substance to perform certain actions freely chosen by the second person of the Trinity. And we could provide an account of the unity of person in the incarnation. But it is not so clear to me that this account would be sufficient for the divine person's actually *being* human (much as the knife-user is not a knife, even if the knife is as much a part of her as a Scissorhands-style blade would be). But we might posit that a person who is somehow dependent on a whole complex of human parts would count as a human person. On this view the Word would be *passive* relative to the relevant causal activity of the human parts, much as I am passive relative to the relevant causal activity of my organs: they cause my survival. So we could put the

---

[15] On this, see Cross (1998: 68–9).

theological issue more bluntly: the human substance in the incarnation is something like a *cause* of the continued human persistence of the second person of the Trinity: it performs a function, relative to the second person of the Trinity, analogous to that of (say) an incubator relative to a premature baby, or an artificial heart relative to someone with end-stage heart failure (bearing in mind that on Scotus's account these devices would count as *parts* of the person).

Now, I claimed above that the fact that a whole animal stands in a certain causal relation to its various parts (be they natural or artificial) is necessary for the continued existence of the whole animal. Clearly, it is accidental to the existence of the divine person that he exists (for a time) as a human being. So these parts are not necessary for his existence, even if they are necessary for his being human. But could we claim that having a human nature as the relevant kind of organ—one with an efficiently causal role in explaining the person's continued *human* existence—is *sufficient* for being human, and not merely necessary? I do not see why not. Consider a standard case. In such a case, possession of the whole array of relevant human parts is sufficient for being human, and the efficient causality of such parts is in some sense sufficient for human persistence. (For convenience, I am bracketing out environmental conditions, but the theory could take account of these too, *mutatis mutandis*.) It would be the same in the case of divine person: the efficient causality of the whole array of relevant human parts is sufficient for the human persistence of the divine person. The human life *piggybacks* onto the divine person: the divine person *borrows* it from the human substance.[16] How might the human substance, or the whole array or relevant human parts, come to perform such a function? I suppose one obvious thought is that God, or a divine person, can put himself into whatever causal relations with the creation that he wishes. Certainly Hervaeus's straightforward instrumentality account requires something like this: God can use whatever he wishes as an instrument, and *a fortiori* can use a human substance as one. What I am suggesting is that, in addition to this active causal relation, God, or a divine person, can allow himself to be affected in whatever way he choose, and can begin to stand in a causal relation to a human substance analogous to that had by a human substance relative to an incubator.[17]

---

[16] It is a problem in certain sorts of christology that there are some cases of parthood in which the properties of the parts piggyback onto the whole, and some cases in which they do not. I do not know a principle that governs these various cases. For a good introduction to the christological application of the notion that a whole can borrow properties from its parts, see Stump (2003: 412–15).

[17] I ignore questions about divine passibility and passivity in such cases, because it seems to me that any doctrine of the incarnation has to allow that God can be affected by creatures, is passible, and is passive in relation to various creaturely activities and attributes.

This account has some important consequences for the metaphysics of personhood. I noted above that a substance that satisfies all the requirements for being an instrument of a divine person lacks some feature that we might label 'personhood'. As Hervaeus might think of it, a person is a human substance that fails to be an instrument in the kind of total sense that I have been trying to outline. It is not the case that a person is *always* an instrument in the conscious intentional activity of another agent, and it is not the case that it is *always* an efficient cause of the human survival of some other substance. And this seems plausible enough. In this sense, a person is *independent*. But we see too that there are other senses in which persons are *dependent*: paradigmatically, the divine person is dependent, for his human survival, on the causal activity of a human substance; and all human persons are dependent on body parts. Furthermore, if the Scotus-style account of identity is correct, it makes no difference to the identity of such dependent persons whether their survival is contingent on internal (to the organic body) or external, or natural or artificial, causes.

INCARNATIONAL INSTRUMENTALITY AND CHRIST'S HUMAN WILL

In Peter Lombard's *Sentences*, the discussion of Christ's human will occurs in distinction 17 of book 3. Book 3 of Hervaeus's *Sentence* commentary ends before a discussion of distinction 17, and thus lacks a treatment of Christ's human will. So it is not clear what his discussion might have included. But there seems to be an obvious objection to his instrumentality account. The human substance joined to the second person of the Trinity has, according to Christian orthodoxy, a will of its own. And this seems to be what Scotus calls a form 'active *in esse quieto*': the human substance is such that it can (contingently) put itself into situations where it causes unless prevented. Clearly, such a substance could be an instrument of another, and it could be so voluntarily; but it could also be so *involuntarily*, and in either case there would be a failure of instrumentality: the second person of the Trinity could not control the human will. A human substance is not the kind of thing that can be a *total* instrument of another substance in this sense—one whose actions are totally under the control of another substance. Scotus certainly argues as much—it is the key component in his rejection of Hervaeus-style christologies. When discussing Christ's human will, Scotus objects to the view that there could be such a will on the grounds that (in effect) the human substance is a total instrument, and nothing that is a total instrument could possess a will:

It is shown that there are not two wills in Christ...on the grounds that every will is the master of its act; but if there were two wills in Christ, one would not be a will, because it would not be the master of its acts. Proof: that power which follows the motion of another power is not the master of its act, but is subordinated to another in respect of its act. But if there were a created will in Christ, that [will] would follow in its action the motion of the uncreated will of the Word, because the Word would bring about the operation of the human nature. Therefore [there is no created will in Christ].[18]

Scotus accepts that there is a human will in Christ, since the alternative is unorthodox. So he argues rather, *tollendo tollens*, that the human substance cannot be a total instrument of the Word:

I concede the major premise, that every will is the master of its act. But when it is said in the minor premise that a will that follows the motion of another power is subordinate to that power, and not its own master, I say—as elsewhere, in the first question of this third [book]—that the Word has no causality over the act of the created will in Christ that is not had by the whole Trinity: and for this reason the created will in the Word is not deprived, on account of the union to the Word, of its mastery in relation to its acts any more than it would be if it were not united to [the Word].[19]

The conclusion is startling: the relation between human and divine wills is just a standard case of secondary causality.

Hervaeus's account of the incarnation is—arguably—an attempt to develop certain insights from Aquinas. Aquinas himself simply claims that human wills can be instruments, even total instruments:

The human will in Christ had a certain determinate mode from the fact that it was in the divine hypostasis: namely, that it was moved always according to the nod of the divine will.[20]

Aquinas's view of the will generally tends more to the compatibilist than Scotus's does: and presumably Aquinas could give an account of this total instrumentality by simply positing that God causes, whether directly or not, only those desires that eventuate in good actions. But the position for Scotus is a bit harder, since Scotus explicitly denies that desires—inclinations of the will—*determine* the will's decision.[21] Self-mastery requires both the capacity

---

[18] Scotus, *Ord.* 3.17.un., n. 2 (Vatican, IX, 563).
[19] Scotus, *Ord.* 3.17.un., n. 16 (Vatican, IX, 569).
[20] Aquinas, *ST* III/1, 114b–115a.
[21] See, e.g., Scotus, *Quaestiones super libros metaphysicorum* 9.15, nn. 21–2, nn. 31–2, 34, in Scotus, *Opera philosophica*, ed. Girard J. Etzkorn et al., 5 vols (St Bonaventure, NY: St Bonaventure Press, 1995–2006), IV, 680–1, 683–4.

and the opportunity to choose between different desires. I return to this in a moment.

If total instrumentality seems hard to square with the presence of a will, Scotus's preferred option seems to tend radically towards the opposite error: if God has no more influence over Christ's human will than he has over mine, does it really make sense to think of the Word as a human person at all? Scotus, of course, has an easy reply: what makes the Word a human person is the fact that the human substance non-causally depends on him. As I noted above, this account lacks much explanatory power. But even if we accept it, Scotus's claims about Christ's human will seem to lead to a problem. Autonomous human substances have been known to sin, and if Christ's human will is subject to no more direct divine control than (say) mine, it seems hard to see how the human substance could be impeccable; and if the human substance is not impeccable, neither is the second person of the Trinity (since on Scotus's account the activities of that substance piggyback to the second person of the Trinity).[22] Scotus attempts to reply to this without having to appeal to instrumentality:

> The nature that [the Word] assumed, was of itself peccable and able to sin, because it was not beatified from the union alone, and had free will—and was thus able to aim either way (*vertibilis erat ad utrumque*); but it was confirmed from the first instant, through beatitude, such that it is impeccable, just as the other *beati* are impeccable.[23]

Given that, as he believes, Christ's human nature enjoyed the beatific vision, Scotus argues (parsimoniously) that the same account of impeccability can be given in Christ's case as can be given in the case of any of the blessed—supposing the generally accepted theological position that the blessed are impeccable. The basic idea is that such a substance retains the power to sin, but is (somehow) deprived of the opportunity to exercise this power:

> It is clear that someone blessed is impeccable in the composed sense, i.e. he cannot simultaneously be blessed and sin. But the divided sense, 'that someone remaining blessed does not have a power or possibility for sinning' can be understood in two ways: either [that he does not have this power] because of something intrinsic to him that excludes this power, or because of some extrinsic cause that excludes from him the proximate potency [for sinning]: e.g. even if someone having sight has an intrinsic power for seeing any body, nevertheless it can be made, through some extrinsic cause, perpetually impossible, for him to see by proximate potency, as in the case that the cause brings about perpetual distance between the sight and the body: just as, if there were a perpetual obstacle between the heavenly empyreum and the eye of a damned

---

[22] On this, see Cross (2002: 198–203).
[23] Scotus, *Ord.* 3.12.un., n. 13 (Vatican, IX, 383).

person, that eye could not see the heavenly empyreum (talking about proximate potency), and this because of some extrinsic cause perpetually preventing the power. But it could see by intrinsic and remote potency, such that there is no intrinsic cause of the impossibility.

So I say that in the will of Michael [the archangel], now blessed, there is no intrinsic cause through which the power for sinning at some other time is excluded, in the divided sense, for there is no intrinsic cause preventing this power from being reduced to act. But it is, in virtue of an extrinsic cause, impossible for this power to be a proximate [power] for sinning, viz. by the will of God going ahead of (*praevenientem*) the will such that it always continues its act of enjoyment, such that it can never reduce its remote power for not enjoying, or for sinning, to act: even though if the secondary cause were never led (*praeventa*) by a higher agent cause to one option, the proximate potency could go to the other option.[24]

The blocks on sinning are *extrinsic* to the agent: God somehow prevents it from sinning. Scotus does not explain what the relevant mechanism is, but presumably one obvious way would be for God to bring it about that the will is only ever subject to good desires, such that, whichever desire it acts on, the agent's activity will be good. God 'goes ahead' of the will by causing the good desires on the basis of which the will chooses. And we could think of this as analogous to the damned person's obstacle, preventing him seeing the sky. God prevents bad desires in the blessed, by causing only good ones.

This view, it seems to me, satisfies Scotus's requirement that a free agent has self-mastery. As he sees it, self-mastery amounts to an ability to choose between different desires; and this account does not require any commitment to a specific view of just how the relevant desires were produced. But what could we say on the assumption that the human substance is a total instrument of the second person of the Trinity? The point of this christology, of course, is to deny that the human substance has self-mastery. Given that orthodoxy requires that Christ have a human will, the question is whether it would be possible for there to be a human will—with libertarian freedom—that nevertheless was such that it was always necessitated by antecedent causal conditions (in this case the causal determination of the divine person). The idea is that the relevant human substance is such that it is always *made* to choose whichever alternative is chosen. If this situation—its always being made to choose—was a necessary feature of its, we would certainly want to say that the substance lacked human free will (understood in Scotus's incompatibilist sense). But perhaps the human substance united to the Word was not like this. It is the *union* that causes the human substance to be such that it is made to will such-and-such. But suppose it is a contingent matter

---

[24] Scotus, *Ord*. 4.49.6, n. 11 (Wadding, X, 455).

that this human substance is united to the Word—something that seems wholly plausible, since the union is simply a matter of the Word's putting himself into certain causal relations with a human substance. In this case, it seems that we should claim that the human substance indeed has free will, even if it is not in a situation in which it can exercise its autonomous freedom. *De dicto*, it is not possible that a human substance united to the second person of the Trinity act freely. But *de re*, it is possible, because the Word could cease to use the human substance as an instrument, and in this case the substance could begin to exercise autonomous agency.[25]

Does this instrumentality clash with the view that Christ's human substance felt the pull of human appetites incompatible with the divine will? Not at all; nothing about this view requires that Christ's human substance not have all sorts of such desires. All that the view requires is that the *choice* between the desires is made by the divine person. The case contrasts nicely with that of the blessed. In the blessed, God is the causal explanation of the *desires*, not of the choice between them; in Christ, the desires can arise in the normal way; the *choice* is made by the second person of the Trinity. Equally, it may well be the case that the human substance was not aware that it lacked ultimate autonomy. But this does not seem to be an insuperable problem. Even supposing that each of us has such ultimate autonomy, it is not clear that we can tell as much simply by introspection. For all we know, compatibilism is true; and this is so even if it seems to us, introspectively, that compatibilism is false. And the *de re* possibility of the autonomous activity of the assumed human substance in Christ is sufficient to secure the presence of a genuinely free will.

INCARNATIONAL INSTRUMENTALITY AND THE NATURE OF GOD'S TRINITARIAN CAUSAL ACTIVITY

As we have already seen, Scotus holds that 'the Word has no causality over the act of the created will in Christ that is not had by the whole Trinity'. His reason for this is that he holds the Augustinian axiom that 'Father, Son, and Holy Spirit...operate inseparably':[26]

---

[25] In fact, the view that the human substance is only contingently united to the second person of the Trinity is, as is well known, one of the key innovations of Scotus's christology: on this, see Cross (2002: 299–300, 302–8).

[26] Augustine, *De trinitate* [= *De trin.*] 1.4.7, ed. W. J. Mountain, CCSL 50/50A (Turnhout: Brepols, 1968), 36; see too e.g. Augustine, *De trin.* 2.2.3 (p. 83); *De trin.* 5.14.15 (p. 223), which last Scotus cites at *Quodlibet* [= *Quod.*] 8, n. 3 (Wadding, XII, 205).

The relation [between the human nature and the Word] is one of order in one of the related extremes. But it is not one of caused to cause, because that is common to the whole Trinity.[27]

Why think that the Augustinian axiom is true? Scotus holds that the divine persons share intellect and will, and he holds that shared mentality entails shared agency:

> The formal and proximate basis for causation in God is the intellect or the will, or some act of intellect or will. But the intellect of the three persons is the same and the will [of the three persons] is the same, and consequently entirely the same act of understanding and willing is theirs, and the same object, whether primary or secondary. Therefore too the same formal basis of causing—even the proximate [formal basis]—is common to the three persons.[28]

So this depends on the view that the divine persons necessarily have shared mentality. One common medieval reason for holding this view is that, following Augustine, the medievals generally held that the only features that distinguish the persons are their relations of origin: the causal relations that they have to each other. If the only features that distinguish the persons are causal relations among themselves, it follows that they must have shared mentality: mental states are not relations of origin, and have some plausible claim on being monadic properties, not relations at all. Curiously, it is Scotus himself who has the resources for rejecting the relation theory of the constitution of a divine person, and thus for allowing there to be distinct mental lives and hence causal powers in the divine persons.

A standard reason for accepting the relation theory of the constitution of a divine person is that denying it entails the possibility that one person could exist without the other, and thus that (at best) tri-theism is true, given that one quick and easy way of distinguishing Trinitarianism from tri-theism is that in the former, but not in the latter, each person requires the existence of the other two. Thus Henry of Ghent:

> If there is a *suppositum* in God, it is necessary that it is constituted by a respective *ratio* founded in the essence, which does not bring about any determination of the thing considered in itself (because it [viz. the relation] does not determine the essence), but [brings about the determination] only of the thing compared to another according to relative opposition, which is [a determination] of the related thing, which is itself constituted as it were from essence and relation, and itself determined and distinct.[29]

---

[27] Scotus, *Ord.* 3.1.1.1, n. 14 (Vatican, IX, 6).
[28] Scotus, *Quod.* 8, n. 6 (Wadding, XII, 205).
[29] Henry of Ghent, *Summa quaestionum ordinariarum* 53.6, 2 vols (Paris, 1520), II, fo. 68rH.

Now, this view does not entail that the persons have no *other* distinguishing features, although Henry (along with all of the medievals) in fact assumes that this is the case. But be that as it may, Scotus disagrees with Henry's relation theory, and in so doing allows a fortiori for the possibility of there being non-relational distinguishing features such as intellect and will:

I say that if we posit that the persons are relational, it is necessary to posit that they are truly subsistents and that the same undivided nature is in them. This cannot be posited on account of some imperfection of the persons in [their manner of] subsisting, for they are posited to be as truly subsistent as they would be if they were absolute. Therefore it must be posited on account of the infinity of the essence which is in the subsistents. But the infinity of the essence would be the same if the persons were absolute. Therefore it would not be necessary for the nature to be divided in that case, just as now the [relational personal] property does not [divide the nature]. Therefore let this be proved: 'Every nature, common to absolute *supposita*, is distinguished in them'. For this is true in creatures, but in the case at hand it begs the principal conclusion.[30]

The relevant requirement of orthodoxy is that tri-theism is false: that is, as Scotus sees it, that 'the same undivided nature is in' all three persons. Scotus does not see that satisfying this principle requires positing that the persons are distinct by relations, since it could just as well be the case that the same undivided nature were in all three persons on the assumption that what distinguishes the persons is some non-relational feature. As Scotus sees it, it is the infinity of the essence that entails its being numerically the same in all three persons. This does not mean that the persons might not also have necessary causal relations to each other— for example, to satisfy the inseparability requirement. The aim is merely to show that it is possible for the persons to have non-relational individual properties too. And developing this line of thought would allow for the possession of distinct causal powers, and thus for the possibility that Christ's human nature is genuinely an instrument *merely* of the second person of the Trinity. Again, Scotus's rich philosophical theology has resources sufficient to develop views that he himself might have found objectionable.

CONCLUSION

On the account that I am describing, the second person of the Trinity extends himself to include a human substance. He does this in two ways, according to

---

[30] Scotus, *Ord.* 1.26.un., n. 82 (Vatican, VI, 37).

the two different accounts that I highlighted in Scotus's discussions of instrumentality. The first—an active causal relation—explains Christ's consciously chosen human activity; the second—a passive causal relation or capacity—explains Christ's organic bodily functioning. I take it that the second of these could be developed to include the divine person's relation to the mental states of the human substance: not just that he has access to these, but that these mental states count in some sense as *his*. After all, on the Extended Mind kind of view that I am describing, the human mind really becomes a part of the second person of the Trinity, and its thoughts are his thoughts. Whether the model can give a fully worked-out account of the causal mechanisms relevant here, I am not sure. But this is a problem not merely for the view that I am describing, but for all two-substance views.

11

The metaphysics of the Extended Mind in ontological entanglements[1]

Anna Marmodoro

INTRODUCTION

This essay explores the prospects of understanding the incarnation of God the Son in Jesus as a philosophically possible phenomenon in light of recent developments in the study of the philosophy of mind—the Extended Mind theory first put forward by Clark and Chalmers in 1998.

The question that the Extended Mind theory addresses is: 'Where does the mind stop and the rest of the world begin?' One's mind, even in ordinary situations of everyday life, is enabled to carry out a variety of cognitive processes by relying on mechanisms or devices external to the brain; for example, when doing complex mathematical calculations using a calculator. The Extended Mind theory holds that in doing so (with qualifications to follow) the mind can, and indeed does, 'extend' beyond the outer limit of one's skin and skull. *The mind 'extends' into the world.*[2]

Roughly put, the thought that motivates the present essay is that it might be fruitful to think of God the Son's incarnation in Jesus along the lines of a

---

[1] The research findings presented in this essay are part of the output of a research project supported by the Leverhulme Trust and based at the University of Oxford. The author would like to thank for helpful comments Brian Leftow and Richard Swinburne in Oxford, and the audiences of conferences at Notre Dame and Oxford, where versions of this essay were presented. (Thanks are owed in particular to Joseph Jedwab who responded to the presentation in Notre Dame.)

[2] The Extended Mind theory is also described by its own authors as *Active Externalism* (1998: 7, 8) because the environment plays an active role in driving one's mental activities. This is another aspect of the theory that might be helpful towards understanding the incarnation: Jesus is the device that God the Son uses for his mental activities, but *qua* device Jesus has an active role in enabling those mental activities—humanity contributes actively to its salvation.

(divine) mind 'extending' onto an external device (Jesus) to carry out (some of) its mental activities (with qualifications to follow). It will be argued that there are possible cases of extension of the human mind into the world which raise metaphysical difficulties parallel to the difficulties we encounter in accounting for the incarnation. If so, there might be a common analysis of what is required for a solution.

For the purposes of this essay God the Son is here assumed to be an essentially spiritual—that is non-physical—being. The assumption is motivated by the orthodox requirement that God the Father and God the Son are divine. God the Father is essentially spiritual and hence non-physical, and his divine nature is shared by God the Son. Nevertheless, we need to find a way of relating physicality to God the Son, without compromising the nature he shares with God the Father on the one hand, while offering an explanation of the phenomenon of the incarnation of God the Son on the other. This essay looks at the incarnation from a philosophical perspective only, asking whether and how an essentially spiritual being can constitutionally partake of the material world.

The conclusion that will be argued for is that while God the Son cannot become physical, for he is essentially a spiritual being, he can become *entangled* with the physical in such ways that the nature of his mental activities and possibly his own nature may be *modified by the dependence*—through 'extending' into the world and onto Jesus. In this sense it is philosophically possible to hold that God the Son is both divine and human.

I will first examine, beyond what has already been done in the Extended Mind theory literature, various degrees to which a mind can extend into the world, and investigate whether *varying degrees of extension and ways of extending* the mind into the world is a matter of quantitative variation only or also qualitative variation. By 'quantitative' I mean that the number of extended mental activities or their range can vary. By 'qualitative' I mean that extension can vary with respect to the type of activity that is extended. Furthermore, I will explore the question of whether *variation in extension reaches a metaphysical threshold*.

I will focus in particular on cases of what I call 'extreme extension', the types of entanglement they give rise to, and the effect that the entanglements have on the nature and identity of what is entangled. I will investigate whether, and how, high degrees of extension affect the nature of the extended activity, and can also affect the nature of the extended subject itself. In particular, I wish to consider whether the *direction of extension* between the mind and the world can switch as we consider various cases of entanglement, resulting in the entangled entity having the nature, not of the mind, but of what the mind extends into.

The analysis of various cases of extension that I offer in this essay is also a contribution to the philosophy of mind literature, for it examines the consequences of multiple extensions of one organism into its environment.

THE EXTENDED MIND THEORY

In their seminal and well-known article 'The extended mind' (1998), Clark and Chalmers explore whether systematic reliance on external mechanisms can extend the mind's cognitive states/processes into the world, by extending the boundaries of the body for the type of work that the brain and peripheral systems do for the agent.

The boundaries of the agent's body extend when the agent systematically relies on external devices which perform for the agent tasks that replace activities normally carried out within the boundaries of the body. In such cases the agent usually has the choice of whether to rely on inner or outer resources. But in other cases, the external activities may enable the agent to perform tasks that her/his body does not enable her/him to perform.

Clark and Chalmers offer the following example for the former type of case.[3] Consider three cases of human problem-solving in playing Tetris: how does one go about assessing whether a given Tetris block will fit in a socket of a certain shape? There are at least three ways:[4]

1. By mentally rotating the Tetris blocks;
2. By choosing either to rotate the images physically on the screen or to rotate them mentally;
3. By having a neural implant which can perform the rotation (with choice of using it or not).

Clark and Chalmers comment: 'How much cognition is present in these cases? We suggest that all the three cases are similar' (1998: 7).

In further cases, the external activities may enable the agent to perform tasks that their body does not, contingently or even in principle, enable them to perform. The very well-known example Clark and Chalmers give to illustrate this point is Otto, a person who suffers from Alzheimer's disease.

Like many Alzheimer's patients he relies on information in the environment to help structure his life. Otto carries a notebook around with him everywhere he goes. When

---

[3] Clark and Chalmers (1998: 7–8).
[4] There may be more but not relevant to the present inquiry.

he learns new information, he writes it down. When he needs some old information, he looks it up. For Otto, his notebook plays the role usually played by a biological memory... The information in the notebook functions just like the information constituting an ordinary non-occurrent belief; it just happens that this information lies beyond the skin.[5]

The conclusion Clark and Chalmers argue for in their 1998 article is that '*beliefs* can be constituted partly by features of the environment, when those features play the right sort of role in driving cognitive processes. *If so, the mind extends into the world.*'[6]

The original Clark and Chalmers hypothesis concerns cognitive processes; hence it has been called the Extended Cognition hypothesis. But Chalmers himself and others find it natural to apply the Extended Cognition hypothesis to a wider range of mental activities and states:

It is natural to ask whether the extended mind thesis might itself be extended. What about extended desires, extended reasoning, extended perception, and extended emotions? I think that there is something to be said for each of these.[7]

So from now onwards I will simply refer to the Extended Mind theory to include all the mental states and activities mentioned in the quote above.

The Extended Mind theory is a variety of Vehicle Externalism. Susan Hurley explains it thus:

Other varieties of externalism aim to explain how—by what processes or mechanisms or 'vehicles'—mental states are enabled. Enabling processes can be explained in terms of computation, neural networks, dynamical systems, and so on. What are the boundaries of the relevant enabling processes? Can enabling processes extend beyond exclusively internal neural processes into the body and its environment? Enabling externalism (or how-externalism, or vehicle externalism) answers 'yes'.

We should distinguish externalism about processes that enable intentional content from externalism about processes that enable phenomenal quality. Arguments for content-enabling externalism have often proceeded under the headings of 'extended mind' or 'embodied, situated cognition'. For example, an Alzheimer patient's cognitive processes arguably extend to a notebook he uses in place of reliable neural memory processes (Clark and Chalmers 1998...); an accountant's cognitive processes may include her use of pen and paper in complex calculations. Arguments for quality-enabling externalism have tended to appeal to embodied, situated interactions with natural environments, often under the heading of 'sensorimotor dynamics' [e.g. Noë].[8]

---

[5] Clark and Chalmers (1998: 12–13).   [6] Clark and Chalmers (1998: 12), my emphasis.
[7] Chalmers, Foreword to Clark (2008: xiv). Elsewhere Chalmers mentions 'the extension of our bodies, the extension of our senses, and crucially, the use of language as a tool to extend our thought' (Foreword to Clark (2008: ix)).
[8] Hurley (forthcoming).

Pivotal to the Extended Mind hypothesis is the following *Parity Principle*:

If, as we are confronted with a task, a part of the world functions as a process which, *were it done in the head*, we would have no hesitation in recognizing as part of the cognitive process, then that part of the world *is* (so we claim) part of the cognitive process.[9]

The analysis of degrees of extension offered below will show that this principle requires qualifications.

Let us investigate further into what the Principle says. In Chalmers's words:

A month ago, I bought an iPhone. The iPhone has already taken over some of the central functions of my brain ... Friends joke that I should get the iPhone implanted into my brain. But if Andy Clark is right, all this would do is speed up the processing, and free up my hands. The iPhone is part of my mind already.

... [Clark] defends the thesis that in at least some of these cases, the world is not serving as a mere instrument for the mind. Rather, the relevant parts of the world have become parts of my mind. My iPhone is not my tool, or at least it is not wholly my tool. Parts of it have become parts of me.

This is the thesis of the extended mind: *when parts of the environment are coupled to the brain in the right way, they become parts of the mind*. My iPhone is not my tool, or at least not wholly my tool. Parts of it have become parts of me.[10]

What does 'coupled in the right way' mean? Clark and Chalmers explain it in the case of Otto thus:

First, the notebook is a *constant* in Otto's life—in cases where the information in the notebook would be relevant, he will rarely take action without consulting it. Second, the information in the notebook is *directly available without difficulty*. Third, upon retrieving information from the notebook he *automatically* endorses it.[11]

The agent 'extends' into the world not when he/she is simply assisted in performing some functions and tasks by various external devices, but only, in short, when she/he *depends systematically* on the external mechanisms for the performance of these tasks. Otto, for example, extends his body onto the notebook by systematically depending on it for remembering information he cannot store in his biological memory.

The *systematic dependence* on such devices is such that one ceases to think of them as instruments which, for example, Otto uses, but comes to think of them as *parts* of Otto, on a par with the parts of Otto's body through which he engages in daily activities.

---

[9] Clark and Chalmers (1998: 8).   [10] Foreword to Clark (2008: ix), my emphasis.
[11] Clark and Chalmers (1998: 17).

What I want to draw attention to and further explore is that dependence between the agent and the device is *mutual* and comes in *degrees*, and accordingly different types of ontological entanglements come about.

A TWO-WAY ONTOLOGICAL ENTANGLEMENT

In the classic scenario by Clark and Chalmers the notebook is an enabler for Otto. It allows him to retrieve information he cannot remember on his own, and to act on it. What is more, he does so systematically; Otto has come to depend on the notebook for the provision of information he needs, and the notebook is part of his daily life plan. In that sense, the notebook functions as a part of Otto's body, enabling Otto to fulfil mental tasks, such as remembering an address, he would not have been able to carry out without it.

But *the notebook does not itself carry out Otto's mental activities*. It is not the notebook that has the belief that the Museum of Modern Art is on 53rd Street. Any mental activity that is performed is performed by Otto. Otto is and remains the thinking agent. To put it in general terms, the external item does *not* do the thinking for the agent. Rather, the external item makes available information that would normally be available to one through the use of their senses or other brain functions.[12] In Clark's and Chalmers's words:

> The key claim... is that *a subject's beliefs* can be partly constituted by features of the environment, when those features play the right sort of role in driving cognitive processes. A bit more generally and precisely, the claim is that sometimes *a subject has a mental state* (e.g., believing that the Museum is on 53rd Street) partly *in virtue* of external processes, and in particular in virtue of these external processes playing the right sort of role in driving cognitive processes. Here, 'in virtue of' should be understood constitutively rather than causally.[13]

So, in Clark's and Chalmers's example, the notebook carries out tasks that would have otherwise been carried out by a part of Otto's brain. Otto thereby enhances his capacities and is able to perform tasks which he would not have been able to perform without the notebook. But the ownership of the relevant cognitive process/states remains with Otto, despite the functional involvement of the notebook.

---

[12] Examples of this could be the use of a notebook rather than one's own memory to remember data; the use of prosthetic devices to gain information about the layout of the immediate environment around one; knowing the way to a place by looking at the road signs.

[13] Clark and Chalmers (1998: 12), my emphasis.

The notebook also depends on Otto to be a vehicle of cognition. The notebook has been taken over by Otto to serve as a memory vehicle. As if it were a part of Otto's body, the notebook becomes functionally if not organically engaged with his body. Yet, the notebook is not dependent on Otto in the way he is dependent on it. Otto is and remains what he is, namely the thinking agent— even when relying on the notebook. The notebook depends on Otto *to be what it becomes,* namely a memory/cognition vehicle. Through Otto's use of it, the notebook becomes part of his remembering process, *because of the purpose it serves.*

In more general terms, an *ontological entanglement* between an agent and an external device is formed. The external device becomes *constitutionally appropriated* by the agent, enabling her to carry out activities that she has either lost the capacity to carry out by herself, or which she could not have carried out without reliance on the device. On the other hand, the agent interferes with the device, determining what it becomes through the use she puts the device to.[14]

THE METAPHYSICS OF EXTENSION

In very general terms, in cases of extension the entity that is being extended engages in an activity that is enabled by some other activity in the external environment of that entity. In the original Clark and Chalmers case, Otto acquires a belief regarding the location of the Museum of Modern Art (namely, that it is on 53rd Street) by extending his belief-formation activity onto the notebook, which he uses to remember the address. So the extension of Otto's mind is determined by the *goal* of the extended activity (in this case, belief formation about the museum address), as well as by the *means* through which the activity is implemented in the environment (through the use of the notebook). The entanglement, for example, of Otto and the notebook, is ontologically bound together by one entity systematically providing the goal, and the other entity providing the means for the realization of an activity.

I will argue that the introduction of a *goal-means entanglement* in the activities of two entities can affect the identities of the activities,[15] and in extreme cases of extension even the nature and the number of the entities

---

[14] The device might in some cases become simply qualified in a certain way, but in others it might become a different type of thing from what it was before.

[15] This is because the causal structure of the implementation of the activities is altered by the extension, and it can thereby change either the nature or the goal of the activities, or both.

themselves (meaning that one of the two entities engaged in the entanglement might become part of the other). The line of thinking behind this conclusion is that within a Kripkean metaphysical framework, which I assume, the identity of a substance depends on the sort or kind of substance it is, which is determined by the substance's constitution, activity, and functionality. Thus, for example, we know what a cat is when we know its make-up and its characteristic activities. If then an entity's activities are put to the service of the activities of another entity, this may interfere with the identity of the activities, and ultimately with the identity of the entities themselves.

In what follows I will address questions that arise from 'extreme' cases of extension. Do the extended agent and the device become parts, the one of the other? Is the task performed by the agent, by the device, by both, or by some new resulting entity? Does the nature of the extended and extending activities change? Does the nature of the extended and extending entities change?

I will discuss these questions by presenting a series of thought experiments to study the types of dependence, and hence the types of entanglement in which we are interested for the purpose of explaining the phenomenon of the incarnation.

DEEP BLUE VERSUS KASPAROV

Let us consider a series of cases of ontological entanglement brought about by 'extreme' extension that I take to bear analogies to the incarnation case. Deep Blue was a chess-playing computer developed by IBM, and was the first computer system to defeat a world champion, Garry Kasparov, in a match under standard chess tournament time controls, in 1997.[16] For the present purposes, I make the assumption that during that match Deep Blue and Kasparov played the same game.[17] Deep Blue beat Kasparov, just as it had been beaten by Kasparov in previous contests.

---

[16] More details may be found on IBM's official website research pages: <http://www.research.ibm.com/deepblue/>.

[17] Deep Blue and Kasparov are both behaving like chess players. Whether it is the same or a similar activity they perform depends on how activities are individuated: at the level of their general function, or of their micro-causal network. For the purposes of this discussion I follow the spirit of the Parity Principle mentioned above, according to which reading the diary is an implementation of remembering for Otto. Correspondingly, were the activities of Deep Blue performed within the boundaries of skin and skull, on the Extended Mind hypothesis we would have no hesitation in recognizing them as part of the chess-playing process. This point will be developed further in what follows.

Kasparov being swapped with Deep Blue

What I wish to explore is whether Deep Blue and Kasparov can extend onto one another, and to which degree, while retaining their numerical distinctness, or whether either of the two can merge with the other. I will first consider a scenario that will allow us to clarify what sort of case we are interested in here, and what not.

Can Deep Blue become Kasparov? The assumption made is that Deep Blue can engage in the same activities as Kasparov and pursue the same goals as Kasparov, for example, to play and win a chess game. We can imagine now that Deep Blue could engage in carrying out certain further tasks of Kasparov's, such as to instruct as well as train young aspiring chess players and prepare them for competing. Gradually, Deep Blue could learn to carry out, in appropriate set-ups, many of Kasparov's professional activities, becoming a *'virtual Kasparov'*.

Virtual Kasparov is basically an enhanced Deep Blue, which can engage in a wider range of chess-playing-related activities, which Kasparov would engage in. Let us then imagine this further enhancement of Deep Blue and swapping Kasparov for the further enhanced Deep Blue. We can suppose that an opportunist agent wishes to replace Kasparov in public life, as the old master is beginning to age. Let us further suppose that scientists build newer versions of Deep Blue, combining computing and robotics, in an attempt to create a machine that looks and acts like Kasparov. They use all the available medical and prosthetic know-how to imitate human behaviour as faithfully as possible, and even feed Kasparov's game tactics, personality traits, and memories into the further enhanced Deep Blue. The final product, let us call it *Deep Blue-K*, would be a robot that looked like Kasparov, behaved like him, and played chess like Kasparov. Let us further assume in this thought experiment that Kasparov retires from public life and the Deep Blue-K steps into his public role.

What exactly would the relation between Deep Blue-K and Kasparov be in this case? Clearly they would be numerically different substances, coexisting and possibly even interacting with each other. So the question is how similar the two could be. The stuff the two are made out of is different. The one is carbon-based and the other is silicon-based. Hence, their causal histories and origins are different as well. Within a Kripkean metaphysical framework, such cases are governed by metaphysical necessity. Kripke has shown that the type of constitution and the origin of natural kinds are essential to them.[18] His well-known example was the discovery of a 'tiger' that is not a mammal:

---

[18] Being a tiger or a reptile is a natural kind; being non-physical is not a kind. No assumption is made that God is a natural kind by assuming that God is essentially non-physical. Nor are natural kinds arguments needed to establish that God is essentially non-physical.

Suppose we discover an animal which, though having all external appearances of a tiger as described here, has an internal structure completely different from that of the tiger... We might find animals in some part of the world which, though they look just like a tiger, on examination were discovered not even to be mammals. Let's say they were in fact very peculiar looking reptiles. Do we then conclude on the basis of this description that some tigers are reptiles? We don't. We would rather conclude that these animals, though they have the external marks by which we originally identified tigers, are not in fact tigers, because they are not of the same species as the species which we called 'the species of tigers'.[19]

Humans are essentially organic, *qua* belonging to a natural kind of such a type, while Deep Blue-K is essentially electronic, *qua* artefact of such a constitution. So Deep Blue cannot become/be another Kasparov. On Kripke's argument, a human being *cannot be embodied* in a computer, since a human being cannot be constituted of silicon.

So, how similar can Deep Blue-K and Kasparov become? How close can Deep Blue get to being Kasparov? What Deep Blue and Kasparov can share in common are activities and states. But how *similarly* do they act with each other, when they engage in the *same* activities?

In the case under consideration, Deep Blue-K carries out the type of activities that Kasparov would have engaged in. By that I mean that at a certain level of generality, their activities are *functionally* the same. But for the purposes of our thought experiment we will assume that Deep Blue-K carries out these activities in the way that a super-computer-cum-robot could do them. That is, at the level of micro-causal activity, what goes on in Deep Blue-K is very different from what would have gone on in Kasparov in the same circumstances. The reason is that silicon circuitry activity is different from neuron activity. At that level of microstructure, the activities of Deep Blue-K and Kasparov are different, even if at a higher level of description their activities are functionally the same. Can they, then, be engaged in exactly similar activities? *Macro-functionally, yes; micro-causally, no.*

A point of clarification. Instead of stipulating, as I am doing, that Deep Blue-K carries out Kasparov's activities in the way that a super-computer-cum-robot could do them, one can imagine that Deep Blue-K is so constructed that it replicates not only the macro-functional activities of Kasparov, but also that it exactly replicates his micro-causal activities. In this case, the similarity between Deep Blue-K and Kasparov is, of course, even stronger. On Chalmers's view of conscious experiences, which according to him arise from fine-grained functional organization, if Deep Blue-K replicated exactly the micro-causal

---

[19] Kripke (1980: 120).

functionality of Kasparov, it would in principle be able to have a mental life just like Kasparov's mental life. Chalmers holds the following Principle of Organizational Invariance:

Given any system that has conscious experiences, then any system that has the *same fine-grained functional organization* will have *qualitatively identical experiences.* According to this principle, consciousness is an organizational invariant: a property that remains constant over all functional isomorphs of a given system. Whether the organization is realized in silicon chips, in the population of China, or in beer cans and ping pong balls does not matter. As long as the functional organization is right, conscious experience will be determined.[20]

On this view, with micro-causal identity, Deep Blue-K would have experiences that would be qualitatively exactly the same as Kasparov's experiences, not only the same in content, so it would be truly a Virtual Kasparov, although not a human being. The difference in make-up—carbon or silicon—between Kasparov and Deep Blue-K would be irrelevant to their being in qualitatively exactly the same mental states. *But this qualitative sameness, due to their micro-causal identity, would not suffice to make Deep Blue-K into a human being, for the reasons given by Kripke's argument.* It would, though, make Deep Blue-K much more similar to a human being and to Kasparov than envisaged above with mere macro-functional identity.

I do not pursue this high degree of similarity hypothesis here, and I stipulate that Deep Blue-K is different at the micro-causal level from Kasparov. This is because ultimately, I assume, micro-causal identity is not an open possibility in the case of God the Son and Jesus—which is the case I want to illuminate with the Kasparov–Deep Blue thought experiments. On the assumption that there is causation in the divine constitution of the Son, it seems plausible to assume that Jesus' physical structure cannot replicate the causal make-up of the Son. I am here assuming that divine mental life is not replicable by human mental life. I will come back to this point later.

We have so far seen that *functional sameness of activities does not guarantee sameness of kind of the agents.* The reason is that functional sameness does not come with a specified degree of coarseness/fineness level. Despite their functional sameness, Deep Blue-K and Kasparov are different in essential kind because of their constitutional (and micro-causal) differences. Kripke's argument shows that even though at some level of description the functions of two organisms (for example, reproducing, or playing chess) are the same, their internal

---

[20] Chalmers (1996: 249), my emphasis. Ping pong balls can deliver the same type of experience despite natural laws because the law connection is between functional organization and experience rather than substratum and experience.

structure, origins, and causal history might set them apart in kind, as individuals of two different species (for example, a tiger and a tiger-looking reptile, or a human and Deep Blue-K).

PROSTHETIC DEEP BLUE

How can the numerical gap between Kasparov and Deep Blue-K be bridged? In the thought experiment discussed above they remained numerically distinct, coexisting as two separate substances. Just increasing their functional similarity through different means would not undermine their numerical distinctness. To explore whether and how their numerical distinctness can be compromised, we need to look at more entangled ontological complexes than the Deep Blue-K case described above.

A more intimate ontological entanglement can be envisaged starting with the following type of case that is standard medical practice. Consider the situation where a patient has a prosthetic arm attached to her body. Here the arm becomes an organ which the patient uses to carry out tasks of her own. The micro-activities are not of the same type as when the patient could use her arm, but they serve generally the same functions. The difference with the swapping scenario of Deep Blue-K given above is that here the prosthetic arm replaces a part of the body of the patient, thereby becoming part of the patient herself.

This is a type of extension of the body of the patient, by the inclusion of the prosthetic arm alongside the material organs that enable her to carry out daily life activities. The relation of the patient to the prosthetic arm is different from her relation to a percolator, for example, because of the intimate and direct causal connection between her body and the prosthetic arm; and because of her higher degree of dependence on the prosthetic arm for her daily activities.

Returning now to our thought experiment with Deep Blue and Kasparov, let us consider a future, aging Kasparov, whom his agent does not wish to let go of. So she puts into action a scheme whereby she implants and appropriately connects a mini version of Deep Blue in Kasparov. Gradually, Kasparov's chess playing and chess teaching and training abilities—as he weakens—will be totally due to Deep Blue's abilities. Let us further imagine in this thought experiment that the aging Kasparov gradually needs additional help to cope with life, and so the shrewd agent provides all the prosthetic and other devices that Kasparov needs, coordinated by Deep Blue in Kasparov, thereby enhancing or replacing the various life-sustaining powers and activities of Kasparov's constitution.

Let us use from now on '*Deep Blue*' to refer collectively to the powerful computer implanted in Kasparov and all the prosthetic devices it coordinates in Kasparov's body. Let us use '*Kasparov/100*' to refer to Kasparov when he is around one hundred years old and progressively weakens even further. What is the metaphysics of Kasparov/100? He is constituted of the body of Kasparov, which is kept alive and active by Deep Blue. The functionality of Kasparov/100, his vital life activities and his actions, are due to Deep Blue.

When he becomes one hundred years old and more, who is he: Kasparov, Deep Blue, or neither? Has either taken over the other? Has either extended themselves into the other?

Since Deep Blue keeps Kasparov's body alive and functioning through its life-sustaining activities, Kripke's argument does not apply to Kasparov/100, because the constitution of Kasparov/100 is still a human constitution, his body, be it ailing and weakened. In other words, enough of the human internal structure remains in Kasparov/100 to be a human. But as increasingly more life-sustaining activities are passed on to Deep Blue, the body becomes an outer shell that has less and less functional role to play in the whole. It gradually becomes the 'clothing' of Kasparov/100. Ultimately, a robot will be the engine of a human cover.

I assume here, as mentioned before, that the way Deep Blue operates at the micro-causal level is different from the way Kasparov would operate at that level: their functions are the same only at a coarse level of description.[21] The reason why I make such stipulation is that, as said above, on the assumption that there is causation in the divine constitution of the Son, it seems plausible also to assume that Jesus cannot replicate the mental causal structure of the Son. If Deep Blue and Kasparov functioned in exactly the same way at the micro-level, this would not be a scenario that is relevant for the problem of the incarnation. When Jesus becomes a vehicle for the activities of the Son within human society, Jesus' activity and functionality in society do not replicate the Son's mode of operation.[22]

In what follows, I will look at three cases of different degrees of extension and examine their impact on the identity of the extended entity. We have seen that extension is a type of systematic dependence, and it comes in degrees and in a variety of types. The difference in the degree and the type of extension has

---

[21] One line of thought which I will not pursue here is the possibility of molecule-by-molecule replacement of Kasparov's body with silicon chips done in such a way that preserves the exact patterns of causal interaction during the replacement process.

[22] For the same reasons, I will not consider scenarios where Deep Blue is programmed with the personality features of Kasparov, since we are not interested in the possibility of exact replication (of the Son by Jesus), but only in functional facilitation (at the level of social activity, as it were) of the Son by Jesus.

an impact on the ontological entanglement that comes about as a result of the dependency relation. Extreme variations in the degree and the type of the dependence may even switch the roles of the *means* and the *end*, thereby switching the direction of dependency, and hence, of the extension.

1. *Kasparov/100 is Deep Blue*

Let us imagine the following case involving Kasparov/100 and Deep Blue, the enhanced mini-computer implanted in him. Suppose that at first, Kasparov is extending only his chess-playing thinking onto Deep Blue, by making Deep Blue part of his enabling process. But as the years go by, the life activities as well as the decisions and social activities and actions of Kasparov/100 are orchestrated in their design and execution by Deep Blue. There comes a point when Kasparov/100 consists of a shell of flesh and bones plus Deep Blue, where the flesh and bones are kept alive on account of the activities of Deep Blue, and Kasparov/100 acts in the social domain as coordinated by Deep Blue. Is Kasparov/100 Kasparov? Is Kasparov/100 a human being at all?

Since the body of Kasparov is retained alive, the entanglement of Kasparov and Deep Blue satisfies the minimal requirements for constituting a human being. Both the constitutional and the historical features of Kasparov, which are essential to him, are preserved.[23]

What is significant for the current investigation is that gradually, and increasingly so, the functionality of Kasparov, which at first was only enhanced by Deep Blue, begins to be shaped by the abilities of Deep Blue.

The chess-playing thinking of Kasparov, his physical vitality, his social activity and interaction, will all be shaped by what is possible to enable him to carry out through Deep Blue. Even if he satisfies the minimal requirements for being a human being, increasingly less and less of Kasparov's characteristic activities will survive in Kasparov/100. More and more, Deep Blue will show its presence in the shape that the entanglement will be taking.

This is a scenario in which (nearly) total reliance of one substance on another for its survival and its functionality *reverses the direction of extension*. We saw above that the extended substance determines the extending activity by setting the goal to be achieved through the activity, while the enabling

---

[23] Much more detail would need to be added to address the question of the preservation of the personal identity of Kasparov, but as I said earlier on, I shall not explore the question of personal identity as it is not relevant to my interests in this paper; the distinction between nature and personal identity does not apply to the Son. Although the Trinity involves three persons, all of whom have the nature of God, what makes each into a different person is not their personal identity, but the internal interrelations.

substance determines the means for the implementation of the activity. But when the reliance of the extended substance on the enabler is considerable, or even nearly total, the nature of the activities and even to some degree the goal achieved by the activities are shaped and determined more by the enabler's capacities than by the extended substance's goals for this activity. *Extreme dependence of one substance on enablers endows the enablers with the power to shape the nature and goal of the activity that extends the substance.*

Hence, where the reliance on the enabler is nearly total, the effect of the enabler's abilities on the nature of the enabled extended substance is significant. The means eventually determine the goal and the nature of the activities. On this scenario, Kasparov/100 becomes increasingly a robotic organism, undermining not only Kasparov's personal identity but even his status as a human being.

2. *Kasparov/100 is neither Kasparov nor Deep Blue*

On the second scenario I propose to consider, Kasparov/100 does rely on Deep Blue, but the degree of reliance is more moderate than in the previous case. Kasparov's body is better preserved, allowing Kasparov/100 to determine more of the activities to be carried out by Deep Blue. It is still a human frame powered by a robot, but here it gives rise to a new compound with a *sui generis* constitution. On this view, Kasparov/100 is *neither* Kasparov nor Deep Blue, but a compound created by the combination of the two. Their roles are not symmetrical. The goal of the activities is set by the needs of Kasparov/100; but in this case, as opposed to the previous scenario, the nature of many activities remains what it has been, while for other activities, their nature is ultimately determined by the enabler—i.e., by what it is possible for Deep Blue to achieve. The result is an amalgam of Kasparov/Deep Blue activity, of *human/robotic* activity and nature.[24]

3. *Kasparov/100 is Kasparov*

On the third and last scenario, let us assume that medicine's developments during the Kasparov/100 period are such that they manage to keep Deep

---

[24] Their ontological entanglement, in more Aristotelian terms, involves the final cause being set by the needs of Kasparov/100's frame and of his social persona, the formal cause being determined by either Kasparov's body or Deep Blue, and the efficient cause being supplied mainly by Deep Blue. Together they make up a compound that is constitutionally different from Kasparov and teleologically different from Deep Blue, while formally being a combination of both.

Blue's role to the original, only partially enabling one. Here the goal of the activities of Kasparov/100 is set by Kasparov/100, but also, due to the stronger condition of his constitution, the nature of the activities is determined by Kasparov/100 as well. Deep Blue provides only the means for the pursuit of these activities. In such a scenario, there would be little reason to think that Kasparov/100 is any less a human being than Kasparov. Kasparov/100 would be like a person incapacitated by illness in the hospital, and being assisted by medical instruments to survive. In such a case there would be no reason to question the humanity of their nature. Similarly here, Kasparov/100 is fully a human being.

The three cases above also suggest what follows from repeated extensions of an organism into the environment. When nearly the totality of the mental activities of Kasparov are carried out by Deep Blue, it becomes a case of replacement rather than enabling. In replacement, if the causal network is exactly similar to the original one, then the phenomenal content of the experiences is preserved[25] but not the constitution of the organism.[26] Hence, even in the best cases of exact functional similarity, the organism does not survive, although its mental life does (for example, the person survives but not the human being). This presents a natural limit to the applicability of Clark and Chalmers Parity Principle. Although the enabling conditions are of the same type as the condition they enable (or replace), the original organism is lost.

Who is Kasparov/100? What is Kasparov/100? How many is/are Kasparov/100?

Each of the three cases considered above suggests a different set of answers to these questions. On the first scenario, for all intents and purposes, Kasparov/100 is Deep Blue. He is a single individual, a robotic organism. On the third scenario, Kasparov/100 is equally clearly a single individual, a human being. On the second scenario—neither Deep Blue nor Kasparov—the situation is more complex. The entanglement of Kasparov/100 and Deep Blue may be thought of as a single individual, a new kind, something in between a human and a robot. Alternatively, their compound might be thought of as two distinct but interdependent individuals, a human and a robot. Whether we count them as one or two will depend on the context within which we ask how

---

[25] See Chalmers's Principle of Organizational Invariance above, p. 215.
[26] See Kripke's argument above, pp. 213–14.

many they are, and the degree of detail in the description of their interaction. The closer we get, the more we distinguish the two, while the more remote our viewpoint, the more they seem to be one whole. In a different context, Chalmers notes what would apply in our case too:

> As Clark suggests... we can flip back and forth between both ways of looking at things. We have a sort of Necker Cube effect, with mental states counting as extended or not depending on our perspective and our purposes.[27]

What we see, therefore, from our thought experiments is that *variations in the dependency relation* between the two substances, the extended one and the enabling one, *make an important difference to the ontology of their entanglement*. They make an important difference *to the identity and number of the entities in the entanglement*. In view of the fact that the differences between the three cases are gradual differences of degree, considering the connection, dependency, discontinuity, etc. in the entanglement gives rise to powerful considerations that support *alternative viewpoints on the identity and number of entities within it*.

It is far from clear that it would be possible in an actual situation to distinguish between these three scenarios, and decide which one of the three we are confronted with, if we were to meet Kasparov/100 with a mini Deep Blue implanted in him. The reason is that which scenario holds depends on how much the nature of how many activities in the entanglement is changed by the enabler to such a degree that it disqualifies them, individually or collectively, as human activities. Changing the nature of a large proportion of the activities to a large enough degree can have an effect on the resulting nature or natures in the entanglement, and hence on the identity and number of the substances involved in it.

I conclude that the arguments and considerations we have at our disposal in determining the identity of things around us are not designed to handle ontological entanglements of the kind we encountered in the case of Kasparov/100. We are divided as to who, what, and how many it is. But if this is how things are, we should recognize them to be such, and not expect a clear, firm answer to the ontological description of the entanglement. We are divided about the entanglement's identity and number, and will remain so for as long as we do not have a theory of the ontology of entanglements. The resolution of the puzzle requires *innovation* on the sortals and on the identity criteria we employ, rather than careful application of the existing ones.

---

[27] Foreword to Clark (2008: xiii).

INCARNATION UNDERSTOOD THROUGH THE KASPAROV-DEEP BLUE MODEL

I have assumed for the present purposes that God the Son is essentially a spiritual, that is, non-physical being. On this basis, it follows that the Son cannot *come to be* a material being, but has to come to be *in* a material being. I take this to be the problem of the 'Incarnation'. Substantial constitution, in the Aristotelian tradition that extends onto David Lewis and David Armstrong and that I endorse in this essay, treats the type of substratum of a substance as essential to the substantial unity. Thus a human being is essentially constituted of flesh and bones. And if God the Son is non-physical, then he cannot come to be constituted of something physical. The Son cannot come to be constituted of matter any more than what is essentially made of flesh and blood can come to be constituted of cables and electronic chips. This means that the body of Jesus cannot come to *constitute* God the Son. This is not a metaphysically possible relation between Jesus and God. Incarnation cannot be understood as God the Son being constituted of the matter of Jesus.

What I propose in this essay is that it might be fruitful to think of the incarnation of the Son in Jesus in terms of extension, instead of constitution. Extension requires only the very weak functionalism captured by the Clark and Chalmers Parity Principle. Namely, extension requires only functional equivalence between the activity performed by the extended entity and the activity of the enabler it extends onto, even if there are different implementations of the activities, for example, thinking about a chess-game move or being directed by Deep Blue as to how to move the mechanical pawn. Depending on Deep Blue for the chess-game move does not change the nature of Kasparov into that of a robot, which would be his demise; rather, it enables Kasparov and thereby extends him. Although Kasparov, *qua* human, cannot be constituted of chips and electronic cables, his incorporation of Deep Blue's activity (which extends Kasparov) does implement Kasparov's 'chess playing' in electronic circuitry. A tension results between Kasparov's nature and the nature of his extension, which is what I explored in the three cases I examined above. We saw in the entanglement cases above that extension can bring about, in extreme cases of dependence, *modification* of the *nature*, of the *number*, and of the *identity* of the entities involved.

In the following sections I will propose a way of understanding how God the Son and Jesus are ontologically related using the metaphysics of the entanglement of Kasparov/100 and Deep Blue as a model.

It is difficult to engage in details about the nature of the *interdependence* between God the Son and Jesus, since the phenomenon of incarnation and the nature of God are significantly underdescribed. The general directive in my investigation is that the Son has certain soteriological goals to fulfil with regard to humanity, which require him to engage with the human social reality. The type of involvement of God in the human social reality is speculative, due to the underdescribed status of the incarnation phenomenon and of God's nature. But the purpose of the forthcoming sections is to give a framework within which various speculative ways of understanding the incarnation phenomenon could be examined and compared.

1. The incarnate Son is Jesus

On one conception of their relation, God the Son is extensively empowered by Jesus within the human social reality. Substantial empowerment could occur only if Jesus' constitution could ground the extension of a great variety of God the Son's mental activities. There are three metaphysical considerations in relation to this degree and variety of extension. The first is whether mental activities other than cognitive ones (e.g. emotional states) can be extended. The second is whether divine mental states can be constituted of (mental or material) human states. The third, and very speculative, is whether Jesus can enable the Son to have types of experience that the Son is not capable of having on his own, e.g. physical pain.

The first consideration regards the possibility of extension of non-cognitive experiences. This is a controversial issue and currently very much in the forefront of research in the area of the philosophy of mind. As I said above, the original Clark and Chalmers hypothesis concerns cognitive processes; hence it has been called the Extended Cognition hypothesis. But Chalmers himself and others find it natural to apply the Extended Cognition hypothesis to a wider range of mental activities and states:

It is natural to ask whether the extended mind thesis might itself be extended. What about extended desires, extended reasoning, extended perception, and extended emotions? I think that there is something to be said for each of these.[28]

On the second consideration, whether divine mental states can be constituted of human mental or physical states, according to Chalmers's Principle of Organizational Invariance quoted above it is possible to implement a mental state on a variety of grounds, and even replicate its phenomenal aspects so long

---

[28] Foreword to Clark (2008: xiv). Elsewhere, Chalmers mentions 'the extension of our bodies, the extension of our senses, and crucially, the use of language as a tool to extend our thought' (Foreword to Clark (2008: ix)).

as the functional organization is the same, not just at the macro-, but also at the micro-levels. But the phenomenal aspects of divine consciousness are far too speculative a topic to consider. I know of no reason blocking our speculation that God's mental states could be at least in part constituted of Jesus' mental or physical states, just as Otto's beliefs were partially constituted of the notebook's, and Kasparov's of Deep Blue's, unless realizability is not a metaphysical option for God's states (as it is not for Aristotle's God, who is non-composite).

The third issue is whether Jesus can extend the range of experience of the Son. Can Jesus empower the Son to experience mental states that the Son is not on his own capable of experiencing, such as physical pain? This too is very speculative, and I mention it only because it touches on questions that may become relevant to extension in the philosophy of mind. There is an experiment which has taken place in cognitive science which bears relevance to this question. A blind patient is fitted with TVSS as follows. A TV camera (mounted on spectacle frames) sends signals through electronic circuitry to an array of small vibrators which is strapped against the subject's skin. The pattern of tactile stimulation corresponds roughly to a greatly enlarged visual image.[29] In these experiments, blind subjects extend their perception through television cameras which generate *tactile* sensations that give rise to semi-*visual* experiences. There is, of course, a difference between this case and the pain case we are envisaging, since the subjects in this experiment had been *capable* of *sight* before becoming blind. It would be reasonable to assume that God the Son in the non-incarnate state is not capable of physical pain because (as per assumption) he is an essentially non-physical being. Nevertheless, this experiment shows a limited way in which one can enrich the types of experience by extension.

It is conceivable, I submit, that Jesus could enable God the Son to feel physical pain if two conditions were to be met. First God the Son would need access to a brain structure that has the micro-causal structure of pain. And this, Jesus can provide. But secondly, this brain structure would need to be

---

[29] 'In a well-known series of studies by Bach-y-Rita (1972, 1984, 1996; Sampaio et al. 2001), blind patients are outfitted with a tactilevision substitution system (TVSS). Vibrators or electrodes on the back, thigh, or tongue receive inputs from a camera fitted on the subject's head or shoulder. Visual input to the camera produces tactile stimulation of the skin, which in turn gives rise to activity in somatosensory cortex, and to tactile experience. After a period of adaptation (as short as a few minutes), subjects report perceptual experiences that are distinctively non-tactile and quasi-visual. For example, objects are reported to be perceived as arrayed at a distance from the body in space and as standing in perceptible spatial relations such as "in front of" or "partially blocking the view of," etc. However, Bach-y-Rita emphasizes that the transition to quasi-visual perception depends on the subject's exercising active control of the camera (1984, 149). If the camera is stationary, or if someone else controls it while the subject passively receives tactile inputs from the camera, subjects report only tactile sensation' (Hurley and Noë 2003: 142).

'hooked up' to God the Son in a micro-causally identical way in which the pain parts of Jesus' brain are hooked up to his own brain. At this point we can proceed no further because we do not have any theory about the causal structure of God the Son's mind and what it would mean to talk about hooking up to a non-physical substance. But we can imagine this case applied to Kasparov and Deep Blue, with Deep Blue providing a chip with the micro-causal pain structure and connecting it appropriately to Kasparov, thereby enabling Kasparov to feel pain sensations.

As is clear, the limits of a significant empowerment of God the Son by Jesus, through a variety of extensions of the Son's mental states onto Jesus, are difficult even to contemplate. The reason is that they concern very speculative areas of what we can say about the incarnation, and also, they raise questions that have only just begun to be investigated in the philosophy of mind in relation to the extension of the mind. We shall therefore leave this scenario underdescribed, and retain only that it is exploring the greatest degree of extension of the Son onto Jesus that metaphysical constraints would allow. Our interest in this scenario is that it has the potential of *maximally humanizing* the Son's mental life by possibly affecting the nature and range of experiences of the Son through extensive reliance on Jesus.[30]

2. The incarnate Son is neither Jesus nor God

On a second possible conception, there is a less intimate entanglement between God the Son and Jesus than described above. As a consequence, the extension of God the Son's mental activities onto Jesus does affect the nature of the activities, but not to the degree envisaged in the previous scenario. For instance, the Son's decisions are carried out through the human actions of Jesus, and are thus subject to human success and failure. This is a compromise on the activities of the Son, rendering them vulnerable in a human way. The result is that Christ is an entanglement that has a life characterized by both divine and human activities, or activities that are an 'amalgam' of the two.

---

[30] One scenario I will not discuss is that God the Son experiences Jesus' pain. The extended mind model does not explain such a change of subjects of a mental state. It would be possible to entertain such a scenario in connection with the three cases discussed here, but the underdetermination of the incarnation phenomenon makes such speculation unfruitful.

3. The incarnate Son is God

The third conception of the incarnation entanglement I want to suggest is one where God the Son's extension onto Jesus is limited. Jesus provides, strictly, means towards the fulfilment of certain goals of the Son. God the Son is assisted in some respects by Jesus in engaging with human reality, but the reliance on Jesus is very restricted, instrumental for the activities of God the Son. Here, the life of Jesus is external and parallel to the life of God the Son. Their entanglement is minimal, and hence the distinctness of the two individuals uncompromised.

CONCLUSIONS

The suggestion put forward in this essay is to understand incarnation as an ontological entanglement brought about by the extension of one substance's activities onto another substance's activities. What I have tried to show above is that the extension, while systematic, can be to different degrees and in a variety of ways. The significance of the variation in degree and manner of extension is that the enabling substance can have varying effects on the extended substance. Minimally, it can simply assist it in carrying out certain tasks by making a partial contribution to the means for the realization of its activities. But maximally, it can contribute so extensively to the execution of the tasks that it can change the nature of the *activities*, although their function remains the same. If this happens to a maximal extent with respect to the majority of the activities of the extended substance, it can affect the *nature of the substance itself*. As a consequence, *extension can have an effect on the identity and distinctness of the substances involved in it, so that varying degrees, extent, and varieties of extension may result in different ways in which one can individuate and count entities in the entanglement*, whether this is Kasparov/100 or Christ.

Each of the three entanglement cases described above gives us a way of viewing the incarnation of the Son in Jesus. Yet, for each of the three cases, there are slippery slopes of ontological dependence which we encounter in attempting to individuate the entangled substances and evaluate their distinctness. The problem is that the incarnation entanglements fall in between clear-cut models of substancehood, because of the dependencies they involve between the entangled entities, and further because of the continuities or discontinuities between the entangled entities and what is external to the entanglement. Being in the borderlines, and sliding along the slopes, allows us to evaluate the weightiness of various aspects of the ontology of the entanglements in *different* ways, and thereby follow different criteria of individuation in each case. The metaphysical slopes also generate epistemological slopes.

Ultimately what is needed in order to address questions of number in ontological entanglements is a theory of identity and individuation that explains how different types of dependency undermine or threaten the numerical distinctness of things. Such a theory would provide a *codification of ontological dependence* that would relate types of dependence to types of distinctness of things. But, of course, slippery slopes are known for defying codification.

None of the models described in each of the cases above delivers *the* metaphysics of the incarnation entanglement, because there is no such unique metaphysics. But what the entanglements give us is a way of understanding how *use* can affect the nature of the *user*. Instead of seeking to fit incarnation into the mould of constitution, which faces metaphysical difficulties, I sought to fit incarnation into the mould of user-used, or means-end, which the Extended Mind theory explores. But what we discovered along the way was that the relation is *reversible*: if the extension is radical, the means can determine the end—the vehicle can determine the extended. And that is sufficient to deliver an intelligible conception of incarnation, in which:

The incarnate nature is affected by the means which realize the extension of all its activities.

What is of further interest is that the incarnation problems are not restricted to the divine domain, but are vividly present in the human–computer entanglements as well, as they would also be in any number of scenarios of extensions.

12

Multiple incarnations and distributed persons

Robin Le Poidevin

THE SCANDAL OF PARTICULARITY

The idea of incarnate deity is not peculiar to Christianity. Greek mythology has many instances of gods coming down to Earth in human form, often with dubious intentions. It is also a recognized phenomenon in that branch of Hinduism according to which the god Vishnu is supposed to have had many incarnations, not all of them human. What is peculiar to Christianity is the *uniqueness* of incarnation, the fact that it is supposed to have occurred just once (something which is often signalled by capitalizing the first letter: the Incarnation). It is this uniqueness within the doctrine of incarnation that provokes an objection often described as the 'scandal of particularity'. The particularity is that in becoming incarnate God intervened in human history at a particular time and place in a way that was unique to that time and place, never having happened before and never to be repeated. The 'scandal' is attached to what this particularity appears to entail, namely that a certain group of people were favoured above others: the chosen people, the children of Israel.[1]

The scandal of particularity provides a moral objection to the incarnation, as the orthodox conceive of it. If the purpose of the incarnation was to save mankind by entering into a closer relationship with humanity than was

---

[1] It could also be said (though this is not a specifically incarnational issue) that Jesus himself showed an unwarranted particularity, first in choosing Jewish disciples to broadcast his message, and second in apparently addressing himself specifically to the Jews, not the Gentiles. See, for instance, Matthew 10: 5–6: 'These twelve Jesus sent forth, and commanded them, saying, "Go not into the way of the Gentiles, and into any city of the Samaritans enter ye not; but go rather to the lost sheep of the house of Israel."' This is an embarrassment to those who want to portray him as a universal saviour.

hitherto possible, then in choosing to become incarnate only once God would have failed to enter into a close relationship with the whole human race, doing so instead only with one particular historical group. Here is one way of putting the point: the saving power of the incarnation for some population is in proportion to the directness of the incarnate God's encounter with that population. But God would have no reason to exercise his saving power in an unequal way, or rather, any inequality in the exercise of that power would have itself to be determined by some moral principle, not by entirely arbitrary considerations of time and place. On the assumption that no moral principle would select first-century Israel (or indeed any other time and place) as the most fitting context for the saving power of the incarnation to be felt in its full force, bringing about an incarnational event then and there but at no other time and place would be morally indefensible. If we balk at the idea of God's being *obliged* to visit all ages with the saving grace of incarnation, we could instead express the key idea in terms of the natural expression of God's love, which would not focus itself in the way that a unique incarnation apparently implies, but would rather embrace all mankind equally.

Why, then, resist the idea of multiple incarnations? Perhaps God did indeed become incarnate on more than one occasion. But to concede the possibility of more than one incarnation may be to invite a Trojan Horse through the gates. If more than one incarnation, why not many? And if many, why should everyone who has ever existed, or exists or will exist, not be God incarnate?[2] But then if *everyone* is God incarnate, then it seems that the entire human race (and perhaps not just the human race) is just one person, namely God. And that would mean, surely, that God would not have a human creation to take care of. There might, perhaps, still be a plurality of beings of some sort, but these could hardly count as God's *creation*, except that he would have created the human bodies whose flesh he then took on. So if multiple incarnations are possible, there must only be a limited number of incarnations—but then any particular number would be entirely arbitrary.

Responses to the moral objection to uniqueness fall into three main categories.[3] One kind of response is to find an opposing moral argument in *favour* of uniqueness. The second concedes the moral case against a unique incarnation and opts for a non-incarnational christology, in which the language of incarnation, interpreted as a metaphor for God's relationship with us, is

---

[2] See, e.g., Wiles (1979: 7–8), discussed under 'Other objections', below.
[3] Within, that is, a recognizably Christian, or at least religious framework. The atheist might point to the scandal of particularity as a reason to reject that particular religion.

retained, and indeed continues to occupy a central place, but is no longer taken to express a metaphysical doctrine.[4] A third kind also concedes the moral case, but finds other, non-moral, reasons for ruling out multiple incarnations. It is that third strategy that will concern us, and in particular Brian Hebblethwaite's suggestion that multiple incarnations would be logically impossible. Hebblethwaite argues that since the incarnation of God requires *numerical identity* between God (more precisely, in Christian theology, the second person of the Trinity) and the being who is God's incarnation on Earth, and since such identity with God cannot be multiply instantiated, it follows that there can at most be one incarnation. After offering a detailed reconstruction of this line of thought, I argue that we can make metaphysical sense of multiple incarnations of a single deity by exploiting the notion of distributed persons.

HEBBLETHWAITE'S OBJECTION TO MULTIPLE INCARNATIONS

Brian Hebblethwaite concedes that if multiple incarnations were a possibility, then there would indeed be a moral objection against uniqueness, but argues that multiple incarnations are logically, or metaphysically, impossible. Here is his initial presentation of the argument:

The suggestion that Jesus might have been one of many incarnations of God in human history betrays a complete failure to appreciate what the doctrine of the incarnation, in classical Christian faith, has been held to state. If God himself, in one of the modes of his being, has come into our world in person, to make himself personally known and to make himself vulnerable to the world's evil, in order to win our love and bind us to himself, we cannot suppose that he might have done so more than once. For only one man can actually be God to us, if God himself is one. We are to posit relation in God, but not a split personality. Only one actual human person can be the vehicle and expression of the one God on earth.[5]

The logical point is made more explicit in a later piece:

---

[4] For attempts to articulate a non-incarnational christology, see the essays in Hick (1977). In his essay for the volume, Wiles compares belief in a metaphysical incarnation as standing to contemporary Christianity rather as beliefs in the virgin birth and transubstantiation do: that is, as something once thought essential to being a Christian, but now seen in a different light (1977: 2–3).

[5] Hebblethwaite (1987: 50).

If Jesus was the same person as God the Son, so would other incarnations be. They would all have to be the same person. That makes no sense, least of all if they exist simultaneously...[6]

There is more than one objection here, but the logical argument appears to be this. Assume for *reductio* that both Jesus and Jeff are incarnations of the Son.

(1) If the Son is incarnate in x then the Son = x.
(2) Identity is both symmetric and transitive, so that $((x = y) \& (x = z)) \rightarrow (y = z)$.
(3) If x and y are different incarnations, then $x \neq y$.
(4) If the Son is incarnate in both Jesus and Jeff, then Jesus = Jeff (From (1) and (2)).
(5) But since Jesus and Jeff are different incarnations, then Jesus $\neq$ Jeff (From (3)).
(6) Therefore at most only one of Jesus and Jeff is the Son incarnate (From (4) and (5)).

Generalizing, there can at most be one incarnation. So the moral problem raised by a unique incarnation may turn out to have a logico-metaphysical solution.

Let us take a look at the three premises of the argument. (1) is implied by the traditional doctrine of the incarnation: incarnation is identity (though note that this would be false on one understanding of the composite model: see below). (2), I take it, is non-negotiable. So the focus should be on (3). Do we have to accept that different incarnations would be different individuals? Consider first *simultaneous* incarnations. There is undoubtedly a strong intuition that simultaneous incarnations are impossible, and it is not difficult to discover principles behind this intuition. Incarnations are persons, and one person first cannot be in two places at once, and second should at any one time exhibit unity of consciousness. Call these 'the impossibility of multiple location principle' and 'the unity of consciousness principle' respectively. The first of these is a restriction that applies to at least some sortals, but perhaps not to all. We might, for example, suppose that universals can be multiply located: that they are wholly in each of their instances.[7] But it is entirely plausible that persons are no exceptions to the rule. The unity of consciousness principle need not imply transparency (that

---

[6] Hebblethwaite (2001: 327).
[7] As Joseph Jedwab has pointed out to me, in the orthodox Catholic view of the Eucharist, Christ's body is wholly present in all pieces of the communion bread.

one is at any time conscious of every mental state one is in at that time), but only that, if x and y are two simultaneous conscious states of a single mind, then there is a state which is the consciousness of both x and y. But individuals constituting putatively multiple yet simultaneous incarnations of a single being would fail to satisfy both of these principles, and indeed it is this very failure to satisfy those principles that leads to our talking of multiple incarnations: they occupy different places, and there is no state which is the consciousness of the conscious states of both individuals. They are, then, different persons.

Since these two principles concern only simultaneous states of affairs, they do not touch the possibility of successive incarnations. What would justify (3) in the case where x and y are successive would be a failure of the usual criteria of identity—for example (since we are dealing here with persons) the criterion of psychological continuity. But even if x and y were not psychologically continuous with each other, they could be psychologically continuous with God the Son, and this would be sufficient, given the logical properties of identity, to guarantee their identity with each other.

Now, if successive incarnations are logically possible but simultaneous ones not, this gives us a non-arbitrary way of limiting the number of incarnations: there is precisely one *at* any time, but *over* time as many as are needed for the rest of human history. However, it might be thought that the possibility of successive incarnations implies the possibility of simultaneous ones. And since simultaneous ones are impossible, so are successive ones. How might the possibility of successive incarnations imply the possibility of simultaneous ones? The case for treating successive incarnations of the Son as identical would rest on their satisfying some non-circular criterion of identity. If, for example, they were both psychologically continuous with the Son, though not necessarily with each other, both could be identified with the Son. From which it would follow, given the logical properties of identity, that they were identical with each other. (Here we are treating psychological continuity as sufficient, but not necessary, for identity.) But this same criterion could be satisfied by simultaneous incarnations.

It might be objected that what criteria we use to decide questions of identity is a purely epistemological matter. Metaphysically speaking, identity is primitive, and is necessarily one-to-one. This may permit successive incarnations, but it clearly rules out simultaneous incarnations. To which the reply is that, as Parfit taught us, what matters in identity is precisely the kinds of psychological connection on which our judgements of identity are made.[8]

---

[8] Parfit (1984: chs 12 and 13).

It is what links our past, present, and future selves. Without it, it is not clear why we should *care* about identity. A primitive identity that could obtain in the absence of any other connection would make no difference to anything. And the same applies to the incarnation: if the identity of Christ and the Son had no implications of any other kind, moral or psychological, it would not matter.

But perhaps there is a way of strengthening the psychological continuity criterion to prevent multiple simultaneous incarnations without having to appeal to primitive identity? The general issue here is familiar: it is the reduplication problem posed by Bernard Williams, here presented in a theological context. Williams's argument is that the psychological continuity criterion of identity permits fission. Continuity can be branching, identity not, therefore continuity $\neq$ identity.[9] A common reply by defenders of continuity is to say that identity is *non-branching* continuity: $x = y$ if and only if y is continuous with x *and* there is no z existing simultaneously with y that is also continuous with x. The objection to this is that identity should be an *intrinsic* matter: that is, whether x and y are identical is something determined entirely by the state of x and y, and not on the state or existence of any other individual. Whatever intuitive force this point has is strengthened when applied to the incarnation. How can whether Jesus is the Son depend on the existence or non-existence of someone else?

So, assuming that any informative and plausible criterion of personal identity will not guarantee that identity is necessarily one-to-one, letting in successive incarnations will open the door to simultaneous ones.

That concludes my reconstruction of Hebblethwaite's logical objection to multiple incarnations. I hasten to emphasize that a number of the moves made here are neither explicit nor implicit in Hebblethwaite's own somewhat brief presentations of the objection, but I submit that something like the line of thought I have suggested—and it would require more development—is required to explain and defend that objection.[10] How might it be resisted? We will look at three strategies, which exploit, respectively, the thesis of relative identity, the composite model of the incarnation, and the idea of distributed persons. The first two, which have been the subject of detailed treatments elsewhere, will only receive the briefest of glances. I shall have most to say about the third of these.

---

[9] Williams (1956–7).
[10] Oliver Crisp, however, has offered a rather different reconstruction of Hebblethwaite's argument, in which a key assumption is that a divine person can have at most one divine nature (2008: 219–22).

RELATIVE IDENTITY

At one point Hebblethwaite is prepared to contemplate relative identity as a solution to incarnational paradox:

> The claim that Jesus of Nazareth is the same person as God the Son raises grave problems of identity, especially if, as Morris does, one espouses a strict Leibnizian theory of identity. If, however, one espouses, with P. T. Geach, a theory of relative identity, things get easier.[11]

According to Geach, unqualified identity assertions are incomplete. 'x is identical to y' is elliptical for 'x is the same F as y', and the substitution of a particular sortal for F completes the expression.[12] Thus identity is relative to a sortal. It is compatible with this thesis that if there is a sortal F such that x is the same F as y, then for any sortal G, x is the same G as y. But what motivates the relative identity thesis, what gives it its point, is the existence of cases where it is apparently appropriate to say that, although x and y are both Fs and Gs and x is the same F as y, x is not the same G as y. Take a bronze statue, a, that is melted down and fashioned into a different statue, b. Then a is the *same lump of bronze* as b but not the *same statue* as b. Believers in absolute identity have an answer to this kind of case, that the appearance of relative identity is due to the linguistic behaviour of certain phase sortals (sortals that are applicable at particular stages of a thing's existence), not indicative of some logical or metaphysical aspect of identity itself. But there are other cases where relative identity comes into its own, so to speak. It was put by Geach to theological use in expounding the doctrine of the Trinity: the Son is the *same God* as the Father, but not the *same person*.[13] This now looks like a substantial, metaphysical thesis.

However, Hebblethwaite may be ill-advised to flirt with the thesis of relative identity, as that thesis threatens to defuse the reconstruction of his objection to multiple incarnations. For the identity in each premise would need to be relativized to a sortal, and it could be argued that (1) and (3) should be relativized to different sortals, making the argument fallacious. (1), for instance, might become:

(1') If the Son is incarnate in x, then the Son is the *same person* as x.

(3), in contrast, could become:

(3') If x and y are different (human) incarnations, then x is not the *same human being* as y.

---

[11] Hebblethwaite (2001: 328).
[12] Geach (1967–8: 3).
[13] Geach and Anscombe (1968: 86–8, 118–20).

The assumption that Jesus and Jeff are both incarnations of the Son would then no longer lead to the contradiction that Jesus both was and was not the same person as Jeff. (1') and (3') lead instead to the non-contradictory, though perhaps not entirely palatable, conclusion that Jesus and Jeff are the same person, but different human beings.

Of course, relative identity would be a thesis too far for many incarnational theorists. I will not pursue the problems it raises here, but will just make the *ad hominem* remark, before moving on, that Hebblethwaite can only damage his own case against multiple incarnations by appealing to it to solve the conundrum of how two incompatible natures can reside in the one person of Jesus.[14]

THE COMPOSITE ACCOUNT

Brian Leftow (2002) and Eleonore Stump (2002) have defended a view of the incarnation in which a single composite being has a divine part and a human part (which itself consists of two further parts, a human soul and a human body). This neatly solves the problem of the two natures of Christ, since each nature will reside in a different part of the composite whole, which on the face of it should be no more contradictory than an apple having red skin but white flesh.

Depending on whether we identify the Son with the composite, or with only a part of the composite, this offers another way out of the argument against multiple incarnations. Take the first premise:

(1) If the Son is incarnate in x then the Son = x.

On the composite account, or rather one version of it, the Son becomes incarnate by becoming part of a composite whole whose other parts include a human body and a human soul. We could say that the Son is incarnate 'in' the body, by virtue of the Son and the body being parts of a whole, or we could say that Son becomes incarnate 'in' the composite, by virtue of being a part of that composite. Both of those seem acceptable ways of construing the phrase 'incarnate in'. But neither of them implies that the Son is identical to what he becomes incarnate in: he need be neither the human body, nor the composite which contains the body as a part. The first premise, then, is false on this

---

[14] Hebblethwaite does see a possible connection between relative identity and multiple incarnations, but denies that accepting the former implies accepting the latter, since multiple incarnations involve different individuals of the same species (2001: 328). This does not, it seems to me, dispose of the point being made here.

view. It is a moot point whether we identify Jesus with the composite, or with the divine part or the human part of the composite, but whatever we say (provided we are consistent) we are not obliged to say *both* that Jesus is identical with Jeff *and* that Jesus is not identical with Jeff, by virtue of the fact that both Jesus and Jeff are God incarnate. The composite account of multiple incarnations will posit two or more composites that share a divine part. They are *different* incarnations in that they are different composites. They are incarnations of the *same* God in that they share a divine part.

Unlike the thesis of relative identity, the composite model does not make any metaphysically revisionary claim. But it does make it harder to stay within the bounds of theological orthodoxy. Here are the different things we might say about the relation between the Son, Jesus, and the composite of divine and human parts: (2) Jesus is identical to the composite, and the Son is the divine part of that composite. But then Jesus, contrary to the orthodox view of the incarnation, is not identical to the Son. (2) Jesus is the human part of the composite and the Son is the divine part. But then again Jesus is not the Son. (3) Jesus is the Son, and both are identical to the composite. But then the Son existed before the composite did, and since there is nothing intrinsically to distinguish between the pre-incarnate Son and the divine part of the composite, then assuming that identity between *x* and *y* is intrinsic, not depending on the existence of any other object, it follows that the Son is identical *both* to the composite and to the divine part of that composite which, of course, is incoherent. (4) Jesus is the Son, and both are the divine part of the composite. But then either the composite is a person, and Jesus and the Son are merely parts of a person (unlike us, who are persons in our own right), or the Son and Jesus are persons but (again, unlike us) are only embodied by virtue of being part of something that is not a person.[15]

DISTRIBUTED PERSONS

Let us now turn to the third strategy. Recall the principles supporting the intuition that simultaneous incarnations of a single divine person are impossible:

---

[15] It could be said that this is our own position. On the Cartesian view, I am essentially a soul, and contingently embodied by virtue of being part of a composite of soul and body. But the relationship between soul and body, as Descartes recognizes, is a peculiarly intimate one—hence his remark that I am not lodged in my body like a pilot in his ship. My soul has a single perspective on the world which is that of my body. It is not at all clear that this could be said of the divine part of the incarnational composite.

The impossibility of multiple location: a person cannot be in two or more places at once.
The unity of consciousness: a person exhibits unity of consciousness at any one time.

We could simply deny that these principles apply to divine persons, as opposed to human persons. But this is not only too quick, it also looks less satisfactory in the context of the incarnation, for whatever we might want to say about disembodied deities, incarnate deities cannot violate too many principles governing ordinary human beings without undermining the belief that they are genuinely incarnate (as opposed to merely controlling a human body from a distance). But perhaps we can accept these two principles, even as applied to incarnate divine persons, and still allow for multiple simultaneous incarnations. The rather unusual idea I want to introduce now is that of a distributed person. A *distributed person* (DP) is a person whose body occupies two or more spatially separated regions such that there is no spatial pathway linking them which is wholly within the spatial boundaries of that body. On the usual assumption that a person is wherever his or her body is, the person him or herself occupies two or more discontinuous regions. Clearly, we are not (typically!) distributed persons in this sense. Take any two spatial regions which at least overlap with your body. One region might contain your left hand and another region your right foot. There will not fail to be a pathway between these that remains within the boundaries of your body. But this may be a purely contingent feature of yours: things might have been otherwise.

How could a single person be distributed? There are two ways in which this might be realized:

Parts model: different parts of the DP occupy the different regions.[16]
No-parts model: the DP *as a whole* occupies the different regions—that is, the DP is wholly located at those regions.

A case to which the Parts model might apply is that of a split brain where there is a greater-than-usual spatial separation between the hemispheres (perhaps involving transplantation). Here, especially if the separation were temporary, we would prefer to talk of a single person having a peculiarly dissociated mental life, rather than of two persons. But, because of that dissociation, it would be appropriate to think of different parts of the person occupying different regions. The possibility of a distributed person along the

---

[16] It is an entirely legitimate question what sense of division permits us to talk of persons having parts. Are we, for instance, talking of spatial parts here? I am going to remain neutral on this question, since it is the No Parts model that I wish to pursue, a model which, of course, sits entirely comfortably with the observation that talk of 'parts' has no application to persons.

lines of the Parts model is also suggested by the Extended Mind hypothesis. If the mind (and hence, the person?) can be extended beyond the boundaries of the body by such artificial devices as PCs and mobile phones, what would be the grounds for disallowing gaps in the spatial region occupied by that mind?

A case for which the No-parts model might be appropriate is one in which what appear to be two persons are in complete mental communication with each other, so that their thoughts constitute a unified mental life. (Perhaps the spatial information received by the two sets of sense organs is integrated into a single coherent image, rather than being presented as mutually exclusive perspectives.) Something like this is portrayed by John Wyndham's *The Midwich Cuckoos*. So one could satisfy unity of consciousness while at the same time violating the impossibility of multiple location. And, arguably, deliverances of the first principle trump deliverances of the second.

If simultaneous incarnations constitute a distributed person, which of the two models above is the appropriate one? Intuitively, the Parts model, since we imagine simultaneous incarnations not to have a unified mental life. But then each incarnation (including, note, Jesus) would count only as part of the whole person. And that seems very strange. Was Jesus then not a person, neither a human person nor a divine one?

However, there may be a way of construing simultaneous incarnations on the No-parts model, even with the lack of mental unity between the different incarnations. This makes use of a suggestion by Barry Dainton in his treatment of fission cases.[17] A fission case is where one spatially unified individual splits into two separate individuals. This is the way the amoeba reproduces, for instance. It is not a method of reproduction characteristic of higher organisms, but it is not logically impossible that it should be. Imagine, then, a person whose body somehow splits in two in such a way that two whole bodies are generated. Has one person become two persons? Or were there always two persons there, even before the fission, only somehow occupying exactly the same space? One approach to the case that is normally ruled out from the start is the idea that the person existing pre-fission is *numerically identical* to each of the persons post-fission. For then, given the logical properties of identity, we would have to identify as one single person the two post-fission individuals. And this is supposed to be absurd, given their spatial separation and their increasingly divergent lives. But, suggests Dainton, there is a way of describing the fission case that offers to remove the appearance of absurdity.

[17] Dainton (1992).

Dainton exploits David Lewis's distinction between *external* time and *personal* time.[18] External time is just time. Personal time is the way in which time is registered by a changing object (typically, but not only, by a person). Imagine someone undergoing cryogenic suspension for a period. The normal biological processes (heart beat, breathing, hair growth, etc.) are slowed right down. One could say of such an individual that during an external time period of ten years, only one year of personal time had passed, meaning that the changes they had undergone were those that would in ordinary circumstances take one year. What is unusual about the persons who undergo fission is that they have a *disunified personal time*: their mental life divides into branches, where there is no connection between one branch and the other that allows us to locate them at a single personal time.[19]

What difference does this distinction make? The two principles to which we appeal in judging the two individuals to be different persons both quantify over times. We would naturally assume that the times in question are external times:

The impossibility of multiple location: no person can be in two places at the same *external* time.

The unity of consciousness: a single person exhibits unity of consciousness at any one *external* time.

But suppose instead we take the principles to quantify over *personal* times:

No person can be in two places at the same *personal* time.

A single person exhibits unity of consciousness at any one *personal* time.

Thus construed, the principles no longer have the consequence that post-fission individuals must be two different persons, for if we treat them as a single person with a branching personal time we will not find a moment in personal time where that person is in two places, or exhibits a disunified consciousness. And that is a significant result for our present discussion, as the post-fission individuals can be described as a distributed person. Conversely, simultaneous incarnations can be seen as the result of fission.

---

[18] Lewis (1976).

[19] It also permits us to talk of a time traveller meeting her earlier self (or even a series of earlier selves if they are permitted to travel with her!). Lewis's own description of this case, however, makes use of the notion of temporal parts or stages: 'A time traveller who talks to himself, on the telephone perhaps, looks for all the world like two different people talking to each other... What's true is that he, unlike the rest of us, has two different complete stages located at the same time in different places' (1976: 147). The two stages, although coincident in external time, have different locations in personal time.

If the notion of a distributed person is coherent—and the substitution of personal time for external time in the understanding of the two principles suggests that it is—then the motivation for premise (3) of the argument against multiple incarnations collapses.

OTHER OBJECTIONS TO MULTIPLE INCARNATIONS

Finally, we should distinguish (as do Hebblethwaite, Thomas V. Morris (1986), and Oliver Crisp (2008)) between the logical possibility of multiple incarnations and their actualization. There may be non-logical obstacles to the latter, and the first passage we quoted from Hebblethwaite above clearly indicates that his objection to multiple incarnations is not limited to his logical argument. Non-logical objections to multiple incarnations fall into three broad types:

Epistemological: even if the concept of distributed persons is a coherent one, our ordinary criteria for identity are such that any assertion that multiple incarnations had taken place would be self-defeating, since the claim of anyone to be the Son would be undermined by the plurality of other claimants.

Psychological: if different incarnations have different personalities (as we would suppose them to have, given differences of time, place, and culture), God would not speak with one voice. As Hebblethwaite puts it, multiple incarnations would involve attributing a 'split personality' to God.[20]

Theological: the incarnation was intended as a once-for-all atonement for our sins, and a reconciliation between God and humanity. If the relationship between God and man has indeed been restored by the incarnation, then it has been restored for all time, and repeated incarnations would be redundant.[21]

Hebblethwaite points out that the idea of a *relationship* between God and man is quite distinct from the idea of an identity between God and a man. God draws near to us by becoming *a* man. It makes no sense to suppose that his way of drawing close to someone is by becoming that person. Here Hebblethwaite is responding to Maurice Wiles's own statement of the moral objection to the uniqueness of the incarnation, and the encounter

---

[20] Hebblethwaite (1987: 50).
[21] See Crisp (2008: 230–5) for a detailed account of the theological case against multiple incarnations.

shows that not all statements of the moral objection to uniqueness are equally compelling. Here, first, is Wiles:

> ... if it is logically conceivable (as Hebblethwaite's view of the incarnation insists that it is) for God to be actually identified with a human person without in any way taking away from the full and genuine humanity of that human person, it follows that God does not, in fact, draw near to us as individual men and women or share our suffering as directly as apparently he could.[22]

And Hebblethwaite's response:

> God draws near to us in Jesus. He is himself present and active precisely there. But he does not become you and me. To suggest that he might is not only a nonsense in itself. It makes nonsense of the purpose of the incarnation, namely, the restoration of a *relationship* between God and ourselves.[23]

This observation about the divine purpose of the incarnation is unaffected by the failure of the logical objection to multiple incarnations which was the topic of this paper.[24]

---

[22] Wiles (1979: 7–8).   [23] Hebblethwaite (1987: 52).

[24] Many thanks to participants at the 'Metaphysics of the incarnation' conference for discussion after the talk on which this paper was based. I am particularly grateful to Joseph Jebwab for his detailed and immensely helpful comments on an early draft.

References

Ackrill, J. L. (ed.) (1963), *Aristotle's Categories and* De interpretatione (Oxford: Oxford University Press).
Adams, M. M. (1999), *What Sort of Human Nature? Medieval Philosophy and the Systematics of Christology* (Milwaukee, WI: Marquette University Press).
──── (2006), *Christ and Horrors* (Cambridge: Cambridge University Press).
Altizer, T. (1966), *The Gospel of Christian Atheism* (Philadelphia, PA: Westminster).
Aquinas, T. (1952–6), *Summa theologiae*, ed. P. Caramello, 3 vols (Turin and Rome: Marietti).
Armstrong, D. (1999), *The Mind–Body Problem* (Boulder, CO: Westview).
Augustine (1968), *De trinitate*, ed. W. J. Mountain, CCSL 50/50A (Turnhout: Brepols).
Balić, C. et al. (eds) (1950–), *Scotus. Opera omnia* (Vatican City: Vatican Press).
Bayne, T. (2001), 'The inclusion model of the incarnation: problems and prospects', *Religious Studies* 37: 125–41.
──── (2003), 'Inclusion and incarnation: a reply to Sturch', *Religious Studies* 39: 107–9.
──── (2007), 'The unity of consciousness and the split-brain problem', *Journal of Philosophy* 105: 277–300.
──── (2008a), 'Hypnosis and the unity of consciousness', in Jamieson (2008: 93–109).
──── (2008b), 'The phenomenology of agency', *Philosophy Compass* 3: 182–202.
Bayne, T. and Chalmers, D. (2001), 'What is the unity of consciousness?', in Cleeremans (2001: 23–58).
Bealer, G. and Koons, R. (eds) (2009), *The Waning of Materialism* (Oxford: Oxford University Press).
Bird, A. (2007), *Nature's Metaphysics: Laws and Properties* (Oxford: Clarendon).
Block, N. (2002), 'Concepts of consciousness', in Chalmers (2002: 206–18).
Block, N., Flanagan, O., and Güzeldere, G. (eds) (1997), *The Nature of Consciousness* (Cambridge, MA: MIT Press).
Bonhoeffer, D. (1966), *Christ the Center*, trans. J. Bowden (New York: Harper & Row).
Brower, J. (2004a), 'The problem with social Trinitarianism: a reply to Wierenga', *Faith and Philosophy* 21: 295–303.
──── (2004b), 'Abelard on the Trinity', in Brower and Guilfoy (2004: 223–57).
──── (forthcoming), 'Aristotelian endurantism: a new solution to the problem of temporary intrinsics', *Mind*.
Brower, J. and Guilfoy, K. (eds) (2004), *The Cambridge Companion to Abelard* (Cambridge: Cambridge University Press).
Brower, J. and Rea, M. (2005), 'Material constitution and the Trinity', *Faith and Philosophy* 22: 487–505.
Butterworth, G. (ed.) (1966), *On First Principles* (New York: Harper & Row).

Chaillot, C. and Belopopsky, A. (eds) (1998), *Towards Unity: The Theological Dialogue between the Orthodox Church and the Oriental Orthodox Churches* (Geneva: Inter-Orthodox Dialogue).

Chalmers, D. (1996), *The Conscious Mind: In Search of a Fundamental Theory* (Oxford: Oxford University Press).

—— (1997), 'Availability: the cognitive basis of experience?' in Block, Flanagan, and Güzeldere (1997: 421–4).

Chalmers, D. (ed.) (2002), *Philosophy of Mind* (Oxford: Oxford University Press).

Chisholm, R. (1991), 'On the simplicity of the soul', in Tomberlin (1991: 157–81).

Clark, A. (2008), *Supersizing the Mind* (Oxford: Oxford University Press).

Clark, A. and Chalmers, D. (1998), 'The extended mind', *Analysis* 58: 7–19.

Cleeremans, A. (ed.) (2001), *Unity of Consciousness* (Oxford: Oxford University Press).

Coakley, S. (2002), 'What Chalcedon solved and didn't solve', in Davis, Kendall, and O'Collins (2002: ch. 7).

Corcoran, K. (ed.) (2001), *Body, Soul and Survival* (Ithaca, NY: Cornell University Press).

Craig, W. (2003), *Philosophical Foundations of a Christian Worldview* (Downer's Grove, IL: Inter-Varsity).

—— (2005), 'Does the problem of material constitution illuminate the doctrine of the Trinity?', *Faith and Philosophy* 22: 77–86.

Crane, T. (2001), *Elements of Mind* (Oxford: Oxford University Press).

Crisp, O. (2007), *Divinity and Humanity: The Incarnation Reconsidered* (Cambridge: Cambridge University Press).

—— (2008), 'Multiple incarnations', in Stone (2008: 217–36).

—— (2009), *God Incarnate: Explorations in Christology* (London: T&T Clark).

Crisp, T., Davidson, M., and Vander Laan, D. (eds) (2006), *Knowledge and Reality: Essays in Honor of Alvin Plantinga* (Dordrecht: Springer).

Cross, R. (1998), *The Physics of Duns Scotus: The Scientific Context of a Theological Vision* (Oxford: Clarendon).

—— (2002), *The Metaphysics of the Incarnation* (Oxford: Oxford University Press).

—— (2003), 'Incarnation, omnipresence and action at a distance', *Neue Zeitschrift für Systematische Theologie* 45: 293–312.

—— (2009), 'The incarnation', in Flint and Rea (2009: 452–75).

Cunliffe-Jones, H. (1978), *A History of Christian Doctrine* (Edinburgh: T&T Clark).

Dainton, B. (1992), 'Time and division', *Ratio* 5: 102–28.

—— (2000), *Streams of Consciousness* (London: Routledge).

Daley, B. (2002), 'Nature and the "mode of union": late patristic models for the unity of Christ', in Davis, Kendall, and O'Collins (2002: 164–96).

Davis, S. (1983), *Logic and the Nature of God* (London: Macmillan).

—— (ed.) (1988), *Encountering Jesus: A Debate on Christology* (Atlanta, GA: Westminster John Knox).

—— (1999), 'John Hick on incarnation and Trinity', in Davis, Kendall, and O'Collins (1999: 251–72).

Davis, S. (2006a), 'Is kenosis orthodox?', in Evans (2006b: 112–38).
—— (2006b), *Christian Philosophical Theology* (Oxford: Oxford University Press).
Davis, S., Kendall, D., and O'Collins, G. (eds) (1999), *The Trinity: An Interdisciplinary Symposium on the Trinity* (Oxford: Oxford University Press).
—— (eds) (2002), *The Incarnation: An Interdisciplinary Symposium on the Incarnation of the Son of God* (Oxford: Oxford University Press).
Driver, G. and Hodgson, L. (eds) (1925), *The Bazaar of Heracleides* (Oxford: Clarendon).
Etzkorn G. J. et al. (eds) (1995–2006), *Scotus. Opera philosophica*, 5 vols (St Bonaventure, NY: St Bonaventure Press).
Evans, C. (2002), 'The self-emptying of love: some thoughts on kenotic christology', in Davis, Kendall, and O'Collins (2002: 246–72).
—— (2006a), 'Kenotic christology and the nature of God', in Evans (2006b: 190–217).
Evans, C. (ed.) (2006b), *Exploring Kenotic Christology: The Self-emptying of God* (Oxford: Oxford University Press).
Evans, G. (ed.) (2004a), *The First Christian Theologians: An Introduction to Theology in the Early Church* (Oxford: Blackwell).
Evans, G. (2004b), 'Eutyches, Nestorius, and Chalcedon', in Evans (2004a: 243–7).
Feenstra, R. (1989), 'Reconsidering kenotic christology', in Feenstra and Plantinga (1989: 128–52).
Feenstra, R. and Plantinga, C. (eds) (1989), *Trinity, Incarnation, and Atonement* (South Bend, IN: University of Notre Dame Press).
Fine, K. (1999), 'Things and their parts', *Midwest Studies in Philosophy* 23: 61–74.
—— (2008), 'Coincidence and form', in *Proceedings of the Aristotelian Society* Supp. 82: 101–18.
Flint, T. (2001), 'A death he freely accepted: Molinist reflections on the incarnation', *Faith and Philosophy* 18: 3–20.
—— (2004), 'Risky business: open theism and the incarnation', *Philosophia Christi* 6: 213–33.
Flint, T. and Rea, M. (eds) (2009), *The Oxford Handbook of Philosophical Theology* (Oxford: Oxford University Press).
Forrest, P. (2000), 'The Incarnation: a philosophical case for kenosis', in *Religious Studies* 36: 127–40.
Foster, J. (1991), *The Immaterial Self* (London: Routledge).
Frank, W. (1992), 'Duns Scotus on autonomous freedom and divine co-causality', in *Medieval Philosophy and Theology* 2: 142–64.
Freddoso, A. (1983), 'Logic, ontology, and Ockham's christology', in *The New Scholasticism* 57: 293–330.
—— (1986), 'Human nature, potency and the incarnation', in *Faith and Philosophy* 3: 27–53.
Frend, W. H. C. (1972), *The Rise of the Monophysite Movement* (Cambridge: Cambridge University Press).
Ganssle, G. and Woodruff, D. (eds) (2002), *God and Time: Essays on the Divine Nature* (Oxford: Oxford University Press).

Geach, P. (1967–8), 'Identity', in *Review of Metaphysics* 21: 3–12.
—— (1977), *Providence and Evil* (Cambridge: Cambridge University Press).
—— (1980), *Reference and Generality* (Ithaca, NY: Cornell University Press).
Geach, P. and Anscombe, G. E. M. (1968), *Three Philosophers* (Oxford: Blackwell).
Gore, C. (1896), *The Incarnation of the Son of God* (London: Murray).
Goulder, M. (ed.) (1979), *Incarnation and Myth: The Debate Continued* (London: SCM).
Gregg, R. (ed.) (1985), *Arianism: Historical and Theological Reassessments* (Cambridge, MA: Philadelphia Patristic Foundation).
Griffin, N. (1977), *Relative Identity* (Oxford: Clarendon).
Hadden, A. (ed.) (1873), *On the Trinity* (Edinburgh: T&T Clark).
Hanson, A. (1984), 'Two consciousnesses: the modern version of Chalcedon', *Scottish Journal of Theology* 37: 471–83.
Hanson, R. (1985), 'The Arian doctrine of the incarnation', in Gregg (1985: 181–211).
Hardy, E. (ed.) (1954), *Christology of the Later Fathers* (Philadelphia, PA: Westminster).
Hasker, W. (forthcoming), 'Constitution and the Trinity: the Brower-Rea proposal', *Faith and Philosophy*.
Hebblethwaite, B. (1987), *The Incarnation: Collected Essays in Christology* (Cambridge: Cambridge University Press).
—— (2001), 'The impossibility of multiple incarnations', *Theology* 104: 323–34.
Henry of Ghent (1520), *Summa quaestionum ordinariarum*, 2 vols (Paris).
Hervaeus, N. (1513), *Quodlibeta* 3.6 (Paris).
—— (1647), *In quatuor libros sententiarum commentaria* (Paris).
Hick, J. (ed.) (1977), *The Myth of God Incarnate* (London: SCM).
—— (1989), 'The logic of God incarnate', *Religious Studies* 25: 409–23.
—— (1993), *The Metaphor of God Incarnate* (London: SCM).
Hight, M. and Bohannon, J. (2010), 'The Son more visible: immaterialism and the incarnation', *Modern Theology* 26.1: 120–48.
Hill, C. (1991), *Sensations* (Cambridge: Cambridge University Press).
Hovorun, C. (2008), *Will, Action, and Freedom: Christological Controversies in the Seventh Century* (Leiden: Brill).
Hudson, H. (2005), *The Metaphysics of Hyperspace* (Oxford: Oxford University Press).
Hurley, S. (forthcoming), 'The varieties of externalism', in Menary (forthcoming).
—— and Noë, A. (2003), 'Neural plasticity and consciousness', *Biology and Philosophy* 18: 131–68.
Jamieson, G. (ed.) (2008), *Hypnosis and Conscious States* (Oxford: Oxford University Press).
Jedwab, J. (2008), 'The metaphysics of the Trinity and the incarnation', D. Phil thesis, University of Oxford.
Johnston, M. (2006), 'Hylomorphism', *Journal of Philosophy* 103: 652–98.
Kelly, J. N. D. (1977), *Early Christian Doctrines*, 5th edition (London: A&C Black).
Koslicki, K. (2008), *The Structure of Objects* (Oxford: Oxford University Press).
Kripke, S. (1980), *Naming and Necessity* (Cambridge, MA: Harvard University Press).
Leftow, B. (1997), 'Divine action and embodiment', *Proceedings of the ACPA* 71: 113–24.

Leftow, B. (2001), 'Souls dipped in dust: Aquinas on soul and body', in Corcoran (2001: 120–38).
—— (2002), 'A timeless God incarnate', in Davis, Kendall, and O'Collins (2002: 273–99).
—— (2004), 'A Latin Trinity', *Faith and Philosophy* 21: 304–33.
—— (2009), 'Soul, mind and brain', in Bealer and Koons (2009: 395–416).
Le Poidevin, R. (2009), 'Identity and the composite Christ: an incarnational dilemma', *Religious Studies* 45: 167–86.
Lewis, D. (1976), 'The paradoxes of time travel', *American Philosophical Quarterly* 13: 145–52.
—— (1983), 'New work for a theory of universals', *Australasian Journal of Philosophy* 61: 343–77.
Lockwood, M. (1989), *Mind, Brain, and the Quantum* (Oxford: Blackwell).
Loux, M. (1991), *Primary Ousia* (Ithaca, NY: Cornell University Press).
Luna, Concetta (1990–1),'La Reportatio della lettura di Egidio Romano sul Libro III delle Sentenze (Clm. 8005) e il problema dell'autenticita dell' Ordinatio', Documenti e studi sulla tradizione filosofica medievale, 1 (1990), 113–225; 2 (1991), 75–126.
MacBride, F. (2005), 'The universal-particular distinction: a dogma of metaphysics?', *Mind* 114: 555–614.
McDaniel, K. (2009), 'Structure-making', *Australasian Journal of Philosophy* 87: 251–74.
McKitrick, J. (2003), 'A case for extrinsic dispositions', *Australasian Journal of Philosophy* 81: 155–74.
Marmodoro, A. and Hill, J. (2009), 'Modeling the metaphysics of the incarnation', *Philosophy and Theology* 20: 1–2.
Martin, R. and Dodd, B. (eds) (1998), *Where Christology Began: Essays on Philippians 2* (Louisville, KY: Westminster John Knox).
Menary, R. (ed.) (forthcoming), *The Extended Mind* (Aldershot: Ashgate).
Merricks, T. (2006), 'Split brains and the Godhead', in Crisp, Davidson, and Vander Laan (2006: 299–326).
—— (2007), 'The Word made flesh: dualism, physicalism, and the incarnation', in Van Inwagen and Zimmerman (2007: 281–300).
Molnar, G. (2003), *Powers: A Study in Metaphysics*, ed. S. Mumford (Oxford: Oxford University Press).
Morris, T. (1983), 'Divinity, humanity, and death', *Religious Studies* 19: 451–8.
—— (1986), *The Logic of God Incarnate* (Ithaca, NY: Cornell University Press).
Morris, T. (ed.) (1988), *Philosophy and the Christian Faith* (Notre Dame, IN: University of Notre Dame Press).
Nieden, M. (1997), Organum deitatis: *Die Christologie des Thomas de Vio Cajetan* (Leiden, New York, Cologne: Brill).
Norris, R. (ed.) (1980), *The Christological Controversy* (Philadelphia, PA: Fortress).
O'Connor, T. (1999), 'Simplicity and creation', *Faith and Philosophy* 16: 405–12.
O'Neil, C. (ed.) (1975), *Summa contra gentiles, vol. 4* (Notre Dame, IN: University of Notre Dame Press).

Oberman, H. (1963), *The Harvest of Medieval Theology: Gabriel Biel and Late Medieval Nominalism* (Cambridge, MA: Harvard University Press).
Olson, E. (2006), 'The paradox of increase', *The Monist* 89: 390–417.
Padgett, A. (ed.) (1994), *Reason and the Christian Religion: Essays in Honour of Richard Swinburne* (Oxford: Clarendon).
Pannenberg, W. (1977), *Jesus—God and Man*, trans. L. Wilkins and D. Priebe (Philadelphia, PA: Westminster).
Parfit, D. (1984), *Reasons and Persons* (Oxford: Oxford University Press).
Parsons, J. (2007), 'Theories of location', *Oxford Studies in Metaphysics* 3: 201–32.
Percival, H. (ed.) (1994), *The Seven Ecumenical Councils* (Peabody, MA: Hendrickson).
Plantinga, A. (1974), *The Nature of Necessity* (Oxford: Oxford University Press).
—— (1999), 'On heresy, mind and truth', *Faith and Philosophy* 16: 182–93.
Ramsey, F. P. (1925), 'Universals', *Mind* 34: 401–17. Reprinted in Ramsey (1990: 8–30).
—— (1990), *Philosophical Papers*, ed. D. Mellor (Cambridge: Cambridge University Press).
Rea, M. C. (ed.) (1997), *Material Constitution* (Lanham, MD: Rowman and Littlefield).
Rea, M. C. (1998a), 'Sameness without identity: an Aristotelian solution to the problem of material constitution', *Ratio* 11: 316–28.
—— (1998b), 'Temporal parts unmotivated', *The Philosophical Review* 107: 225–60.
—— (2003), 'Relative identity and the doctrine of the Trinity', *Philosophia Christi* 5: 431–46.
—— (2006), 'Polytheism and Christian belief', *Journal of Theological Studies* 57: 133–48.
—— (2009), 'The Trinity', in Flint and Rea (2009: 403–29).
Rosemann, P. (2004), *Peter Lombard* (Oxford: Oxford University Press).
Russell, N. (ed.) (2000), *Cyril of Alexandria* (New York: Routledge).
Scotus, D., *Ordinatio*, in Balić et al. (1950).
Sedley, D. (1982), 'The Stoic criterion of identity', *Phronesis* 27: 255–75.
Senor, T. (1991), 'God, supernatural kinds, and the incarnation', *Religious Studies* 27: 353–70.
—— (2002), 'Incarnation, timelessness, and Leibniz's Law problems', in Ganssle and Woodruff (2002: 220–35).
—— (2007), 'The compositional account of the incarnation', *Faith and Philosophy* 24: 52–71.
Sider, T. (2001), 'Maximality and intrinsic properties', *Philosophy and Phenomenological Research* 63: 357–64.
Sorabji, R. (2006), *Self. Ancient and Modern Insights about Individuality, Life, and Death* (Oxford: Clarendon).
Stone, M. (ed.) (2008), *Reason, Faith and History: Philosophical Essays for Paul Helm* (Aldershot: Ashgate).
Stump, E. (2002), 'Aquinas' metaphysics of the incarnation', in Davis, Kendall, and O'Collins (2002: 197–218).
—— (2003), *Aquinas* (London: Routledge).

Sturch, R. (2003), 'Inclusion and incarnation: a reply to Bayne', *Religious Studies* 39: 107–9.
Swinburne, R. (1986), *The Evolution of the Soul* (Oxford: Oxford University Press). Revised edition (Oxford: Clarendon, 1997).
—— (1993), *The Coherence of Theism* (Oxford: Oxford University Press).
—— (1994), *The Christian God* (Oxford: Clarendon).
—— (2007), 'From mental/physical identity to substance dualism', in Van Inwagen and Zimmerman (2007: 142–65).
—— (2008), *Was Jesus God?* (Oxford: Oxford University Press).
Tanner, N. (ed.) (1990), *Decrees of the Ecumenical Councils* (London: Sheed & Ward; Washington, DC: Georgetown University Press).
Thompson, T. (2006), 'Nineteenth-century kenotic christology: the waxing, waning, and weighing of a quest for a coherent orthodoxy', in Evans (2006b: 74–111).
Tixeront, J. (1923), *History of Dogmas, vol. 2* (St Louis, MO: Herder).
Tomberlin, J. (ed.) (1991), *Philosophical Perspectives 5* (Aterscadero, CA: Ridgeview).
Torrance, I. (1988), *Christology after Chalcedon: Severus of Antioch and Sergius the Monophysite* (Norwich: Canterbury).
Van Inwagen, P. (1988), 'And yet they are not three Gods but one God', in Morris (1988: 241–78).
—— (1994), 'Not by confusion of substance, but by unity of person', in Padgett (1994: 201–26).
—— (1995), *God, Knowledge, and Mystery* (Ithaca, NY: Cornell University Press).
—— (1998), 'Incarnation and christology', in E. Craig (ed.), *Routledge Encyclopedia of Philosophy* (London: Routledge). Retrieved 18 March 2009, from <http://www.rep.routledge.com/article/KO38SECT3>.
Van Inwagen, P. and Zimmerman, D. (eds) (2007), *Persons: Human and Divine* (Oxford: Clarendon).
Von Balthasar, H. (1990), *Mysterium Paschale: The Mystery of Easter*, trans. A. Nichols (Edinburgh: T&T Clark).
—— (1992), *Theo-drama III: The Dramatis Personae: The Person in Christ*, trans. G. Harrison (San Francisco, CA: Ignatius).
—— (1994), *Theo-drama IV: The Action*, trans. G. Harrison (San Francisco: Ignatius).
Wadding L. (ed.) (1649), Scotus. *Opera omnia*, 12 vols (Lyon).
Waterlow, S. (1982), *Nature, Change, and Agency in Aristotle's Physics* (Oxford: Clarendon).
Welch, C. (ed.) (1965), *God and Incarnation in Mid-nineteenth-century German Theology* (Oxford: Oxford University Press).
Wessel, S. (2004), *Cyril of Alexandria and the Nestorian Controversy: The Making of a Saint and a Heretic* (Oxford: Oxford University Press).
West, J. L. A. (2007), 'Aquinas on Peter Lombard and the metaphysical status of Christ's human nature', *Gregorianum* 88: 557–86.
Weston, F. (1907), *The One Christ: An Enquiry into the Manner of the Incarnation* (London: Longmans Green).

White, T. (2008), 'Dyotheletism and the instrumental human consciousness of Jesus', *Pro ecclesia* 17: 397–422.
Whitehead, A. N. (1978), *Process and Reality* (New York: Free).
Wiggins, D. (1980), *Sameness and Substance* (Oxford: Blackwell).
Wiles, M. (1977), 'Christianity without incarnation?', in Hick (1977: 1–10).
────── (1979), 'A survey of issues in the *Myth* debate', in Goulder (1979: 1–12).
Williams, B. (1956–7), 'Personal identity and individuation', *Proceedings of the Aristotelian Society* 57: 229–52.
Witt, C. (1989), *Substance and Essence in Aristotle* (Ithaca, NY: Cornell University Press).
────── (2003), *Ways of Being: Potentiality and Actuality in Aristotle's* Metaphysics (Ithaca, NY: Cornell University Press).

Index

Ackrill, J.L. 117n.
Adams, M.M. 46n., 47n., 64n., 135n., 159n., 160n.
Alexander III, Pope 47n.
Almeider, Michael 87n.
Altizer, Thomas 9
Anscombe, G.E.M. 234n.
Antognazza, Maria Rosa 134n.
Apollinarius of Laodicea 9–10, 95
Aquinas, Thomas 14, 20n., 27, 29, 41, 44n., 46, 47n., 48, 59n., 71, 81n., 82n., 87, 90, 95, 116n., 130, 131, 156, 157, 159, 186, 187, 198
Aristotle 19, 52n., 75, 76, 115, 117, 135, 136–8, 139n., 140, 148, 156, 158, 219n., 222, 224
Armstrong, David 184n., 222
Augustine of Hippo 156, 167n., 201–2

Bailey, Andrew 134n.
Bauckham, Richard 126n.
Bayne, Tim 15n., 172n., 176n., 179n., 181n., 185n.
Belopopsky, Alexander 155n.
Berkeley, George 46n.
Bird, Alexander 140n., 141n.
Block, Ned 170–1
Bohannon, Joshua 46n.
Bonhoeffer, Dietrich 119n.
Brower, Jeffrey 75n., 134n., 136, 147, 148n.
Butterworth, G.W. 158n.

Chaillot, Christine 155n.
Chalmers, David 171, 172n., 176n., 190n., 205, 207–8, 209, 210, 211, 214, 215, 220, 221, 222, 223
Chisholm, Roderick 55n.
Clark, Andy 190n., 205, 207–8, 209, 210, 211, 220, 221, 222, 223
Coakley, Sarah 4
Cottingham, John 44n.
Craig, William 76n., 129n., 180n.
Crane, Tim 174n.
Crisp, Oliver 13n., 19, 45n., 46n., 57n., 63n., 82n., 87n., 113n., 135n., 151n., 233n., 240

Cross, Richard 2n., 5n., 11n., 19, 20n., 22, 31, 43n., 46n., 47n., 50n., 53n., 57n., 62, 66n., 67n., 71n., 79n., 81n., 82n., 84n., 117n., 135n., 195n., 199n., 201n.
Cunliffe-Jones, Hubert 67n., 84n.
Cyril of Alexandria 16n.

D'Costa, Gavin 66n.
Dainton, Barry 171n., 172n., 238–9
Daley, Brian 157n.
Damasus I, Pope 95
Davis, Stephen 3n., 17, 19, 90, 104n., 105, 114n., 119n., 127n., 128n., 129n.
Dodd, Brian 126n.
Dougherty, Trent 134n.
Driver, G.R. 2n.

Eutyches 2n.
Evans, C. Stephen 17n., 104n., 90, 115, 119n.,
Evans, G. 2n.

Feenstra, Ronald 90, 104n., 105n., 115
Fine, Kit 138n.
Flint, Thomas 12n., 13n., 19, 26, 44n., 46n., 50n., 51n., 66n., 69n., 82n., 113n., 135n., 181
Forrest, Peter 17n., 121n., 124n.
Forsyth, P.T. 115
Foster, John 25, 172n.
Frank, William 191
Freddoso, Alfred 46n., 71n., 72n., 82n., 159n.
Frend, W.H.C. 2n.

Geach, Peter 7n., 58, 60, 122, 234
Gess, W.F. 103, 115
Giles of Rome 187n.
Gore, Charles 17n., 115
Gregory of Nyssa 155, 157
Griffin, Nicholas 7n.

Hadden, A.W. 167n.
Hanson, A. 14n.
Hanson, R. 10n.
Hardy, Edward 155n.
Hare, John 85n., 87n.
Hasker, William 76n.

Hawking, Stephen 61, 63, 65
Hebblethwaite, Brian 115, 230–1, 233, 234, 235, 240–1
Helm, Paul 66n.
Henry of Ghent 202–3
Hervaeus Natalis 187–9, 190–1, 193, 194, 195, 196, 197, 198
Hick, John 57n., 94, 95, 127n., 230n.
Hight, Mark 46n.
Hill, Christopher 172n.
Hill, Jonathan 8n.
Hodgson, Leonard 2n.
Hovorun, Cyril 162n.
Howard-Snyder, Daniel 113n., 134n.
Hudson, Hud 21n., 144n., 134n.
Hunt, David 87n.
Hurley, Susan 208, 224n.

Irenaeus of Lyon 67n.

Jedwab, Joseph 14n., 15, 19, 20n., 25n., 44n., 52n., 66n., 87n., 134n., 205n., 231n., 241n.
John Paul II, Pope 154
Johnston, Mark 138n., 142

Kasparov, Garry 212–21, 222, 224, 225, 226
Kelly, J.N.D. 158n.
Kleinschmidt, Shieva 134n.
Koslicki, Kathrin 136n., 138n.
Kowalski, Dean 87n.
Kreitzer, Larry 126n.
Kripke, Saul 212, 213–4, 215, 217, 220n.

Lampe, G.W.H. 67n.
Le Poidevin, Robin 7n., 19, 73n., 185n.
Leftow, Brian 8n., 11n., 13n., 19, 22n., 38n., 39n., 41n., 44n., 46n., 47, 48, 50n., 53, 56n., 58, 59, 60, 61, 66n., 72n., 79, 80, 81n., 87n., 90, 96, 97–8, 111, 113n., 134n., 160n., 180n., 185n., 205n., 235
Lewis, David 74, 139n., 222, 239
Lizza, John 185n.
Lockwood, Michael 172n.
Loux, Michael 136n., 138n.

MacBride, Fraser 149n.
McDaniel, Kris 138n.
MacKintosh, H.R. 115
McKitrick, Jennifer 141n.
Marmodoro, Anna 8n., 9n., 19, 113n., 134n., 190n.

Martin, Jennifer 134n.
Martin, Ralph 126n.
Mawson, Tim 44n.
Maximus the Confessor 156
Merricks, Trenton 8–9, 20n., 23, 31, 32, 37–8, 39–40, 41, 44n., 51, 52n., 135n., 180n.
Molnar, George 139, 140n., 141n.
Morris, Thomas 6n., 14, 16–7, 18n., 90–5, 96, 101–2, 104n., 107, 110, 111, 120, 121, 125, 129n., 234, 240

Nestorius 2n., 16n., 50n., 118, 131–2,
Nieden, Marcel 187n.
Noë, Alva 208, 224n.
Norris, Richard 10n.

O'Connor, Timothy 174n.
O'Neil, Charles 14n.
Oberman, Heiko 47n.
Ockham, William of 159n.
Olson, Eric 72n., 75n., 77
Origen 158

Pannenberg, Wolfhart 119n.
Parfit, Derek 179–80, 232
Parsons, Josh 144n.
Paul 103, 115, 125–6
Percival, Henry 30n., 37n.
Peter Lombard
Plantinga, Alvin 11n., 25, 67n., 87n., 117n.
Plantinga, Cornelius 115
Plato 22, 23, 25–9, 42, 43, 156
Potter, Luke 134n.
Prosphonetus 37n.
Pruss, Alex 134n.

Ramsay, F.P. 149n.
Rea, Michael 19, 20n., 21n., 44n., 75n., 87n., 113n., 148n., 151n.
Rosemann, Philipp 8n.
Russell, Norman 16n.

Scotus, John Duns 46, 62n., 79, 81n., 159n., 186–7, 188, 189–95, 196, 197–200, 201–2, 203, 204
Sedley, David 72n.
Senor, Thomas 5–6, 13n., 17, 19, 56–8, 59–60, 98n., 107n., 131, 133n.
Severus of Antioch 2n., 12n.
Shields, Christopher 134n.
Sider, Theodore 32
Skiles, Alex 134n.

Socrates 136–7, 188
Sorabji, Richard 158n.
Stump, Eleonore 18n., 46n., 52n., 56n., 58n., 79n., 90, 95–6, 97, 111, 130, 131, 159n., 196n., 235
Sturch, Richard 15n.
Swinburne, Richard 7n., 10, 14, 19, 30, 31, 38, 39–40, 44, 65, 153n., 157n., 160n., 164n., 185n., 205n.

Tanner, Norman 1n., 4n., 5n., 49n., 53n., 54n., 153n., 163n., 168n.
Theodore of Mopsuestia 53
Thomasius, Gottfried 17, 102, 115
Thompson, Thomas 103n., 115
Tixeront, Joseph 162n.
Torrance, Iain 12n.
Tuggy, Dale 133n.

Van Balthasar, Hans Urs 115
van Dyke, Christina 134n.
van Horn, Luke 134n.
Van Inwagen, Peter 7, 46n., 128, 181

Wasserman, Ryan 134n.
Waterlow, Sarah 136n.
Welch, Claude 17n., 115n.
Wessel, Susan 2n.
West, J.L.A. 47n.
Weston, Frank 115
White, Thomas 14n.
Whitehead, A.N. 115n.
Wiggins, D. 7n.
Wiles, Maurice 229n., 230n., 240–1
Williams, Bernard 233
Witt, Charlotte 136n., 137n., 140n.
Wood, William 31n., 44n.

Milton Keynes UK
Ingram Content Group UK Ltd.
UKHW022106230923
429248UK00004B/69